# The French Revolution
# and the Psychology
# of Revolution

# THE FRENCH REVOLUTION AND THE PSYCHOLOGY OF REVOLUTION

## Gustave LeBon

With a New Introduction by
Robert A. Nye

Transaction Books

New Brunswick (U.S.A) and London (U.K.)

Library of Congress Catalog Number: 78-62691
ISBN: 0-87855-310-X (cloth); 0-87855-697-4 (paper)
Printed in the United States of America

**Library of Congress Cataloging in Publication Data**

LeBon, Gustave, 1841-1931.
    The French Revolution and the psychology of
revolution.

    (The Social science classics series)
    Translation of La révolution française et la
psychologie des révolutions.
    Reprint of the 1913 ed. published by Putnam,
New York under title: The psychology of revolution.
    Includes bibliographical references and index.
    1. France—History—Revolution, 1789-1799—
Causes and character. 2. Revolutions. 3. Social
psychology. I. Title II. Series.
DC149.L3213    1979      301.6'333'0944      78-62691

# INTRODUCTION

## GUSTAVE LEBON'S *PSYCHOLOGY OF REVOLUTION:* HISTORY, SOCIAL SCIENCE, AND POLITICS IN NINETEENTH AND EARLY TWENTIETH CENTURY FRANCE

*Robert A. Nye*

THERE will no doubt be several strategies employed by those who introduce the texts in this social science classics series. None of these presentations, however, is likely to overlook the need to decide exactly what makes a text a classic text. It can be argued that in setting forth the processes by which classics are labeled and preserved as such, one takes a running start on introducing the specific reasons for the success or importance of the text at hand. An examination of these processes seems particularly crucial for our text, owing to its being a kind of bastard of social science and history, and, in addition, a pioneering effort to popularize social science methods.

It has been the usual practice in the discussion of "classic" texts to choose between "presentist" and "historicist" approaches. One can present a social science text as a contribution to the present understanding of its subject matter, or one can examine the historical origins and context of the classic by way of explaining its meaning and appeal to its own age. Of course these are not mutually exclusive aims, though most presentations give a preponderant attention to one or the other. Historically, the need to choose between these approaches has also marked the general history of social theory and of the particular social sciences. A disconcerting number of these "histories" have chosen the "presentist" alternative and made historical background play the unimportant role of local color in the enterprise. This introduction will follow the opposite course, relying more heavily on "historicist" *explanation,* but introducing "presentist" *judgment* where appropriate. Let us begin by discussing the nature of a social science classic.

Through the development of the modern social sciences, the classic texts have served a variety of functions. They have, of course, performed the obvious service of announcing to the specialist community the results of personal research. The elevation of such a text to the "classic" rank is usually the consequence of the text's having "solved" particularly vexing empirical or methodological problems that members of the community had previously puzzled over with no convincing result. Though this "progressive" role of a key text in advancing the work of a research community is often held to be its most important function, it is by no means the only reason why certain texts reach "classic" status and retain it for generations after. One has not, in other words, exhausted the meaning of a social science text by isolating its empirical components or its theoretical contributions. The survival of a social science classic is dependent on a broader ground of appeal than this, both for the generation to which it was first addressed and for our own.

Some aspects of this wider appeal are obvious. During the nineteenth century, before the professional or evaluative standards of special disciplines and sub-disciplines had fully developed, the authors of social science texts pitched their arguments to an audience of generalists whose training was as much philosophical and literary as scientific. On occasion, social scientists might address either the general reading public or particular elite leaderships for whom the author believed the text had a special message. In these cases the success of the text cannot be said to be entirely reliant on its "scientific" content, but in great measure on its general argument, timeliness, affective appeal, literary style, or the author's general reputation. The presence of these factors does not thereby diminish the importance of the "internal" or empirical elements, but it does require some additional analysis of the text's success in articulating the conclusions of formal research with the more general knowledge held by some non-specialized audiences. This is not to say that in addressing a broader set of issues the popular "classic" text thereby forfeits its right to "solve" problems in the same manner as more formal or specialized texts; the more popular text also provides answers to certain problems. These are addressed on a more general level and with less logical rigor, and conclusions are more suggestive than absolute, but the process itself may not be much different from what takes place in more rarified atmospheres.

There are other non-technical factors that account for the "classic" denomination of certain texts. One of these is the increasingly studied matter of the research cluster which comes to surround a particularly eminent figure, and whose members were either educated by

vii

this great man or owed their positions or future prospects to his patronage. Durkheimian sociology is a particularly good example of this phenomenon. Though Durkheim's texts had obvious merits, the existence of a body of devoted acolytes, many of whom were well-placed in the educational network, guaranteed a more sympathetic reception for him than for the texts of some "outsider."[1] To mention yet another factor, Robert Alun Jones has recently argued that classic texts may have a certain "heuristic value" that helps to expand the "sociological imaginations" of later generations.[2] The example of Durkheim again comes to mind in this connection. For all its question-begging, *Suicide* in part reached the dimensions of a classic by virtue of Durkheim's brilliant presentation and demolition of rival theories prior to the introduction of his own arguments. *Suicide* and other texts are assigned to the students of classic sociological theory courses as much for their illustration of methodological and problem-solving techniques as for their empirical findings.

Gustave LeBon's *The French Revolution and the Psychology of Revolution,* first published in 1912, does not owe its "classic" status to its author's ability to distribute academic patronage, for he had none, nor to its solution of pressing empirical or technical problems in studies of collective behavior, for the book was in large measure a rehash of his earlier work. But that the book enjoyed success there can be little doubt. Thirteen thousand copies had been sold by 1914, seventeen thousand by 1924, and the book was still in print at LeBon's death in 1931. English and American editions appeared in 1913 and also saw brisk sales.

Under the title *The Psychology of Revolution,* the book was surpassed in English-speaking editions only by LeBon's enormously successful *Psychology of Socialism* and *The Crowd.* As we shall see, the book still finds mention in the historiography of the French Revolution and by serious students of the theory of revolution. The book's commercial success and general reputation depended, we will argue, on other factors than influence networks or its scientific problem-solving virtues.

But to effectively analyze the remarkable appeal of this book, to scholars and public alike, we must definitely choose between the "historicist" and "presentist" positions. The historicist position has clear advantages in accounting for the success of a work of scientific vulgarization such as this, and though we must ultimately make some judgments about the book's "contributions" to various areas, the largest measure of understanding we will gain of this work must come from an analysis of the historical context to which its message was originally addressed. There are also good reasons for thinking that the "presentist" approach, which insists on assessing only the logical processes that produce scientific results, needs the findings of historical analysis to satisfy *its own criteria* for evaluating the progress of knowledge. Summarizing the arguments for an historicist position, Jones has recently written:

> Thus any claim for or criticism of a contemporary theoretical perspective necessarily implies certain things about its past; and of course, if the particu-lar historical connections thus implied are not

credible, that fact would seem to diminish the credibility of the claim or criticism itself accordingly. One can only look forward to the day when such extended historical investigations designed to unveil the "absolute presuppositions" of such perspectives replace the mythological reconstructions contrived to legitimate them.[3]

It seems impossible to escape the conclusion that certain social science theories have had a definite emotional and ideological appeal to their own age. Alvin Gouldner has written persuasively about the general nature of this appeal.[4] We are, moreover, fascinated with the formulations of earlier thinkers when the problems (and their solutions) of their age seem like ours. But there is a danger that we might accept the implicit ideological orientations and overtones that envelop these theories and transmute them into the present—reading the present, as it were, in terms of past theory. A virtue of studying social science classics might be, then, to help understand the extent to which these works were a response to a certain set of historical circumstances. It may be argued that we would therefore be better positioned to eliminate from them those elements that owe more to the ideological atmosphere of their own age than to the formulations of empirical social science.

None of this guarantees that social scientists will suddenly understand the limitations and strengths of some particular branch of social science theory. Durkheimians and Weberians have not, and probably should not, reject the master's work simply because they happen to discover that he was neurotic, was committed for or against democracy, or favored deductive or post-hoc proofs to experimental ones. Such discoveries, which will be encouraged by series such as these, should, however, serve to raise the aims and methods of social science research to a higher level of self-consciousness than is sometimes the case with practitioners. Social and natural scientists have learned a good deal from recent work in the sociological and social processes of science, and from the study of the cognitive foundations of scientific revolutions. The members of nearly all domains of knowledge with scientific pretensions, and many without them, have become more aware of what it is they are about and what they mean when they use normative terminology.

*The French Revolution and the Psychology of Revolution* may be historically located at the intersection of several vectors, each of which clarifies the nature and meaning of the book in an important way. Among the most important of these vectors were the intentions of the author, Gustave LeBon, a prolific and influential writer on the science and politics of his day. Quentin Skinner has reminded us of the need to examine intentionality in intellectual history as a way of insuring an *understanding* of the texts that rises above the *meaning* in the text.[5] Another of these vectors is the status in LeBon's day of the sort of social science history represented by his book. Did LeBon write a book of great originality, or can its popularity be explained by its resemblance to a *genre* of similar works? Yet another vector deals with the subject of the book itself: revolution, and in particular the French Revolution. Where may one locate LeBon's book in the great flood of writings published by the French on

xi

the greatest trauma of their national past? Lastly, we must attempt to place the book in the historical context of pre-war France and explore the relationship of contemporary politics to the intrusive message one finds in LeBon's book. He was writing, as we shall see, about the dangers and consequences of the revolutionary tradition in his own times, and he openly identified those parties among his contemporaries which he believed were perpetuating the Jacobin Reign of Terror.

LeBon was seventy when his book was published. Born in 1841, he had already written over twenty-five books and nearly two hundred articles on a variety of scientific, medical, and political topics. LeBon took a medical degree in Paris during the last years of the Second Empire, but he never formally practiced, devoting himself instead to research and writing, at first within a range of specialities related to the medical training he had received. Gradually his interests broadened to include physical and cultural anthropology and the study of non-European cultures. In the 1880s he undertook expeditions to Arabia and the Indian subcontinent to examine the history and monuments of those cultures, publishing those studies in handsome editions illustrated by elaborate line drawings and photographs. In 1889 he employed the methods used in these works for an equally ambitious history of the classical cradles of civilization, *Les Premières Civilisations*.[6] His anthropological work in the late 1870s and early 1880s had convinced him of the benefits of studying the adaptation of organisms to their physical environment. As an enthusiastic supporter of a materialistic Darwinian evolution,

LeBon reasoned that these adaptive processes applied with equal force to human societies and the varieties of culture they displayed. A profound belief in a positivistic monism encouraged him to reduce cultural manifestations to biological terms in a way that made his explanations of social change rigidly deterministic. As a consequence race was his all-important analytical category, encompassing within its sway "sentiment," "character," and other intellectual factors, all of which were themselves permanent adaptive variations that had at some point ensured the survival of the racial stock.[7]

Such explanations of the ingredients and nature of cultural evolution were by no means unusual for this period. Bagehot and Spencer in England, Taine, Vacher de la Pouge, and Charles LeTourneau in France, and the *Volkerpsychologie* of Wilhelm Wundt in Germany all depended on similar explanations of the psychological aspect of racial character. The culmination of LeBon's writings on race psychology was *Les Lois psychologiques de l'évolution des peuples* (1894). This volume, a great favorite of Theodore Roosevelt, clearly illustrated the ideological presumptions that underlay all LeBon's work in this area. Each great national people, he opined, had a more or less permanent set of psychological characteristics that had evolved over centuries of interaction between the race and its environment. The culture, laws, and institutions they adopted were the instruments of their collective adaptation to their milieu and were thoroughly rooted in the character of the humblest individual in the group. Where these cultural manifestations had left room for internal social competition and a healthy measure of individual variation, continued evolutionary progress and a creative and vigorous social organism were strong likelihoods. Many formerly great peoples had succumbed, LeBon warned, to restrictive central governments whose suffocating control of public affairs produced an egalitarian herd that was increasingly unfit to survive in a harshly competitive world. The English and Americans, of course, were among the former type, and the French and other "Latin" races among the latter.

The political perspectives that informed these notions derived from LeBon's old-fashioned liberalism, his belief in the virtues of an unregulated civic life, and the beneficent effects of a struggle for survival. He was naturally suspicious of all varieties of social leveling, of *étatisme,* of the modern forms of economic collectivism, and of the first signs of native resistance to imperialism in the European colonies. His anxieties in these matters were characteristic of a whole generation of European liberals whose political, social and economic prerogatives were being challenged by the increasing collectivization of public life. In both Europe and America these liberal figures became ardent defenders of property, free enterprise, and the rule of law, the prototypes for mainstream twentieth century conservatism. The other face of liberal retrenchment was their violent anti-socialism, their stubborn resistance to further extensions of democratic prerogatives to the masses, and their growing tendency to view militarism and nationalism as possible sources for the disciplining and control of the unpredictable masses.

For LeBon these anti-democratic and anti-egalitarian sentiments took the form of a theory of collective behavior. His applications of this theory to the explanation of the problems of modern life occupied LeBon until his death at ninety in 1931. His seminal book in this area was *La Psychologie des foules* (1895). This work, destined to become one of the most reprinted and translated volumes in the social science literature, owed its notable success to the highly synthetic and generalized nature of its argument. LeBon drew both on his own early work in mental medicine and on the work of the Italian writers Sighele and Rossi and his own countrymen Gabriel Tarde and Hippolyte Taine.[8] The theoretical elements that figured in LeBon's theory of collective behavior derived from the French tradition of hypnosis, from organismic social theory, and from psychiatrists' observations of the contagious nature of certain mental states among the inmates of asylums. The roots of collective psychology were located deep within the tradition of medical pathology, a condition which this subdiscipline of social psychology never managed to transcend.

Empirical and observational influences on the early development of collective theory were minimal. LeBon himself witnessed few actual collective manifestations; he drew most of his accounts of crowd phenomena from newspapers, which he used to illustrate aspects of the theory in a more or less anecdotal manner. The high level of abstraction and generalization he employed allowed him to plausibly explain a variety of situations where collective mental states were assumed to be operating. Juries, parliaments, mass meetings, even the dispersed publics influenced by information media could be shown to behave according to the "laws" of collective behavior.[9] The essential touchstone of these laws was the distinction they made between the irrational, suggestible, and emotional behavior of (apparently) rational individuals under the influence of collective states of mind. This distinction had an obvious appeal to the majority of the middle class property-owning electorate, if we can judge from its consistent repetition in the press and popular literature of the 1890s. All forms of socialist or union collective activities, from meetings to strike actions, were pejoratively characterized as "emotional," "savage," or "unconscious" according to the criteria of collective theory.

LeBon continued to apply these principles to various contemporary problems for the next few decades. *La Psychologie du socialisme* appeared in 1898, *La Psychologie de l'éducation* in 1901, and *La Psychologie politique et la défense sociale* in 1910. In 1911 he published *Les Opinions et les croyances,* a general study of the mechanisms of opinion formation in modern society. This book was a kind of loosely argued collective version of Freud's *The Psychopathology of Everyday Life,* LeBon making the general point that rational behavior was much less frequent than behavior dominated by what he called "biological," "mystic," or "affective" logic. The general public interest in studies such as this was considerable in the decades prior to World War I. Henri Ellenberger has brilliantly characterized the European obsession with mysticism, decadence, and eroticism that provided the popular background to the flood of "serious" writings on these topics.[10] The year following *Les Opinions et les croyances,* LeBon published his book on the French Revolution as an application of his "researches" to "the study of concrete instances." At this point we may introduce the second of our vectors of influence on LeBon's book.

*La Révolution française et la psychologie des révolutions* was a serious effort at what we today call "interdisciplinary history." Contemporary historians are likely to believe that the use of social science methods in historical writings is a relatively recent phenomenon and still of a very tentative nature. The latter may still be true, but widespread interest in this kind of synthetic history has been around for many generations. Its theoretical foundations extend back to the Enlightenment, and, ultimately, to Vico. It was only around the turn of the century in France, however, that the use of social science methods in historical investigation became notably widespread. At that time if one posed the question of social science history, it was generally understood that this entailed very broad epistemological claims about the nature of historical knowledge. Historians are trained nowadays in the techniques of social science investigation, with little thought being given to the epistemological consequences of their use. These matters are often assumed to be the province of the philosophers of history and the rare crank among professional historians who agonizes over the scientific status of his work. In LeBon's day historians were thoroughly familiar with these wider issues, and considered the outcome of the debate over them a matter of important consequence for their profession.

xvii

As has so often been the case in French intellectual debate, the sides in the matter of scientific history were drawn between insiders and outsiders, with the professional historians defending the walls of the university against their "interdisciplinary" opponents. But this was not a simple matter of radical "have-nots" challenging the prerogatives of the conservative establishment. Professional historians in the universities and the government-sponsored institutes such as the École pratique des hautes études and the École des chartes, which taught paleography and the analysis of texts, considered their own work "scientific" by standards laid down thirty and forty years earlier. The chief division between the insiders and outsiders, then, was between rival conceptions of what was meant by "scientific" history.

The origins of the professional historian's older conception of scientific history may be traced to the last years of the Second Empire. At that time the prestige of the German school of historical studies was at its peak, and a handful of recent graduates of the École normale supérieure, dissatisfied with what passed for historical scholarship in France, took post-graduate work in Germany with the luminaries of German academic history. Enthusiastic over the great benefits of the methods they learned in German seminars, they prevailed upon Louis Napoleon's education minister, Victor Duruy, to found the École pratique des hautes études where historians could be thoroughly introduced in seminar work to German techniques of historical investigation. This first generation, Gabriel Monod, Ernest Lavisse, Gaston Paris and Alfred Rambaud, eventually reached positions of power in the educational establishment and the political network of the Third Republic from which they dominated the training and placement of historians until World War I. Monod became a professor at the École normale supérieure in 1888, Rambaud was appointed to a professorship at the Sorbonne in 1884, and Lavisse became director of historical studies and professor at the Sorbonne in 1883. Paris was elected to the Collège de France where he lectured until his death in 1903.[11] These men and their second generation disciples—Alphonse Aulard, Philippe Sagnac, Charles Seignobos, and Gabriel Hanotaux—more or less perpetuated the methodological principles they had imbibed from German historical science. They enforced these principles in the scholarly organs they controlled, the *Revue Historique,* founded in 1876 by Monod,[12] and, later, the *Revue d'Histoire Moderne et Contemporaine.* The "science" this first generation had learned consisted of the careful reconstruction of historical evidence from the surviving documentary record. Learning to carefully read texts and to interpret them in terms of their internal meanings and the immediate context of their appearance was a considerable advance over the inconsistent use of texts by earlier historians.

By "getting back to the texts" it was hoped subjective orientations and "imaginative" interpretations would disappear, since, to quote Monod's teacher the German historian Georg Waitz, "every generalization is nothing but a grouping of facts."[13] The desire to eliminate subjective elements in historical writing was intensified by the mood of reaction that followed the

French defeat in the Franco-Prussian war. This was so because it was widely believed that German superiority in science was in large measure the key factor in the victory of Prussian arms. The discipline and habits of mind that were assumed to govern German science and educational institutions had insured the winning margin over the frivolously imaginative French character.[14] For this impressionable young community of historians, the implementation of "scientific" history was to be their contribution to the reshaping of French character and the rebirth of the Fatherland. It would permit the discovery of the "real" historical sources of French national greatness and train Frenchmen in the analytic techniques of disinterested inquiry.

If the contradiction between "objective" and "nationalist" history went largely unchallenged in a country recovering from the humiliation of military defeat, the epistemological claims of scientific reconstruction of the past did not. From the 1880s on criticisms began to appear questioning the notion that the dating and construing of texts qualified as scientific history. These criticisms often included political overtones that challenged the self-satisfied centrist republican stance of the establishment historians from both left and right. An entire generation of monarchist and conservative writers objected to the implicit republicanism of mainstream history; leftist writers were equally concerned by what they took to be an untoward emphasis on the bourgeois accomplishments of the French and European past.

Émile Durkheim developed his criticism of academic history in lectures and writings during his early tenure as professor of social science at the University of Bordeaux. Academic history, he wrote, produced "vile and arbitrary classifications, vain erudition, useless and dead compilations."[15] He argued that reconstructions of past societies needed certain theoretical "idées directrices" which would serve to organize the chaos of facts into a structure from which general laws could be deduced. Durkheim was joined in this line of argument by the founder of a rival school of sociology, René Worms. Worms devoted a part of the opening essay of his new *Revue Internationale de Sociologie* to an attack on academic history and in following years his *Revue* featured numerous examples of the sort of sociological history he advocated.[16]

Another advocate of social science history, Paul Lacombe, wrote an important broadside in 1894, called *De L'Histoire considerée comme science,* wherein he drew the distinction between reconstructing historical reality and understanding it. He argued that only a bold conceptual approach which sought "general truths" about the evolution of social institutions would yield knowledge worth knowing about the past. The most systematic effort of this period to organize the social sciences into a unified program for historical inquiry was that of Henri Berr. His *Revue de Synthèse Historique* (1900) opened its pages to scholars from all disciplines who wished to explore the past from an interdisciplinary perspective. He encouraged both synthetic general history and the development and perfection of the "special" histories of economics, culture, and science. His thoroughly eclectic approach to social science history has been widely recognized as among the most important influences on modern, especially French, interdisciplinary history.[17]

Against this broad array of critics the apologists for the older scientific history could only object that this passion for theorizing would encourage irresponsible and unobjective speculations and threaten the solid work of thirty years of careful archival gleanings. However feeble this response might seem to us today, before 1914 the academic historians were in little danger of having their monopoly on the teaching and training of historians broken. Besides, in the aftermath of the Dreyfus Affair, many of the chief participants in this debate over scientific history found a common republican and Dreyfusard political ground for concerted action. This unity in great measure tempered the acrimony of the debate and encouraged a search for a methodological compromise.[18]

The terms of this political compromise could not effectively moderate the hostility of the "outsiders" on the right, whose objections to academic history were based to a great extent on its tendency to glorify the revolutionary events in the French past and underrate the achievements of the monarchy. In their efforts to undermine this historical apologetics, these historians found as much support in social science sources as did the earlier leftist-oriented group of critics we have already reviewed. It is well known that the theoretical origins of sociology in France arose from a conservative critique of the atomizing and destabilizing social effects of both political modernization (the French Revolution) and economic change.[19] It might thus be expected that late nineteenth century conservatives had a natural link with this supremely organic science. By the 1890s, however, the various branches of the French sociological tradition had either found a niche within the French university system or otherwise made their peace with the republican regime. Solidarism, a moderate republican philosophy of political unity and social peace, found its nourishment primarily in Durkheimian, Wormsian and LePlayan theory.[20] Critics of the republican regime, therefore, generally found their support elsewhere, chiefly in psychology and in the French clinical and medical tradition.

The orientation of this tradition in France was largely toward pathological and abnormal psychology; "experimental" psychology was accordingly often little more than systematic clinical observation and careful classification.[21] Collective and social psychology had deep roots in this tradition and retained a pathological bias throughout the century. This did not prevent early writers on the psychology of society, foremost among them Gabriel Tarde, from elaborating remarkably convincing explanations of complex social processes which rivaled sociological explanations in contemporary celebrity.[22] Conservative historians found the theoretical work of this tradition of individual and group psychology especially useful, particularly in demonstrating the "pathological" origins of modern institutions of which they disapproved. Many of the historical accounts published in this period were written by medical doctors and psychiatrists. Two of these doctors, Nass and Cabanès, published a regular periodical after 1894, *Le Chronique Medical,* devoted to the analysis of the mental problems of (usually) left-wing figures in French and European political history. Using the techniques of the clinic and the collective theory of LeBon and others, doctors and historians analyzed celebrated revolutionaries and identified the pathological sources of collective revolutionary behavior in French history.[23] Of course, the general interpretive outlook of these works was overwhelmingly unfriendly to the radical tradition, but the medical and social theories on which they were constructed were widely accepted by most contemporaries as accurate, even scientific, explanations of aberrant behavior. Thus Henri Berr, whose leadership in the field of interdisciplinary historical inquiry we have already noted, was convinced that collective psychology could "prove to be a precious auxiliary of collective ethnology."[24]

For all the theoretical discussion of these social science and medical methods in historical inquiry, little history was written before 1914 that actually drew upon them. Fustel de Coulanges and Charles Seignobos experimented with some social science techniques, but the best known practitioner in the genre was probably the prolific critic and historian Hippolyte Taine. By 1870 Taine had already acquainted himself with the French psychiatric tradition in his efforts to find methods for making the analysis of literature more scientific.[25] He was a liberal anti-democrat who despaired of the future of "natural" elites and social order in the Third Republic. In 1876 he undertook his ambitious history of the revolutionary period, *Les Origines de la France contemporaine,* in order to reveal the profound mental and moral disorder that accompanied modern experiments with democratic political institutions. In those volumes (1876-1893) Taine explained the fall of the old regime and the rise of the Jacobin dictatorship as a consequence of the spread of the analytic habits of mind of eighteenth century *philosophisme;* their corrosive effects "dissolved" the stabilizing institutions of the old regime and substituted for them abstract and impracticable visions of classical ideals. The effect of these developments on the normally conservative masses was at once uprooting and intoxicating, and Taine described their behavior in the language of the clinic as a ". . . cold or furious monomania, maddened in the destruction of a past it curses, and in the establishment of the millenium it pursues, and all in the name of an imaginary contract, at once anarchical and despotic, which unfetters insurrection and justifies dictatorship; all to end in a social antagonism, resembling now a bacchanalian orgy of madmen, and now a Spartan conventual group."[26]

Descriptions of this nature influenced LeBon and the other proponents of collective psychology in their own characterizations of mob and crowd behavior, but their influence on generations of conservative historians of the Revolution and on the literate public was perhaps even more significant.[27] Taine's political and intellectual influence was so feared by the republicans that the Sorbonne historian Alphonse Aulard wrote a book on Taine as an historian which stated that any doctoral candidate "would disqualify himself if he quoted Taine as an authority on any historical question."[28]

Taine's influence was great enough that all later

applications of the hostile and debunking language of mental pathology to the French Revolution and other popular upheavals owed their own popularity in part to the retrospective aura of his work. LeBon's history of the French Revolution may be placed squarely in the methodological and literary path blazed by Taine. The success of his own book may not be exclusively explained, therefore, by the coming of age of social science history or any special explanatory value it possessed, but to the general sorts of arguments he made and his use of the particular "scientific" and clinical terminology popularized by Taine and others. We can see these things if we turn now to his book.

It is clear from LeBon's text that he thought he was writing history of a sort different from that of those historians who "have generally stopped short at the study of documents . . ." His book was not "scientific" out of some refined exegetical method but because his history contained "applications of science" that allowed him to penetrate beyond mere printed sources "to read men and the motives of conduct."[29] The psychologist, he argued, by virtue of his training as a scientist is intrinsically an objective observer, while the historian, who must at some point be selective in his choice of documentation if he is to avoid writing shapeless chronicles, is tempted by his prejudices to choose self-fulfilling sources.[30]

In *The French Revolution* LeBon is also guilty of a form of self-justifying selection in his application of psychological analysis. He picks from the events of those years precisely those occurrences that may be best described by his theories of collective behavior. Of necessity these are the most dramatic episodes, and in

xxvi

particular the ones, such as the taking of the Bastille or the famous night of August 4 (when the nobles of the Assembly proclaimed the abolition of feudalism) when exaggerated behavior was the rule. LeBon explained these episodes by appealing to the "laws" of collective behavior. Thus, violent or bizarre episodes were a consequence of morbid "suggestions" or "mental contagion" spread by radical leaders, or the effect of crowd "mentalities" in which individuals behave differently than they do when isolated from crowds.[31] He uses these kinds of explanations repeatedly throughout the book, and at a level of generality that allows them to cover a wide variety of phenomena. The revolutionary clubs, the various legislative assemblies, armies, street crowds, and more general groups such as "Latins" or the "French" are protrayed in LeBon's book as acting under the influence of collective states of mind.

For the most violent episodes of the revolution LeBon reserves a supplementary explanation that opens a biological dimension and illustrates in general the vestiges in crowd theory of the body-mind identity that was still a working assumption of French mental pathology. In discussing the "criminal mentality" LeBon writes that:

> All the civilised societies inevitably drag behind them a residue of degenerates, of the unadapted, of persons affected by various taints. Vagabonds, beggars, fugitives from justice, thieves, assassins, and starving creatures that live from day to day, may constitute the criminal population of the great cities. In ordinary times these waste products of civilisation are more or less restrained

by the police. During revolution nothing restrains them, and they can easily gratify their insincts to murder and plunder.[32]

These "degenerates" were responsible for the September massacres, the killing of the Princess de Lamballe, and other bloody acts not easily explained even by the pathological categories of collective theory. Degeneracy was a process of retrograde biological evolution first popularized in French psychiatry by B. H. Morel in his *Traité des dégénéréscences* (1854). Initiated by alcoholism, vice, or genetic accident, this process caused a kind of moral anesthesia in the persons it afflicted, making them particularly vulnerable to violent or morbid stimuli and led them, it was generally believed, to engage in a wide range of anti-social behavior. Not surprisingly, it was held that these individuals concentrated in the poorer quarters of urban areas, and were thus readily available as cohorts for revolutionary activities.

LeBon also reserved some of the technical psychiatric terminology of his day for his descriptions of the most important radical leaders of the Revolution. He argued that under the influence of a strong new belief, the human personality can undergo a dramatic transformation and take entirely unexpected forms, some of these of a decidedly pathological sort. He cites the French psychopathologist Pierre Janet on this phenomenon of "multiple personality" (dissassociation), though in his own work Janet never presumed to uniformly characterize the origins of this process.[33] Robespierre suffered from a "persecution mania;" Fouquier-Tinville was a "very inferior mind" ('une âme très basse'); Billaud-Varenne,

xxviii

the "perfect type of bestial ferocity;" and Marat, a "semi-lunatic ('demi-aliéné') affected by megalomania ('délire des grandeurs') and haunted by fixed ideas."[34] These characterizations were drawn from the psychiatric nosologies of the day, but they are used by LeBon here so generally that they could scarcely be falsified, even if we miraculously possessed a detailed clinical record of these individual's behavior.

It is important to understand that for LeBon the individual and collective pathologies he discusses here are directly related. LeBon, and many other social scientists, men of affairs and politicians of his day, divided, even as we often do now, all kinds of social action into two groups: those regulated by reason and those regulated by instinct (or at least by unnamed processes operating beyond the aegis of reason). Thus, instances of individual and collective pathology were made to fall within a grand spectrum of threatening and disruptive activities which challenged the "rational" and "conscious" exercise of power that prevailed in normal times. As LeBon made abundantly clear, revolutionary episodes destabilized normal personalities and the accompanying collective behavior allowed the atavistic substructure of human character to assert itself.[35] Though the upper classes of society were by no means immune from the threat of this surge of instinct, LeBon generally portrayed the relative possession of reason as a function of class status. Thus, "From the moment when the Revolution descended from the middle to the lower classes of society, it ceased to be a domination of the instinctive by the rational, and became, on the contrary, the effort of the instinctive to overpower the rational."[36]

LeBon's account of the forces that worked to unleash the primitive passions of the masses in the French Revolution was an updating and distinct improvement, as he himself argued, over the theory used by Taine to explain those same processes. It was Taine's belief that the popular violence of the Revolution was a consequence of the spread of Enlightenment rationalism, a kind of lunatic intensification of the utopian allure of eighteenth century political and moral abstractions. Taine argued that this undue regard for the dogmatic conclusions of deductive reasoning swept through the ranks of the Jacobins and other radicals and from there to the broad masses of the people. LeBon quotes Taine at length on this point,[37] but criticizes his account of this rationalist "fever" by adding: "So that although the Jacobin is a great reasoner, this does not mean that he is in the least guided by reason. When he imagines he is being led by reason it is really his passions and his mysticism that lead him."[38] Here and elsewhere LeBon presses the argument, in contradistinction to Taine's more complicated one, that reason was seldom an influence in the motivations of leaders or crowds in the Revolution; their behavior was thus exactly what it appeared to be: irrational, exaggerated, passionate. LeBon's more simple characterization allowed him to escape the absolute hegemony of the anti-revolutionary generation of Edmund Burke and Joseph De Maistre. In their defense of monarchy and tradition, these early reactionaries had to demonstrate the fallacies of the Enlightenment ideas they assumed had weakened the old regime and yet show how these false ideas had nonetheless managed to produce concrete transformations in French life and institutions. The intellectual procedures they had used to formulate these ideas—complete with snippets of romanticism and revelatory Catholicism—washed in their own age, but were wearing thin by the late nineteenth century. LeBon's new formula dressed up the old message in the fashion of the Belle Époque.

With this discussion of Taine it is perhaps time to turn to the third vector within which this book must be located. By the late nineteenth century, the subject of the French Revolution was the most written about event in French history. Popular versions of the revolution abounded, but the "serious" histories were also widely read and sold well. Some of these, put forth by Michelet, Taine, Thiers on the Consulat and Empire, were also distinguished literary efforts and models of French prose for their time. The new "scientific" historians made the study of the French Revolution a province of especial concern, and by the 1880s Alphonse Aulard and others were publishing volume after volume of a monumental documentary "history" of the period. As patriotic republicans these first generations of "scientific" historians were convinced that their archival labors would reveal the wide base of support that existed for institutional change in France in 1789, and in general would minimize the standard right-wing conception of the revolution as a conspiratorial terror directed against monarchy and church. These writers invariably saw all the great benefits of modern enlightenment and progress as originating in the revolutionary years, and explained all the backwardness or ignorance in contemporary France as vestigial aspects of those pre-

Revolutionary institutions that had not been utterly transformed from 1789-1815.

These views did not go unchallenged by conservative historians who were anxious to defend the heritage of the old regime. Taine, Albert Sorel, Albert Vandal, Franz Funck-Brentano, Louis Madelin, and Augustin Cochin wrote books about the revolutionary period that either doubted the universally good effects of the French Revolution or managed to show how certain aspects of traditional society were left untouched by the upheaval. In turn, they explained that these traditional elements provided the small measure of stability present in modern French life.[39] These writers were at a distinct disadvantage in the struggle for influence with the Sorbonne's historical mandarinat. They did not have access to the influence network of teaching positions, scholarly journals, or the selection of "official" textbooks in the public schools. Few of them had been trained in the seminars in which the methods of "scientific" history were taught, and they were systematically reviled as "amateurs" by the spokesmen for the historical establishment. The books of this group were nonetheless very popular with the public. They were generally written in a livelier and less scholarly style, and were unencumbered by the documentary scrupulosity that marked the books of the "scientific" historians. But perhaps the best explanation for the appeal of these turn-of-the-century texts lies in the mode of dramatic emplotment that was invariably built into their narrative structures.

Hayden White has argued that in their narrative accounts historians tend to organize the events of their texts into figurative discourses that take the shape of "culturally provided categories, such as metaphysical concepts, religious beliefs, or story-forms. The effect of such encodations is to familiarize the unfamiliar, and in general this is the way of historiography, whose 'data' are always immediately strange, not to say exotic, simply by virtue of their distance from us in time and their origination in a way of life different from our own."[40] The dramatic mode favored by the conservative was that of tragedy: the fall of the monarchy and the ruin of old France. Without carrying White's argument about the nature of historical narrative any further, there is no denying the appeal of this conservative history on a strictly dramatic and literary level. What is more, the emplotment of the Revolution in a tragic mode had an old and deeply respected history. Men of enormous reputation, the greatest nineteenth century writers on the revolution— De Maistre, Tocqueville, Taine—had cast their histories in this mode. A history of the French Revolution as tragedy was insured a kind of instant literary recognition and a core of loyal readers. LeBon's book, of course, is written in this mode, but, owing to its clinical and social science discourse, *The French Revolution and the Psychology of Revolution* had an appeal that was qualitatively broader than the purely literary efforts of other conservatives.

But what specific evidence did LeBon present in his book that sharpened or strengthened the claims of other conservative historians or which simply enhanced the explanatory force of their general arguments? The conservative historians of LeBon's generation generally stressed the conspiratorial nature of the revolution, and emphasized the decisive role

xxxiii

played by radical leaderships in the assemblies, clubs and the press in provoking popular upheavals.[41] This bias was in part a reaction to idealized portraits of the Revolutionary masses composed by Michelet and, in LeBon's day, Aulard. In Aulard's more friendly version of the revolution, leaders were created by the people themselves, corporeal archetypes of popular visions and ideals. LeBon's role in this conflict of interpretation was to explain how a determined leadership could turn the people in this or that direction, even against the counsels of reason and self-interest. He portrayed the revolutionary leadership employing the various techniques of manipulation available in the grab-bag of crowd psychology: suggestion, repetition, affirmation and appeal to the "mystic" and "religious" logic that dominated the crowd mind. These techniques were adjusted in ways appropriate to the nature of certain audiences, whether newspaper public, political club, parliamentary assembly or street mob.[42]

LeBon's "scientific" explanations of the preponderant role of leadership added an undeniable dimension of appeal to the conservative's argument that the monarchy did not fail because of its own weaknesses so much as through the persistent efforts of a fanatical conspiratorial minority. None of the pre-World War I conservative historians really tried to systematically show how this conspiracy managed to effectively envelop the entire nation, other than to suggest, by extension, that the same fanatical leaders controlled opinion in the countryside through the network of Jacobin clubs and other radical groups. We are still some years from the sort of subtle and situational portrait of rural upheaval one finds in Georges

Lefebvre's *La Grande Peur de 1789*. Nonetheless, LeBon's leader-crowd model did seem to explain events in Paris fairly well. But it is especially in his treatment of the careers of the great parliamentary assemblies of the revolutionary decade that LeBon's explanations added depth to the conservative interpretation; as general political history they have a certain appeal even today.

"The power of a political assembly resides, above all, in the weakness of its adversaries."[43] This dictum, combined with common sense and the notion of parliamentary crowds as "feminine" organisms, allowed LeBon to succinctly characterize the relations of the various executives of the decade (the King, the Committee of Public Safety, the Directory, and the Consulate) with their respective assemblies. The formula *strong executive equals weak assembly,* in not specifying any causal priority, *does* appear to describe executive-legislative relations from 1788-1800. Through threats, which surrounded parliamentarians with an aura of collective fear, or the more subtle blandishments of exhortation, some of the leaders of the period achieved remarkable influence. This LeBon chronicles in some detail.[44]

To modern readers there is one aspect of LeBon's book that, apart from the clinical terminology, appears particularly anachronistic: his conviction that ideas were the great motivating force of the French Revolution. In expressing this belief, however, LeBon was not merely showing his conservative affiliations. Nearly all writers on the revolution in those times would have agreed, the difference between them being their respective attitudes to the ideas.[45] As for the ideas themselves, they were always the same: liberty, equality, fraternity, and the panoply of concepts associated with democratic government and the sovereignty of the people. It was LeBon's task to show how these ideas intrinsically brutalized or deluded the people, just as it was Aulard's task to show how they uplifted and ennobled them. But one cannot disdain the ideas of democratic political sovereignty without having some strong objections to the practice of democracy itself. This is where we must consider, as the last vector of influence, the effect of LeBon's own age on his work.

As a "scientific" historian whose work yielded general laws, LeBon felt free to comment on other times and other places where these laws presumably applied. The examples he chose as special cases of his general laws run from ancient Greece to his own age, but he is most obviously concerned with France in the first decade of the twentieth century. LeBon is at pains to reveal the dire effects of the revolutionary heritage and he subjects the new "Jacobins" to the same withering denunciations he applied to their eighteenth century predecessors. *The French Revolution* is no different in this respect from nearly all of LeBon's previous (and future) books. Each of them enlisted some general principles based on psychological laws in a frontal assault on the political leadership and radical ideologies of his day.[46]

Near the conclusion of the Dreyfus Affair in France a new coalition of republican politicians, inclined toward progressive views in social and economic matters, replaced a more conservative republican *bloc* as the dominant political force in the nation. With the ascension of this coalition of centrists, radicals, and radical socialists, the main issues that had divided the older parties of movement and order—education, church-state relations, monarchy or republic—were more or less brought to a resolution. After 1900 politicians on the left and right of the large pragmatic center divided along the more "modern" lines of socialism vs. private property, capital vs. labor, and anti-militarism vs. nationalism. These new divisions reflected the growing strength of working class electoral organizations and the advances of militant labor. The *Confédération générale du travail,* formed in 1896, coordinated a host of loosely affiliated syndicalist (union) organizations which engaged to an increasing degree in direct action movements. These militant labor groups professed a contempt for parliamentary politics and their leaders showed a growing interest in the tenets of revolutionary syndicalism and its ultimate threat of the general strike. At the same time, however, the various splinter socialist groups in the Chamber of Deputies were enjoying a period of growing working-class support, which belied to some extent the claims of proletarian apoliticality made on the part of the militant syndicalist leadership. These groups coalesced in 1905 into the S.F.I.O. parliamentary union led by the peerless speaker and socialist publicist, Jean Jaurès. The first socialist, the moderate Alexandre Millerand, found a place in the Waldeck-Rousseau cabinet of 1899, and from 1906, radical cabinets regularly proposed a progressive tax on incomes and other social insurance schemes designed for the workers and the poor.

For many Frenchmen, whether long-time opponents of political democracy like LeBon, or

simply property owners concerned about their carefully accumulated patrimonies, these developments
portended a grim future. As we have already seen, most
educated Frenchmen were haunted by the ghost of
battles past; it was only natural that many would find
in the revolutionary history of the nation some analogies with contemporary events. Jacobinism could be
made to seem a by-word for a kind of intensification of
political democracy that was not in itself socialist, but
which certainly lay the foundations for an extension of
*égalité* in the name of democratization. The new
coalition of radical republicans was cast in the role of a
Jacobin dictatorship pandering to an envious and
sinister combination of working men and urban scum.
In the concluding sections of his book, LeBon identi-
fies the new Jacobins and their enemies. There are first
the rationalist "intellectuals" of the academic establishment who shape the educational values of the nation in
their own image. These mandarins are allied with
another elite, the radical and socialist political leaders,
who draw upon rationalist concepts in formulating
their ideologies of progress and democracy, but who
proselytize their ideas by demagogic appeal to the
lowest common denominator of hatred and envy.[47]
These elites, who LeBon imagines to be out of touch
with the "real" France, maintain their position through
their domination of the state bureaucracy, a structure
the Jacobins originally created, of course, to enforce
the Terror.

By the end of the first century of the decade, intellectuals of both the syndicalist left and the anti-democratic right were in agreement on the central shortcomings
of the parliamentary regime.[48] These intellectuals were

on the whole convinced that power could be wrested from the "Jacobins" only through an open competition for mass allegiance in the political marketplace. Implicit in this conviction was a deep faith in the ability of "natural" elites to rouse the masses to appropriate action. For the syndicalist intellectuals the elite was the grassroots labor leadership;[49] the favored model varied on the right from traditional aristocracy and rural notables to LeBon's pseudo-Comtian industrial-scientific elite. LeBon believed inequality to be in the "nature" of things,[50] and, as he ominously warned in the section of his book on Bonaparte, great leaders have a tendency to assume control of events just when anarchy is at high tide.[51]

Around 1900, most of the right, and even, in time, the syndicalists, came to believe in the unifying power of nationalism and in the possibility of achieving their long run objectives under a nationalist banner. LeBon had advocated a national revival in his earlier writings, and by 1912 his dream of patriotic renascence was on the point of becoming a reality.[52] In his *The French Revolution* he made an effort to separate the nationalist ideal from Jacobinism *per se* and to credit nationalism as the inspirational source for the great military achievements of the Revolution. "The multitude," he wrote, "must be shown the road to follow; it is not for them to choose it."[53] That road, followed by a growing proportion of the political class after 1912, led to chauvinism, jingoism, and, finally, war.

The effect of the political context on LeBon's social science cannot be assessed with great precision; yet it seems clear enough that through his career LeBon chose as subjects for his books things that were *problems* for his contemporaries. This is certainly so for *The French Revolution,* which treats the whole issue of the revolution and its heritage as a contemporary political issue. But, as Maurice Mandelbaum has recently argued, the presence of subjective orientations in the author of an historical work cannot therefore lead us to conclude that the work itself is unobjective. The objective status of the work must be addressed separately.[54] We will conclude this introduction with a brief discussion of the contributions LeBon has made to the two principal subjects of his book: the French Revolution and the psychological elements in revolutions.

It cannot be said that LeBon has a secure place in the historiography of the French Revolution. Indeed, most of the French academic history of the Revolution written since World War I has been dominated by the leftists Albert Mathiez, Georges Lefebvre, and Albert Soboul, who have succeeded one another in Aulard's chair at the Sorbonne. These and other historians have pushed the study of collective behavior in the period of the French Revolution to remarkable lengths. Moreover, the Jacobin episode as a whole has received very close and detailed attention by French and other scholars since LeBon's day. The actions of radical leaders and their followers, when viewed in their social, economic, and political settings, no longer appear "irrational" or "pathological" as they did in LeBon's accounts. By reconstructing the immediate context of collective behavior or political extremism, and by examining the social origins and goals of the participants rather than the toll in lives and property of their actions, historians have been able to sensibly explain violent episodes that could previously be explained only by appeal to some "inherent flaw" theory such as LeBon's.

But in revising the concepts of collective behavior LeBon introduced to revolutionary history, these historians have nevertheless taken LeBon and his theory as a starting point. In his 1934 article on revolutionary crowds Georges Lefebvre took exception to LeBon's account at several points: his non-situational and abstract treatment of collective phenomena, his assumption that the process was unconscious and irrational, and the assumption that the collective mentality was somehow bestial or primitive.[55] This did not, however, prevent Lefebvre from finding much of great utility in crowd theory. "Collective mentality," for instance, was a most useful concept for explaining certain manifestations of group solidarity. LeBon's notion of "mental contagion," when studied as a process of "conversion" of individuals, did service as an explanation of the spread of panics. Yet, Lefebvre found he could not do without the terms "suggestion" or "auto-suggestion" in his book on the rural panics of 1789, a fact that indicates the extent of the dominance that clinical language still exercises in this field.[56] Another opponent of LeBon's crowd theory, George Rudé, agrees substantially with Lefebvre's general criticism of LeBon,[57] but he also finds "collective mentality" and the panic-fear syndrome employed by Lefebvre to be useful. He concedes that "leaders" are undoubtedly an important element in collective violence, though he holds they do not play the controlling role assigned to them by Taine and LeBon.

Moreover, in the recent work of Richard Cobb it

might be said that a greater willingness to consider the latent brutality of popular manifestations is reasserting itself:

> Certainly, too, what is so often clothed over and 'historicized' as something called the 'popular movement' . . . was frequently cruel and cowardly, base and vengeful, barbaric and not at all pretty to watch. Professor Rudé's Crowd is somehow altogether too respectable; one hesitates to credit all these worthy shopkeepers and all these honest apprentices, family men too, with such horrors, and, in identifying the assailants, one is in danger of leaving the assailed out of the picture.[58]

In Cobb's new "realism" there is a willingness to reconsider the sanguinary behavior of the radicals in the reign of terror as a consequence of both circumstance and "temperament," though not as an instance of the general laws of collective behavior as was the case with LeBon.[59] The collective "mentality" that shaped the Jacobin outlook has even been characterized recently by Marc Bouloiseau, a student of Mathiez and Lefebvre, as "at base a mystique" of "a religious character" comprised of "an ensemble of images and concepts, a structure of persuasion, an impassioned dynamic, because it intends to convince and convert."[60] We are certainly closer here to some appreciation of the emotional and non-rational components of the Terror than has often been the case in post-World War I historiography. It is of especial interest that the question of emotion vs. reason is no longer politicized as it once was inasmuch as Cobb and Bouloiseau fall somewhere within the orbit of the left.

On the more general problem of the psychological elements in revolutions, the recent literature is too vast to survey here. There seem to be two general areas where LeBon's influence has been recognized as important to later developments. One of these, recently discussed by Isaac Kramnick, is that of the classification of the group psychology of revolutionary movements.[61] Though critical of his work in this area, later commentators have nonetheless used his various works on collective behavior as points of departure.[62] Hagopian appears to agree with Kramnick in believing *The French Revolution and the Psychology of Revolutions* to be an advance on *The Crowd* in its more concrete appreciation of the immediate context of revolutionary episodes and more precise identification of their participants.[63] Following LeBon's lead in a more popular vein, the well-known work of Eric Hoffer, especially *The True Believer,* offers a series of "proofs" of the instability and irrationality of revolutionary movements.

The other major strand of LeBon's influence on theories of revolution seems to lie in the general area of the role of leadership. In this connection the point ought to be made that the English translator of LeBon's book inexplicably chose to translate the French word "élite," which LeBon uses several times in the text, in the English as "elect," thereby giving the impression that leaders are somehow born to the roles they come to fill. Attracted as he was to biological explanation, LeBon nonetheless portrayed the triumphs of leaders as mediated by social situation, which might, as in the case of the French Revolution, produce leaders of a decidely brilliant though morbid

xliii

type. To some extent, then, the problem of revolution was a problem of leadership or competing leaders, the masses being, in any event, the passive tools of elite manipulation. This view has been perpetuated in various forms to the present day, and owes a good deal to the way leader-crowd relations were originally formulated by the early theorists of collective behavior.

Interested as they were in the mechanisms of political leadership, the political sociologists Pareto, Mosca, and Michels relied heavily on these theories of collective behavior.[64] In his *Systèmes Socialistes* (1902), a predecessor of his *Trattato generale di sociologia,* Pareto characterized political power as a struggle between conservative and progressive elites, the latter having a certain advantage in their closer familiarity with the ideas and passions of the masses.[65] This general way of viewing revolutions and social upheaval has had a notable history since the classic works of Pareto, Mosca, and Michels appeared. It has figured in the work of theorists of mass society[66] and is still popular as an historical explanation of the rise of totalitarian dictatorships between the wars.[67]

In this country Harold Lasswell has been the most important social scientist to continue the elite-mass dichotomy in the analysis of revolutionary movements. He concluded his book on propaganda in World War I with the warning: "It is an atomized world, in which individual whims have wider play than ever before, and it requires more strenuous exertion to co-ordinate and unify than formerly. The new antidote to willfulness is propaganda. If the mass will be free of chains of iron, it must accept its chains of silver. If it will not love, honour, and obey, it must not expect to escape seduction."[68] In later works Lasswell explored other components of psychology and power, but in his post World War II writings he has not strayed far from his central proposition that the key to the understanding of both revolutionary and counter-revolutionary movements is the role of elites.[69]

Such a brief review of developments in theories of revolution influenced by nineteenth century theories of collective behavior cannot possibly do justice to the richness of work in this general field. It should suggest, however, the fruitfulness of the social science tradition LeBon helped to found. If the empirical value of LeBon's work has been universally criticized, some of the general propositions that guided his work, and the generally anti-democratic bias in his outlook have been incorporated into later works of social science and history. No doubt the exact influences that worked on LeBon in his own time are not identical to the ones that work on us. In reading his work we are free to accept or reject his assertions in a way he was not. But it may be, as this essay has tried to point out, that whatever else we imagine it to be, our grounds for the selection and popularization of social science theory are more complex in nature than can be exhausted in some strictly empirical verification, even supposing the rules for verification could be universally agreed upon by social scientists. We still read LeBon's texts, and those of other pioneers in social science, because they provoke in us, on many levels, a resonance like the one that insured their original success.

# NOTES

[1] See Terry N. Clark, *Prophets and Patrons: The French University and the Emergence of the Social Sciences* (Cambridge, Mass.: Harvard University Press, 1973), pp. 66-94, 162-98.

[2] Robert Alun Jones, "On Understanding a Sociological Classic," *American Journal of Sociology, 83* (1977), p. 291.

[3] Ibid., p. 311.

[4] See Alvin Gouldner, "Metaphysical Pathos and the Theory of Bureaucracy," *American Political Science Review, 49* (1955), pp. 496-507; and "Romanticism and Classicism: Deep Structures in Social Science," *Diogenes, 82* (1973), pp. 88-107.

[5] Quentin Skinner, "Meaning and Understanding in the History of Ideas," *History and Theory, 8* (1969), pp. 3-53.

[6] Gustave LeBon, *La Civilisation des Arabes* (Paris: Firmin-Didot, 1883); *La Civilisation de l'Inde* (Paris: Firmin-Didot, 1886); *Les Premières Civilisations* (Paris: Marpan et Flammarion, 1889).

[7] Robert A. Nye, *The Origins of Crowd Psychology. Gustave LeBon and the Crisis of Mass Democracy in the Third Republic* (London and Beverly Hills: Sage Publications, 1975), pp. 39-58.

[8] Ibid., pp. 59-81.

[9] Gustave LeBon, *La Psychologie des foules* (Paris: Alcan, 1895), pp. 136-7; Scipio Sighele, *Psychologie des sectes* (Paris: Giard et Briere, 1898), p. 201; Gabriel Tarde, *L'Opinion et la foule* (Paris: Alcan, 1901).

[10] Henri Ellenberger, *The Discovery of the Unconscious. The History and Evolution of Dynamic Psychiatry* (New York: Basic Books, 1970), pp. 254-84.

[11] William R. Keylor, *Academy and Community. The Foundation of the French Historical Profession* (Cambridge, Mass.: Harvard University Press, 1975), pp. 64-8.

[12] The Centenary issue of the *Revue Historique* recently published retrospective articles dealing directly with these issues: Charles-Olivier Carbonelle, "La Naissance de la *Revue Historique*. Une revue de combat," *Revue Historique, 518* (1976), pp. 331-52; Alice Gérard, "Histoire et Politique. *La Revue Historique* face à l'histoire contemporaine (1885-1898)," *Revue Historique, 518* (1976), 353-406.

[13] Keylor, *Academy and Community*, p. 37.

[14] See Claude Digeon, *La Crise allemande du pensée française* (Paris: Presses Universitaires de France, 1959), pp. 155-254; André Bellesort, *Les Intellectuels et l'avènement de la troisième République #1871-1875)* (Paris: Grassett, 1931).

[15] Keylor, *Academy and Community*, p. 113.

[16] On Worms and his sociological "cluster," see Clark, *Prophets and Patrons*, pp. 147-61.

[17] On Berr and the *Revue de Synthèse*, see Keylor, *Academy and Community*, pp. 125-40; Martin Siegel, "Henri Berr's *Revue de Synthèse Historique*," *History and Theory, 9* (1970), pp. 322-34; also the relevant sections in Georg Iggers, *New Directions in European Historiography* (Middletown, Conn.: Wesleyan University Press, 1975); and Traian Stoianovich, *French Historical Method: The Annales Paradigm* (Ithaca, New York: Cornell University Press, 1976).

[18] Keylor, *Academy and Community*, pp. 163-207.

[19] Robert A. Nisbet, "The French Revolution and the Rise of Sociology," *American Journal of Sociology, 18* (1943), pp. 156-64; "Conservatism and Sociology," *American Journal of Sociology, 49* (1952), pp. 167-75; Leon Bramson, *The Political Context of Sociology* (Princeton, N.J.: Princeton University Press, 1961).

[20] Theodore Zeldin, *France 1848-1945*. Vol. I (Oxford: Clarendon Press, 1973), pp. 640-82.

[21] Gardner Murphy, *Historical Introduction to Modern Psychology,* rev. ed. (New York: Harcourt, Brace, 1949), pp. 127-36; Ellenberger, *The Discovery of the Unconscious*, pp. 331-417; Henri Baruk, *La Psychiatrie française de Pinel à nos jours* (Paris: Presses Universitaires de France, 1967).

[22] Terry N. Clark, "Introduction," *Gabriel Tarde. On Communication and Social Influence* (Chicago: University of Chicago Press, 1969), pp. 1-72; Nye, *The Origins of Crowd Psychology*, pp. 59-121.

[23] Dr. Lucien Nass and Dr. Cabanès, *La Névrose révolutionnaire* (Paris, 1906) and *Névroses de l'histoire* (Paris, 1908); Raymond Clauzel, *Les Fanatiques: Maximilien Robespierre* (Paris, 1912); Lucien Nass, *Le Siège de Paris et la Commune. Essais de pathologie historique* (Paris, 1914); Dr. Alexandre Cullerre, "Les Psychoses dans l'histoire," *Archives de Neurologie,* April 1912, 225-49; June 1912, 359-71; July 1912, 23-36; August 1912, 89-110; September 1912, 162-77; October 1912, 211-24.

[24] Henri Berr, *La Synthèse en histoire* (Paris, 1911), pp. 106-107.

[25] Taine's psychological masterpiece was *De L'Intelligence* (Paris, 1870).

[26] Hippolyte Taine, *The Ancient Regime*, Vol. I, trans. John Durand, rev. ed. (New York: Henry Holt, 1891), p. 251. A fine introduction to these volumes may be found in Edward T. Gargan's introduction to Taine's *The Origins of Contemporary France* (Chicago: University of Chicago Press, 1974), pp. xi-xlv.

xlvii

[27] Alfred Cobban, *Aspects of the French Revolution* (New York: Braziller, 1968), p. 44.

[28] Quoted in ibid., p. 18.

[92] LeBon, *The French Revolution and the Psychology of Revolution* (1913 ed., trans. Bernard Miall), pp. 12-3.

[30] Ibid., pp. 134-5.

[31] Ibid., pp. 102-12, 118, 172-5, 187-8, 218-31.

[32] Ibid., p. 99.

[33] Ibid., p. 77.

[34] Ibid., pp. 241-51.

[35] Ibid., pp. 28-9, 60-3.

[36] Ibid., pp. 65-6. See also p. 101.

[37] Ibid., pp. 93-4.

[38] Ibid., p. 95.

[39] Especially important are Franz Funck-Brentano, *L'Ancienne France, Le Roi,* 2nd ed. (Paris: Hachette, 1912); Louis Madelin, *La Révolution* (Paris: Hachette, 1911); Albert Sorel, *L'Europe et la révolution française,* 9 vols. (Paris: Plon, 1885-1911); Albert Vandal, *L'Avènement de Bonaparte,* 2 vols. (Paris: Plon, 1902-1907); Augustin Cochin, *Les Sociétés de pensée et la démocratie. Études d'histoire révolutionnaire,* rev. ed. (Paris, 1921); *La Crise de l'histoire révolutionnaire. Taine et M. Aulard,* 2nd ed. (Paris, 1909).

[40] Hayden White, "The Historical Text as Literary Artifact," *Clio, 3* (1974), p. 283.

[41] This is especially true of the works of Hippolyte Taine, Cochin and Louis Madelin.

[42] LeBon, *The French Revolution,* p. 49, 65, 68-70, 85-6, 109-20, 124.

[43] *Ibid.,* p. 172.

[44] *Ibid.,* pp. 166-212.

[45] Cobban, *Aspects of the French Revolution,* p. 18.

[46] Nye, *The Origins of Crowd Psychology,* pp. 83-122.

[47] LeBon, *The French Revolution,* pp. 293-312.

[48] Robert A. Nye, "Two Paths to a Psychology of Social Action: Gustave LeBon and Georges Sorel," *The Journal of Modern History, 45* (1973), pp. 411-438; Irving Louis Horowitz, *Radicalism and the Revolt Against Reason* (New York: Humanities Press, 1961); Michael Curtis, *Three Against the Third Republic: Sorel, Barrès and Maurras* (Princeton, N.J.: Princeton University Press, 1959).

[49] On the syndicalist left, see F.F. Ridley, *Revolutionary syndicalism in France* (Cambridge: Cambridge University Press, 1973).

[50] The capitalization is LeBon's. *The French Revolution,* p. 297.

[51] *Ibid.,* pp. 265-74.

[52] On the national revival see Eugen Weber, *The Nationalist Revival in France, 1905-1914* (Berkeley, Calif.: The University of California Press, 1959).

[53] LeBon, *The French Revolution,* p. 231.

[54] On this issue see Maurice Mandelbaum, *The Anatomy of Historical Knowledge* (Baltimore: Johns Hopkins University Press, 1977).

[55] Georges Lefebvre, "Les Foules Révolutionnaires," *Les Annales Historiques de la Révolution Française, 11* (1934), pp. 1-26.

[56] Georges Lefebvre, *The Great Fear of 1789. Rural Panic in Revolutionary France,* trans. Joan White (New York: Random House, 1973), pp. 50, 168.

[57] George Rudé's *The Crowd in History: A Study of Popular Disturbances in France and England 1730-1848* (New York: Wiley, 1964), p. 9.

[58] Richard Cobb, "The Revolutionary Mentality in France, 1793-1794," *History, 42* (1957), pp. 181-96; "Quelques aspects de la mentalité révolutionnaire," *Revue d'Histoire Moderne et Contemporaine, 6* (1959), pp. 86-120; *Reactions to the French Revolution* (London: Oxford University Press, 1972), pp. 107-27.

[60] Marc Bouloiseau, *La République jacobine, 10 août 1792 - 9 thermidor an II* (Paris: Editions du Seuil, 1972), p. 38.

[61] Isaac Kramnick, "Reflections on Revolution: Definition and Explanation in Recent Scholarship," *History and Theory, 11* (1972), p. 53.

[62] The most important of these are Roger W. Brown, "Mass Phenomena," Handbook of Social Psychology, Vol. II, ed. Gardner Lindzey (Cambridge, Mass.: Addison-Wesley, 1956), p. 841; Stanley Milgrim and Hans Toch, "Collective Behavior: Crowds and Social Movements," in *The Handbook of Social Psychology,* 2nd ed., eds. Gardner Lindzey and Elliot Aronson (Reading, Mass.: Addison-Wesley, 1969), pp. 507-610; Kurt and Gladys Lang, *Collective Dynamics* (New York: Crowell, 1961).

[63] Mark N. Hagopian, *The Phenomenon of Revolution* (New York: Dodd, Mead, 1974), pp. 308-10.

[64] See Robert A. Nye, *The Anti-Democratic Sources of Elite Theory. Pareto, Mosca, Michels* (London and Beverly Hills: Sage Publications, 1977).

[65] Ibid., pp. 23-5.

[66] For example, James Burnham, *The Machiavellians. Defenders of Freedom* (New York: John Day, 1943); William Kornhauser, *The Politics of Mass Society* (New York: Free Press, 1959); Emil Lederer, *The State of the Masses* (New York: Norton, 1940).

[67] Nye, *The Anti-Democratic Sources of Elite Theory,* pp. 31-47.

xlix

[68] Harold D. Lasswell, *Propaganda Technique in the World War* (New York: Knopf, 1927), p. 222.

[69] Harold Lasswell and Daniel Lerner, *The Comparative Study of Elites* (Stanford: Hoover Institute, 1952); *World Revolutionary Elites* (Cambridge, Mass.: M.I.T. Press, 1965). See also Arnold A. Rogow, ed. *Politics, Personality, and Social Science in the Twentieth Century. Essays in Honor of Harold D. Lasswell* (Chicago and London: University of Chicago Press, 1969).

1

# CONTENTS

5

# Contents

# Contents

7

# Contents

# Contents

## PART III

## *THE RECENT EVOLUTION OF THE REVOLUTIONARY PRINCIPLES*

9

# The
# Psychology of Revolution

## INTRODUCTION

### THE REVISION OF HISTORY

THE present age is not merely an epoch of discovery; it is also a period of revision of the various elements of knowledge. Having recognised that there are no phenomena of which the first cause is still accessible, science has resumed the examination of her ancient certitudes, and has proved their fragility. To-day she sees her ancient principles vanishing one by one. Mechanics is losing its axioms, and matter, formerly the eternal substratum of the worlds, becomes a simple aggregate of ephemeral forces in transitory condensation.

Despite its conjectural side, by virtue of whicn it to some extent escapes the severest form of criticism, history has not been free from this universal revision. There is no longer a single one of its phases of which we can say that it is certainly known. What appeared to be definitely acquired is now once more put in question.

Among the events whose study seemed completed was the French Revolution. Analysed by several generations of writers, one might suppose it to be

# The Psychology of Revolution

perfectly elucidated. What new thing can be said of it, except in modification of some of its details?

And yet its most positive defenders are beginning to hesitate in their judgments. Ancient evidence proves to be far from impeccable. The faith in dogmas once held sacred is shaken. The latest literature of the Revolution betrays these uncertainties. Having related, men are more and more chary of drawing conclusions.

Not only are the heroes of this great drama discussed without indulgence, but thinkers are asking whether the new dispensation which followed the *ancien régime* would not have established itself naturally, without violence, in the course of progressive civilisation. The results obtained no longer seem in correspondence either with their immediate cost or with the remoter consequences which the Revolution evoked from the possibilities of history.

Several causes have led to the revision of this tragic period. Time has calmed passions, numerous documents have gradually emerged from the archives, and the historian is learning to interpret them independently.

But it is perhaps modern psychology that has most effectually influenced our ideas, by enabling us more surely to read men and the motives of their conduct.

Among those of its discoveries which are henceforth applicable to history we must mention, above all, a more profound understanding of ancestral influences, the laws which rule the actions of the crowd, data relating to the disaggregation of personality, mental contagion, the unconscious formation of beliefs, and the distinction between the various forms of logic.

# Introduction

To tell the truth, these applications of science, which are utilised in this book, have not been so utilised hitherto. Historians have generally stopped short at the study of documents, and even that study is sufficient to excite the doubts of which I have spoken.

The great events which shape the destinies of peoples—revolutions, for example, and the outbreak of religious beliefs—are sometimes so difficult to explain that one must limit oneself to a mere statement.

From the time of my first historical researches I have been struck by the impenetrable aspect of certain essential phenomena, those relating to the genesis of beliefs especially; I felt convinced that something fundamental was lacking that was essential to their interpretation. Reason having said all it could say, nothing more could be expected of it, and other means must be sought of comprehending what had not been elucidated.

For a long time these important questions remained obscure to me. Extended travel, devoted to the study of the remnants of vanished civilisations, had not done much to throw light upon them.

Reflecting upon it continually, I was forced to recognise that the problem was composed of a series of other problems, which I should have to study separately. This I did for a period of twenty years, presenting the results of my researches in a succession of volumes.

One of the first was devoted to the study of the psychological laws of the evolution of peoples. Having

13

# The Psychology of Revolution

shown that the historic races—that is, the races formed by the hazards of history—finally acquired psychological characteristics as stable as their anatomical characteristics, I attempted to explain how a people transforms its institutions, its languages, and its arts. I explained in the same work why it was that individual personalities, under the influence of sudden variations of environment, might be entirely disaggregated.

But besides the fixed collectivities formed by the peoples, there are mobile and transitory collectivities known as crowds. Now these crowds or mobs, by the aid of which the great movements of history are accomplished, have characteristics absolutely different from those of the individuals who compose them. What are these characteristics, and how are they evolved? This new problem was examined in *The Psychology of the Crowd*.

Only after these studies did I begin to perceive certain influences which had escaped me.

But this was not all. Among the most important factors of history one was preponderant—the factor of beliefs. How are these beliefs born, and are they really rational and voluntary, as was long taught? Are they not rather unconscious and independent of all reason? A difficult question, which I dealt with in my last book, *Opinions and Beliefs*.

So long as psychology regards beliefs as voluntary and rational they will remain inexplicable. Having proved that they are usually irrational and always involuntary, I was able to propound the solution of this important problem; how it was that beliefs which no reason could justify were admitted without difficulty by the most enlightened spirits of all ages.

The solution of the historical difficulties which had so long been sought was thenceforth obvious. I arrived at the conclusion that beside the rational logic which conditions thought, and was formerly regarded as our sole guide, there exist very different forms of logic : affective logic, collective logic, and mystic logic, which usually overrule the reason and engender the generative impulses of our conduct.

This fact well established, it seemed to me evident that if a great number of historical events are often uncomprehended, it is because we seek to interpret them in the light of a logic which in reality has very little influence upon their genesis.

All these researches, which are here summed up in a few lines, demanded long years for their accomplishment. Despairing of completing them, I abandoned them more than once to return to those labours of the laboratory in which one is always sure of skirting the truth and of acquiring fragments at least of certitude.

But while it is very interesting to explore the world of material phenomena, it is still more so to decipher men, for which reason I have always been led back to psychology.

Certain principles deduced from my researches appearing likely to prove fruitful, I resolved to apply them to the study of concrete instances, and was thus led to deal with the Psychology of Revolutions—notably that of the French Revolution.

Proceeding in the analysis of our great Revolution,

# The Psychology of Revolution

the greater part of the opinions determined by the reading of books deserted me one by one, although I had considered them unshakable.

To explain this period we must consider it as a whole, as many historians have done. It is composed of phenomena simultaneous but independent of one another.

Each of its phases reveals events engendered by psychological laws working with the regularity of clockwork. The actors in this great drama seem to move like the characters of a previously determined drama. Each says what he must say, acts as he is bound to act.

To be sure, the actors in the revolutionary drama differed from those of a written drama in that they had not studied their parts, but these were dictated by invisible forces.

Precisely because they were subjected to the inevitable progression of logics incomprehensible to them we see them as greatly astonished by the events of which they were the heroes as are we ourselves. Never did they suspect the invisible powers which forced them to act. They were the masters neither of their fury nor their weakness. They spoke in the name of reason, pretending to be guided by reason, but in reality it was by no means reason that impelled them.

"The decisions for which we are so greatly reproached," wrote Billaud-Varenne, "were more often than otherwise not intended or desired by us two days or even one day beforehand : the crisis alone evoked them."

Not that we must consider the events of the

16

# Introduction

Revolution as dominated by an imperious fatality. The readers of our works will know that we recognise in the man of superior qualities the *rôle* of averting fatalities. But he can dissociate himself only from a few of such, and is often powerless before the sequence of events which even at their origin could scarcely be ruled. The scientist knows how to destroy the microbe before it has time to act, but he knows himself powerless to prevent the evolution of the resulting malady.

When any question gives rise to violently contradictory opinions we may be sure that it belongs to the province of beliefs and not to that of knowledge.

We have shown in a preceding work that belief, of unconscious origin and independent of all reason, can never be influenced by reason.

The Revolution, the work of believers, has seldom been judged by any but believers. Execrated by some and praised by others, it has remained one of those dogmas which are accepted or rejected as a whole, without the intervention of rational logic.

Although in its beginnings a religious or political revolution may very well be supported by rational elements, it is developed only by the aid of mystic and affective elements which are absolutely foreign to reason.

The historians who have judged the events of the French Revolution in the name of rational logic could not comprehend them, since this form of logic did not dictate them. As the actors of these events themselves understood them but ill, we shall not be far from the truth in saying that our Revolution

# The Psychology of Revolution

was a phenomenon equally misunderstood by those who caused it and by those who have described it. At no period of history did men so little grasp the present, so greatly ignore the past, and so poorly divine the future.

. . . The power of the Revolution did not reside in the principles—which for that matter were anything but novel—which it sought to propagate, nor in the institutions which it sought to found. The people cares very little for institutions and even less for doctrines. That the Revolution was potent indeed, that it made France accept the violence, the murders, the ruin and the horror of a frightful civil war, that finally it defended itself victoriously against a Europe in arms, was due to the fact that it had founded not a new system of government but a new religion. Now history shows us how irresistible is the might of a strong belief. Invincible Rome herself had to bow before the armies of nomad shepherds illuminated by the faith of Mahommed. For the same reason the kings of Europe could not resist the tatterdemalion soldiers of the Convention. Like all apostles, they were ready to immolate themselves in the sole end of propagating their beliefs, which according to their dream were to renew the world.

The religion thus founded had the force of other religions, if not their duration. Yet it did not perish without leaving indelible traces, and its influence is active still.

We shall not consider the Revolution as a clean

# Introduction

sweep in history, as its apostles believed it. We know that to demonstrate their intention of creating a world distinct from the old they initiated a new era and professed to break entirely with all vestiges of the past.

But the past never dies. It is even more truly within us than without us. Against their will the reformers of the Revolution remained saturated with the past, and could only continue, under other names, the traditions of the monarchy, even exaggerating the autocracy and centralisation of the old system. Tocqueville had no difficulty in proving that the Revolution did little but overturn that which was about to fall.

If in reality the Revolution destroyed but little it favoured the fruition of certain ideas which continued thenceforth to develop. The fraternity and liberty which it proclaimed never greatly seduced the peoples, but equality became their gospel: the pivot of socialism and of the entire evolution of modern democratic ideas. We may therefore say that the Revolution did not end with the advent of the Empire, nor with the successive restorations which followed it. Secretly or in the light of day it has slowly unrolled itself and still affects men's minds.

The study of the French Revolution to which a great part of this book is devoted will perhaps deprive the reader of more than one illusion, by proving to him that the books which recount the history of the Revolution contain in reality a mass of legends very remote from reality.

These legends will doubtless retain more life than

history itself. Do not regret this too greatly. It may interest a few philosophers to know the truth, but the peoples will always prefer dreams. Synthetising their ideal, such dreams will always constitute powerful motives of action. One would lose courage were it not sustained by false ideas, said Fontenelle. Joan of Arc, the Giants of the Convention, the Imperial epic—all these dazzling images of the past will always remain sources of hope in the gloomy hours that follow defeat. They form part of that patrimony of illusions left us by our fathers, whose power is often greater than that of reality. The dream, the ideal, the legend—in a word, the unreal —it is that which shapes history.

# PART I

## THE PSYCHOLOGICAL ELEMENTS OF REVOLUTIONARY MOVEMENTS

# BOOK I

## GENERAL CHARACTERISTICS OF REVOLUTIONS

## CHAPTER I

### SCIENTIFIC AND POLITICAL REVOLUTIONS

#### 1. *Classification of Revolutions.*

WE generally apply the term *revolution* to sudden political changes, but the expression may be employed to denote all sudden transformations, or transformations apparently sudden, whether of beliefs, ideas, or doctrines.

We have considered elsewhere the part played by the rational, affective, and mystic factors in the genesis of the opinions and beliefs which determine conduct. We need not therefore return to the subject here.

A revolution may finally become a belief, but it often commences under the action of perfectly rational motives : the suppression of crying abuses, of a detested despotic government, or an unpopular sovereign, &c.

Although the origin of a revolution may be perfectly rational, we must not forget that the reasons invoked in preparing for it do not influence the crowd

23

until they have been transformed into sentiments. Rational logic can point to the abuses to be destroyed, but to move the multitude its hopes must be awakened. This can only be effected by the action of the affective and mystic elements which give man the power to act. At the time of the French Revolution, for example, rational logic, in the hands of the philosophers, demonstrated the inconveniences of the *ancien régime*, and excited the desire to change it. Mystic logic inspired belief in the virtues of a society created in all its members according to certain principles. Affective logic unchained the passions confined by the bonds of ages and led to the worst excesses. Collective logic ruled the clubs and the Assemblies and impelled their members to actions which neither rational nor affective nor mystic logic would ever have caused them to commit.

Whatever its origin, a revolution is not productive of results until it has sunk into the soul of the multitude. Then events acquire special forms resulting from the peculiar psychology of crowds. Popular movements for this reason have characteristics so pronounced that the description of one will enable us to comprehend the others.

The multitude is, therefore, the agent of a revolution ; but not its point of departure. The crowd represents an amorphous being which can do nothing, and will nothing, without a head to lead it. It will quickly exceed the impulse once received, but it never creates it.

The sudden political revolutions which strike the historian most forcibly are often the least important. The great revolutions are those of manners and thought. Changing the name of a government does not transform the mentality of a people. To overthrow the institutions of a people is not to re-shape its soul.

The true revolutions, those which transform the destinies of the peoples, are most frequently accomplished so slowly that the historians can hardly point to their beginnings. The term evolution is, therefore, far more appropriate than revolution.

The various elements we have enumerated as entering into the genesis of the majority of revolutions will not suffice to classify them. Considering only the designed object, we will divide them into scientific revolutions, political revolutions, and religious revolutions.

## 2. *Scientific Revolutions.*

Scientific revolutions are by far the most important. Although they attract but little attention, they are often fraught with remote consequences, such as are not engendered by political revolutions. We will therefore put them first, although we cannot study them here.

For instance, if our conceptions of the universe have profoundly changed since the time of the Revolution, it is because astronomical discoveries and the application of experimental methods have revolutionised them, by demonstrating that phenomena, instead of being conditioned by the caprices of the gods, are ruled by invariable laws.

Such revolutions are fittingly spoken of as evolution, on account of their slowness. But there are others which, although of the same order, deserve the name of revolution by reason of their rapidity : we

# The Psychology of Revolution

may instance the theories of Darwin, overthrowing the whole science of biology in a few years; the discoveries of Pasteur, which revolutionised medicine during the lifetime of their author; and the theory of the dissociation of matter, proving that the atom, formerly supposed to be eternal, is not immune from the laws which condemn all the elements of the universe to decline and perish.

These scientific revolutions in the domain of ideas are purely intellectual. Our sentiments and beliefs do not affect them. Men submit to them without discussing them. Their results being controllable by experience, they escape all criticism.

### 3. *Political Revolutions.*

Beneath and very remote from these scientific revolutions, which generate the progress of civilisations, are the religious and political revolutions, which have no kinship with them. While scientific revolutions derive solely from rational elements, political and religious beliefs are sustained almost exclusively by affective and mystic factors. Reason plays only a feeble part in their genesis.

I insisted at some length in my book *Opinions and Beliefs* on the affective and mystic origin of beliefs, showing that a political or religious belief constitutes an act of faith elaborated in unconsciousness, over which, in spite of all appearances, reason has no hold. I also showed that belief often reaches such a degree of intensity that nothing can be opposed to it. The man hypnotised by his faith becomes an Apostle, ready to sacrifice his interests, his happiness, and even his life for the triumph of his faith. The absurdity of

26

# Scientific and Political Revolutions

his belief matters little ; for him it is a burning reality. Certitudes of mystic origin possess the marvellous power of entire domination over thought, and can only be affected by time.

By the very fact that it is regarded as an absolute truth a belief necessarily becomes intolerant. This explains the violence, hatred, and persecution which were the habitual accompaniments of the great political and religious revolutions, notably of the Reformation and the French Revolution.

Certain periods of French history remain incomprehensible if we forget the affective and mystic origin of beliefs, their necessary intolerance, the impossibility of reconciling them when they come into mutual contact, and, finally, the power conferred by mystic beliefs upon the sentiments which place themselves at their service.

The foregoing conceptions are too novel as yet to have modified the mentality of the historians. They will continue to attempt to explain, by means of rational logic, a host of phenomena which are foreign to it.

Events such as the Reformation, which overwhelmed France for a period of fifty years, were in no wise determined by rational influences. Yet rational influences are always invoked in explanation, even in the most recent works. Thus, in the *General History* of Messrs. Lavisse and Rambaud, we read the following explanation of the Reformation :—

" It was a spontaneous movement, born here and there amidst the people, from the reading of the Gospels and the free individual reflections which were suggested to simple persons by an extremely pious conscience and a very bold reasoning power."

# The Psychology of Revolution

Contrary to the assertion of these historians, we may say with certainty, in the first place, that such movements are never spontaneous, and secondly, that reason takes no part in their elaboration.

The force of the political and religious beliefs which have moved the world resides precisely in the fact that, being born of affective and mystic elements, they are neither created nor directed by reason.

Political or religious beliefs have a common origin and obey the same laws. They are formed not with the aid of reason, but more often contrary to all reason. Buddhism, Islamism, the Reformation, Jacobinism, Socialism, &c., seem very different forms of thought. Yet they have identical affective and mystic bases, and obey a logic that has no affinity with rational logic.

Political revolutions may result from beliefs established in the minds of men, but many other causes produce them. The word discontent sums them up. As soon as discontent is generalised a party is formed which often becomes strong enough to struggle against the Government.

Discontent must generally have been accumulating for a long time in order to produce its effects. For this reason a revolution does not always represent a phenomenon in process of termination followed by another which is commencing, but rather a continuous phenomenon, having somewhat accelerated its evolution. All the modern revolutions, however, have been abrupt movements, entailing the instantaneous overthrow of governments. Such, for example, were the Brazilian, Portuguese, Turkish, and Chinese revolutions.

To the contrary of what might be supposed, the

# Scientific and Political Revolutions

very conservative peoples are addicted to the most violent revolutions. Being conservative, they are not able to evolve slowly, or to adapt themselves to variations of environment, so that when the discrepancy becomes too extreme they are bound to adapt themselves suddenly. This sudden evolution constitutes a revolution.

Peoples able to adapt themselves progressively do not always escape revolution. It was only by means of a revolution that the English, in 1688, were able to terminate the struggle which had dragged on for a century between the monarchy, which sought to make itself absolute, and the nation, which claimed the right to govern itself through the medium of its representatives.

The great revolutions have usually commenced from the top, not from the bottom; but once the people is unchained it is to the people that revolution owes its might.

It is obvious that revolutions have never taken place, and will never take place, save with the aid of an important fraction of the army. Royalty did not disappear in France on the day when Louis XVI. was guillotined, but at the precise moment when his mutinous troops refused to defend him.

It is more particularly by mental contagion that armies become disaffected, being indifferent enough at heart to the established order of things. As soon as the coalition of a few officers had succeeded in overthrowing the Turkish Government the Greek officers thought to imitate them and to change their government, although there was no analogy between the two *régimes.*

# The Psychology of Revolution

A military movement may overthrow a government —and in the Spanish republics the Government is hardly ever destroyed by any other means—but if the revolution is to be productive of great results it must always be based upon general discontent and general hopes.

Unless it is universal and excessive, discontent alone is not sufficient to bring about a revolution. It is easy to lead a handful of men to pillage, destroy, and massacre, but to raise a whole people, or any great portion of that people, calls for the continuous or repeated action of leaders. These exaggerate the discontent; they persuade the discontented that the government is the sole cause of all the trouble, especially of the prevailing dearth, and assure men that the new system proposed by them will engender an age of felicity. These ideas germinate, propagating themselves by suggestion and contagion, and the moment arrives when the revolution is ripe.

In this fashion the Christian Revolution and the French Revolution were prepared. That the latter was effected in a few years, while the first required many, was due to the fact that the French Revolution promptly had an armed force at its disposal, while Christianity was long in winning material power. In the beginning its only adepts were the lowly, the poor, and the slaves, filled with enthusiasm by the prospect of seeing their miserable life transformed into an eternity of delight. By a phenomenon of contagion from below, of which history affords us more than one example, the doctrine finally invaded the upper strata of the nation, but it was a long time before an emperor considered the new faith sufficiently wide-spread to be adopted as the official religion.

### 4. *The Results of Political Revolutions.*

When a political party is triumphant it naturally seeks to organise society in accordance with its interests. The organisation will differ accordingly as the revolution has been effected by the soldiers, the Radicals, or the Conservatives, &c. The new laws and institutions will depend on the interests of the triumphant party and of the classes which have assisted it—the clergy for instance.

If the revolution has triumphed only after a violent struggle, as was the case with the French Revolution, the victors will reject at one sweep the whole arsenal of the old law. The supporters of the fallen *régime* will be persecuted, exiled, or exterminated.

The maximum of violence in these persecutions is attained when the triumphant party is defending a belief in addition to its material interests. Then the conquered need hope for no pity. Thus may be explained the expulsion of the Moors from Spain, the autodafés of the Inquisition, the executions of the Convention, and the recent laws against the religious congregations in France.

The absolute power which is assumed by the victors leads them sometimes to extreme measures, such as the Convention's decree that gold was to be replaced by paper, that goods were to be sold at determined prices, &c. Very soon it runs up against a wall of unavoidable necessities, which turn opinion against its tyranny, and finally leave it defenceless before attack, as befell at the end of the French Revolution. The same thing happened recently to a Socialist Australian ministry composed almost exclusively of working-men. It enacted laws so absurd, and accorded such privileges to the trade unions, that public opinion rebelled against it so unanimously that in three months it was overthrown.

But the cases we have considered are exceptional. The majority of revolutions have been accomplished in order to place a new sovereign in power. Now this sovereign knows very well that the first condition of maintaining his power consists in not too exclusively favouring a single class, but in seeking to conciliate all. To do this he will establish a sort of equilibrium between them, so as not to be dominated by any one of these classes. To allow one class to become predominant is to condemn himself presently to accept that class as his master. This law is one of the most certain of political psychology. The kings of France understood it very well when they struggled so energetically against the encroachments first of the nobility and then of the clergy. If they had not done so their fate would have been that of the German Emperors of the Middle Ages, who, excommunicated by the Pope, were reduced, like Henry IV. at Canossa, to make a pilgrimage and humbly to sue for the Pope's forgiveness.

This same law has continually been verified during the course of history. When at the end of the Roman Empire the military caste became preponderant, the emperors depended entirely upon their soldiers, who appointed and deposed them at will.

It was therefore a great advantage for France that she was so long governed by a monarch almost

# Scientific and Political Revolutions

absolute, supposed to hold his power by divine right, and surrounded therefore by a considerable prestige. Without such an authority he could have controlled neither the feudal nobility, nor the clergy, nor the parliaments. If Poland, towards the end of the sixteenth century, had also possessed an absolute and respected monarchy, she would not have descended the path of decadence which led to her disappearance from the map of Europe.

We have shewn in this chapter that political revolutions may be accompanied by important social transformations. We shall soon see how slight are these transformations compared to those produced by religious revolutions.

# CHAPTER II

## RELIGIOUS REVOLUTIONS

1. *The importance of the study of Religious Revolutions in respect of the comprehension of the great Political Revolutions.*

A PORTION of this work will be devoted to the French Revolution. It was full of acts of violence which naturally had their psychological causes.

These exceptional events will always fill us with astonishment, and we even feel them to be inexplicable. They become comprehensible, however, if we consider that the French Revolution, constituting a new religion, was bound to obey the laws which condition the propagation of all beliefs. Its fury and its hecatombs will then become intelligible.

In studying the history of a great religious revolution, that of the Reformation, we shall see that a number of psychological elements which figured therein were equally active during the French Revolution. In both we observe the insignificant bearing of the rational value of a belief upon its propagation, the inefficacy of persecution, the impossibility of tolerance between contrary beliefs, and the violence and the desperate struggles resulting from the conflict of different faiths. We also observe the exploitation of a belief by interests quite inde-

34

pendent of that belief. Finally we see that it is impossible to modify the convictions of men without also modifying their existence.

These phenomena verified, we shall see plainly why the gospel of the Revolution was propagated by the same methods as all the religious gospels, notably that of Calvin. It could not have been propagated otherwise.

But although there are close analogies between the genesis of a religious revolution, such as the Reformation, and that of a great political revolution like our own, their remote consequences are very different, which explains the difference of duration which they display. In religious revolutions no experience can reveal to the faithful that they are deceived, since they would have to go to heaven to make the discovery. In political revolutions experience quickly demonstrates the error of a false doctrine and forces men to abandon it.

Thus at the end of the Directory the application of Jacobin beliefs had led France to such a degree of ruin, poverty, and despair that the wildest Jacobins themselves had to renounce their system. Nothing survived of their theories except a few principles which cannot be verified by experience, such as the universal happiness which equality should bestow upon humanity.

## 2. *The beginnings of the Reformation and its first disciples.*

The Reformation was finally to exercise a profound influence upon the sentiments and moral ideas of a great proportion of mankind. Modest in its beginnings, it was at first a simple struggle against the abuses of the clergy, and, from a practical point of view, a return to the prescriptions of the Gospel. It never constituted, as has been claimed, an aspiration towards freedom of thought. Calvin was as intolerant as Robespierre, and all the theorists of the age considered that the religion of subjects must be that of the prince who governed them. Indeed in every country where the Reformation was established the sovereign replaced the Pope of Rome, with the same rights and the same powers.

In France, in default of publicity and means of communication, the new faith spread slowly enough at first. It was about 1520 that Luther recruited a few adepts, and only towards 1535 was the new belief sufficiently widespread for men to consider it necessary to burn its disciples.

In conformity with a well-known psychological law, these executions merely favoured the propagation of the Reformation. Its first followers included priests and magistrates, but were principally obscure artisans. Their conversion was effected almost exclusively by mental contagion and suggestion.

As soon as a new belief extends itself, we see grouped round it many persons who are indifferent to the belief, but who find in it a pretext or opportunity for gratifying their passions or their greed. This phenomenon was observed at the time of the Reformation in many countries, notably in Germany and in England. Luther having taught that the clergy had no need of wealth, the German lords found many merits in a faith which enabled them to seize upon the goods of the Church. Henry VIII. enriched himself by a similar operation. Sovereigns who were often molested by the Pope could as a rule only look favourably upon a doctrine which added religious powers to their political powers and made each of them a Pope. Far from diminishing the absolutism of rulers, the Reformation only exaggerated it.

3. *Rational value of the doctrines of the Reformation.*

The Reformation overturned all Europe, and came near to ruining France, of which it made a battle-field for a period of fifty years. Never did a cause so insignificant from the rational point of view produce such great results.

Here is one of the innumerable proofs of the fact that beliefs are propagated independently of all reason. The theological doctrines which aroused men's passions so violently, and notably those of Calvin, are not even worthy of examination in the light of rational logic.

Greatly concerned about his salvation, having an excessive fear of the devil, which his confessor was unable to allay, Luther sought the surest means of pleasing God that he might avoid Hell. Having commenced by denying the Pope the right to sell indulgences, he presently entirely denied his authority, and that of the Church, condemned religious ceremonies, confession, and the worship of the saints, and declared that Christians should have no rules of conduct other than the Bible. He also considered that no one could be saved without the grace of God.

This last theory, known as that of predestination, was in Luther rather uncertain, but was stated precisely by Calvin, who made it the very foundation of a doctrine to which the majority of Protestants are

37

# The Psychology of Revolution

still subservient.　According to him: "From all eternity God has predestined certain men to be burned and others to be saved."　Why this monstrous iniquity?　Simply because "it is the will of God."

Thus according to Calvin, who for that matter merely developed certain assertions of St. Augustine, an all-powerful God would amuse Himself by creating living beings simply in order to burn them during all eternity, without paying any heed to their acts or merits.　It is marvellous that such revolting insanity could for such a length of time subjugate so many minds—marvellous that it does so still.[1]

---

[1] The doctrine of predestination is still taught in Protestant catechisms, as is proved by the following passage extracted from the last edition of an official catechism for which I sent to Edinburgh:

"By the decree of God, for the manifestation of His glory, some men and angels are predestinated unto everlasting life, and others foreordained to everlasting death.

"These angels and men, thus predestinated and foreordained, are particularly and unchangeably designed; and their number is so certain and definite that it cannot be either increased or diminished.

"Those of mankind that are predestinated unto life, God, before the foundation of the world was laid, according to His eternal and immutable purpose, and the secret counsel and good pleasure of His will, hath chosen in Christ unto everlasting glory, out of His mere free grace and love, without any foresight of faith or good works, or perseverance in either of them, or any other thing in the creature, as conditions, or causes moving him thereunto; and all to the praise of his glorious grace.

"As God hath appointed the elect unto glory, so hath He, by the eternal and most free purpose of His will, foreordained all the means thereunto.　Wherefore they who are elected being fallen in Adam, are redeemed by Christ; are effectually called unto faith in Christ by His spirit working in due season; are justified, adopted, sanctified, and kept by His power through faith unto salvation. Neither are any other redeemed by Christ, effectually called, justified, adopted, sanctified, and saved, but the elect only."

# Religious Revolutions

The psychology of Calvin is not without affinity with that of Robespierre. Like the latter, the master of the pure truth, he sent to death those who would not accept his doctrines. God, he stated, wishes "that one should put aside all humanity when it is a question of striving for his glory."

The case of Calvin and his disciples shows that matters which rationally are the most contradictory become perfectly reconciled in minds which are hypnotised by a belief. In the eyes of rational logic, it seems impossible to base a morality upon the theory of predestination, since whatever they do men are sure of being either saved or damned. However, Calvin had no difficulty in erecting a most severe morality upon this totally illogical basis. Considering themselves the elect of God, his disciples were so swollen by pride and the sense of their own dignity that they felt obliged to serve as models in their conduct.

## 4. *Propagation of the Reformation.*

The new faith was propagated not by speech, still less by process of reasoning, but by the mechanism described in our preceding work: that is, by the influence of affirmation, repetition, mental contagion, and prestige. At a much later date revolutionary ideas were spread over France in the same fashion.

Persecution, as we have already remarked, only favoured this propagation. Each execution led to fresh conversions, as was seen in the early years of the Christian Church. Anne Dubourg, Parliamentary councillor, condemned to be burned alive, marched to the stake exhorting the crowd to be converted. "His constancy," says a witness, "made more Protestants among the young men of the colleges than the books of Calvin."

To prevent the condemned from speaking to the people their tongues were cut out before they were burned. The horror of their sufferings was increased by attaching the victims to an iron chain, which enabled the executioners to plunge them into the fire and withdraw them several times in succession.

But nothing induced the Protestants to retract, even the offer of an amnesty after they had felt the fire.

In 1535 Francis I., forsaking his previous tolerance, ordered six fires to be lighted simultaneously in Paris. The Convention, as we know, limited itself to a single guillotine in the same city. It is probable that the sufferings of the victims were not very excruciating ; the insensibility of the Christian martyrs had already been remarked. Believers are hypnotised by their faith, and we know to-day that certain forms of hypnotism engender complete insensibility.

The new faith progressed rapidly. In 1560 there were two thousand reformed churches in France, and many great lords, at first indifferent enough, adhered to the new doctrine.

5. *Conflict between different religious beliefs— Impossibility of tolerance.*

I have already stated that intolerance is always an accompaniment of powerful religious beliefs. Political and religious revolutions furnish us with numerous proofs of this fact, and show us also that the mutual intolerance of sectaries of the same religion is always much greater than that of the defenders of remote and alien faiths, such as Islamism and Christianity. In fact, if we consider the faiths for whose sake France was so long rent asunder, we shall find that they did not differ on any but accessory points. Catholics and Protestants adored exactly the same God, and only differed in their manner of adoring Him. If reason had played the smallest part in the elaboration of their belief, it could easily have proved to them that it must be quite indifferent to God whether He sees men adore Him in this fashion or in that.

Reason being powerless to affect the brain of the convinced, Protestants and Catholics continued their ferocious conflicts. All the efforts of their sovereigns to reconcile them were in vain. Catherine de Medicis, seeing the party of the Reformed Church increasing day by day in spite of persecution, and attracting a considerable number of nobles and magistrates, thought to disarm them by convoking at Poissy, in 1561, an assembly of bishops and pastors with the object of fusing the two doctrines. Such an enterprise indicated that the queen, despite her subtlety, knew nothing of the laws of mystic logic. Not in all history can one cite an example of a belief destroyed or reduced by means of refutation. Catherine did not even know that although toleration is with difficulty possible between individuals, it is impossible between collectivities. Her attempt failed completely. The assembled theologians hurled texts and insults at one another's heads, but no one was moved. Catherine thought to succeed better in 1562 by promulgating an edict according Protestants the

# The Psychology of Revolution

right to unite in the public celebration of their cult.

This tolerance, very admirable from a philosophical point of view, but not at all wise from the political standpoint, had no other result beyond exasperating both parties. In the Midi, where the Protestants were strongest, they persecuted the Catholics, sought to convert them by violence, cut their throats if they did not succeed, and sacked their cathedrals. In the regions where the Catholics were more numerous the Reformers suffered like persecutions.

Such hostilities as these inevitably engendered civil war. Thus arose the so-called religious wars, which so long spilled the blood of France. The cities were ravaged, the inhabitants massacred, and the struggle rapidly assumed that special quality of ferocity peculiar to religious or political conflicts, which, at a later date, was to reappear in the wars of La Vendée.

Old men, women, and children, all were exterminated. A certain Baron d'Oppede, first president of the Parliament of Aix, had already set an example by killing 3,000 persons in the space of ten days, with refinements of cruelty, and destroying three cities and twenty-two villages. Montluc, a worthy forerunner of Carrier, had the Calvinists thrown living into the wells until these were full. The Protestants were no more humane. They did not spare even the Catholic churches, and treated the tombs and statues just as the delegates of the Convention were to treat the royal tombs of Saint Denis.

Under the influence of these conflicts France was progressively disintegrated, and at the end of the reign of Henri III. was parcelled out into veritable

# Religious Revolutions

little confederated municipal republics, forming so many sovereign states. The royal power was vanishing. The States of Blois claimed to dictate their wishes to Henri III., who had fled from his capital. In 1577 the traveller Lippomano, who traversed France, saw important cities—Orleans, Tours, Blois, Poitiers—entirely devastated, the cathedrals and churches in ruins, and the tombs shattered. This was almost the state of France at the end of the Directory.

Among the events of this epoch, that which has left the darkest memory, although it was not perhaps the most murderous, was the massacre of St. Bartholomew in 1572, ordered, according to the historians, by Catherine de Medicis and Charles IX.

One does not require a very profound knowledge of psychology to realise that no sovereign could have ordered such an event. St. Bartholomew's Day was not a royal but a popular crime. Catherine de Medicis, believing her existence and that of the king threatened by a plot directed by four or five Protestant leaders then in Paris, sent men to kill them in their houses, according to the summary fashion of the time. The massacre which followed is very well explained by M. Battifol in the following terms :—

"At the report of what was afoot the rumour immediately ran through Paris that the Huguenots were being massacred; Catholic gentlemen, soldiers of the guard, archers, men of the people, in short all Paris, rushed into the streets, arms in hand, in order to participate in the execution, and the general massacre commenced, to the sound of ferocious

43

# The Psychology of Revolution

cries of 'The Huguenots! Kill, kill!' They were struck down, they were drowned, they were hanged. All that were known as heretics were so served. Two thousand persons were killed in Paris."

By contagion, the people of the provinces imitated those of Paris, and six to eight thousand Protestants were slain.

When time had somewhat cooled religious passions, all the historians, even the Catholics, spoke of St. Bartholomew's Day with indignation. They thus showed how difficult it is for the mentality of one epoch to understand that of another.

Far from being criticised, St. Bartholomew's Day provoked an indescribable enthusiasm throughout the whole of Catholic Europe. Philip II. was delirious with joy when he heard the news, and the King of France received more congratulations than if he had won a great battle.

But it was Pope Gregory XIII. above all who manifested the keenest satisfaction. He had a medal struck to commemorate the happy event,[1] ordered joy-fires to be lit and cannon fired, celebrated several masses, and sent for the painter Vasari to depict on the walls of the Vatican the principal

[1] The medal must have been distributed pretty widely, for the cabinet of medals at the *Bibliothèque Nationale* possesses three examples : one in gold, one in silver, and one in copper. This medal, reproduced by Bonnani in his *Numism. Pontific.* (vol. i. p. 336), represents on one side Gregory XIII., and on the other an angel striking Huguenots with a sword. The exergue is *Ugonotorum strages*, that is, *Massacre of the Huguenots.* (The word *strages* may be translated by carnage or massacre, a sense which it possesses in Cicero and Livy ; or again by disaster, ruin, a sense attributed to it in Virgil and Tacitus.)

scenes of carnage. Further, he sent to the King of France an ambassador instructed to felicitate that monarch upon his fine action. It is historical details of this kind that enable us to comprehend the mind of the believer. The Jacobins of the Terror had a mentality very like that of Gregory XIII.

Naturally the Protestants were not indifferent to such a hecatomb, and they made such progress that in 1576 Henri III. was reduced to granting them, by the Edict of Beaulieu, entire liberty of worship, eight strong places, and, in the Parliaments, Chambers composed half of Catholics and half of Huguenots.

These forced concessions did not lead to peace. A Catholic League was created, having the Duke of Guise at its head, and the conflict continued. But it could not last for ever. We know how Henri IV. put an end to it, at least for a time, by his abjuration in 1593, and by the Edict of Nantes.

The struggle was quieted but not terminated. Under Louis XIII. the Protestants were still restless, and in 1627 Richelieu was obliged to besiege La Rochelle, where 15,000 Protestants perished. Afterwards, possessing more political than religious feeling, the famous Cardinal proved extremely tolerant toward the Reformers.

This tolerance could not last. Contrary beliefs cannot come into contact without seeking to annihilate each other, as soon as one feels capable of dominating the other. Under Louis XIV. the Protestants had become by far the weaker, and were forced to renounce the struggle and live at peace. Their number was then about 1,200,000, and they possessed more than 600 churches, served by about 700 pastors.

# The Psychology of Revolution

The presence of these heretics on French soil was intolerable to the Catholic clergy, who endeavoured to persecute them in various ways. As these persecutions had little result, Louis XIV. resorted to dragonnading them in 1685, when many individuals perished, but without further result. Under the pressure of the clergy, notably of Bossuett, the Edict of Nantes was revoked, and the Protestants were forced to accept conversion or to leave France. This disastrous emigration lasted a long time, and is said to have cost France 400,000 inhabitants, men of notable energy, since they had the courage to listen to their conscience rather than their interests.

### 6. *The results of Religious Revolutions.*

If religious revolutions were judged only by the gloomy story of the Reformation, we should be forced to regard them as highly disastrous. But all have not played a like part, the civilising influence of certain among them being considerable.

By giving a people moral unity they greatly increase its material power. We see this notably when a new faith, brought by Mohammed, transforms the petty and impotent tribes of Arabia into a formidable nation.

Such a new religious belief does not merely render a people homogeneous. It attains a result that no philosophy, no code ever attained : it sensibly transforms what is almost unchangeable, the sentiments of a race.

We see this at the period when the most powerful religious revolution recorded by history overthrew paganism to substitute a God who came from the plains of Galilee. The new ideal demanded the

# Religious Revolutions

renunciation of all the joys of existence in order to acquire the eternal happiness of heaven. No doubt such an ideal was readily accepted by the poor, the enslaved, the disinherited who were deprived of all the joys of life here below, to whom an enchanting future was offered in exchange for a life without hope. But the austere existence so easily embraced by the poor was also embraced by the rich. In this above all was the power of the new faith manifested.

Not only did the Christian revolution transform manners : it also exercised, for a space of two thousand years, a preponderating influence over civilisation. Directly a religious faith triumphs all the elements of civilisation naturally adapt themselves to it, so that civilisation is rapidly transformed. Writers, artists and philosophers merely symbolise, in their works, the ideas of the new faith.

When any religious or political faith whatsoever has triumphed, not only is reason powerless to affect it, but it even finds motives which impel it to interpret and so justify the faith in question, and to strive to impose it upon others. There were probably as many theologians and orators in the time of Moloch, to prove the utility of human sacrifices, as there were at other periods to glorify the Inquisition, the massacre of St. Bartholomew, and the hecatombs of the Terror.

We must not hope to see peoples possessed by strong beliefs readily achieve tolerance. The only people who attained to toleration in the ancient world were the polytheists. The nations which practise toleration at the present time are those that might well be termed polytheistical, since, as in England and America, they are divided into innumerable sects.

# The Psychology of Revolution

Under identical names they really adore very different deities.

The multiplicity of beliefs which results in such toleration finally results also in weakness. We therefore come to a psychological problem not hitherto resolved : how to possess a faith at once powerful and tolerant.

The foregoing brief explanation reveals the large part played by religious revolutions and the power of beliefs. Despite their slight rational value they shape history, and prevent the peoples from remaining a mass of individuals without cohesion or strength. Man has needed them at all times to orientate his thought and guide his conduct. No philosophy has as yet succeeded in replacing them.

# CHAPTER III

### 1. *The feeble resistance of Governments in time of Revolution.*

MANY modern nations—France, Spain, Italy, Austria, Poland, Japan, Turkey, Portugal, &c.—have known revolutions within the last century. These were usually characterised by their instantaneous quality and the facility with which the governments attacked were overthrown.

The instantaneous nature of these revolutions is explained by the rapidity of mental contagion due to modern methods of publicity. The slight resistance of the governments attacked is more surprising. It implies a total inability to comprehend and foresee created by a blind confidence in their own strength.

The facility with which governments fall is not however a new phenomenon. It has been proved more than once, not only in autocratic systems, which are always overturned by palace conspiracies, but also in governments perfectly instructed in the state of public opinion by the press and their own agents.

Among these instantaneous downfalls one of the most striking was that which followed the Ordinances of Charles X. This monarch was, as we know, over-

49

# The Psychology of Revolution

thrown in four days. His minister Polignac had taken no measures of defence, and the king was so confident of the tranquillity of Paris that he had gone hunting. The army was not in the least hostile, as in the reign of Louis XVI., but the troops, badly officered, disbanded before the attacks of a few insurgents.

The overthrow of Louis-Philippe was still more typical, since it did not result from any arbitrary action on the part of the sovereign. This monarch was not surrounded by the hatred which finally surrounded Charles X., and his fall was the result of an insignificant riot which could easily have been repressed.

Historians, who can hardly comprehend how a solidly constituted government, supported by an imposing army, can be overthrown by a few rioters, naturally attributed the fall of Louis-Philippe to deep-seated causes. In reality the incapacity of the generals entrusted with his defence was the real cause of his fall.

This case is one of the most instructive that could be cited, and is worthy of a moment's consideration. It has been perfectly investigated by General Bonnal, in the light of the notes of an eye-witness, General Elchingen. Thirty-six thousand troops were then in Paris, but the weakness and incapacity of their officers made it impossible to use them. Contradictory orders were given, and finally the troops were forbidden to fire on the people, who, moreover—and nothing could have been more dangerous—were permitted to mingle with the troops. The riot succeeded without fighting and forced the king to abdicate.

Applying to the preceding case our knowledge of

the psychology of crowds, General Bonnal shows how easily the riot which overthrew Louis-Philippe could have been controlled. He proves, notably, that if the commanding officers had not completely lost their heads quite a small body of troops could have prevented the insurgents from invading the Chamber of Deputies. This last, composed of monarchists, would certainly have proclaimed the Count of Paris under the regency of his mother.

Similar phenomena were observable in the revolutions of Spain and Portugal.

These facts show the *rôle* of petty accessory circumstances in great events, and prove that one must not speak too readily of the general laws of history. Without the riot which overthrew Louis-Philippe, we should probably have seen neither the Republic of 1848, nor the Second Empire, nor Sedan, nor the invasion, nor the loss of Alsace.

In the revolutions of which I have just been speaking the army was of no assistance to the government, but did not turn against it. It sometimes happens otherwise. It is often the army which effects the revolution, as in Turkey and Portugal. The innumerable revolutions of the Latin republics of America are effected by the army.

When a revolution is effected by an army the new rulers naturally fall under its domination. I have already recalled the fact that this was the case at the end of the Roman Empire, when the emperors were made and unmade by the soldiery.

The same thing has sometimes been witnessed in modern times. The following extract from a news-

The Psychology of Revolution

paper, with reference to the Greek revolution, shows what becomes of a government dominated by its army : —

"One day it was announced that eighty officers of the navy would send in their resignations if the government did not dismiss the leaders of whom they complained. Another time it was the agricultural labourers on a farm (*metairie*) belonging to the Crown Prince who demanded the partition of the soil among them. The navy protested against the promotion promised to Colonel Zorbas. Colonel Zorbas, after a week of discussion with Lieutenant Typaldos, treated with the President of the Council as one power with another. During this time the Federation of the corporations abused the officers of the navy. A deputy demanded that these officers and their families should be treated as brigands. When Commander Miaoulis fired on the rebels, the sailors, who first of all had obeyed Typaldos, returned to duty. This is no longer the harmonious Greece of Pericles and Themistocles. It is a hideous camp of Agramant."

A revolution cannot be effected without the assistance or at least the neutrality of the army, but it often happens that the movement commences without it. This was the case with the revolutions of 1830 and 1848, and that of 1870, which overthrew the Empire after the humiliation of France by the surrender of Sedan.

The majority of revolutions take place in the capitals, and by means of contagion spread through the country ; but this is not a constant rule. We know that during the French Revolution La Vendée,

Brittany, and the Midi revolted spontaneously against Paris.

## 2. *How the resistance of Governments may overcome Revolution.*

In the greater number of the revolutions enumerated above, we have seen governments perish by their weakness. As soon as they were touched they fell.

The Russian Revolution proved that a government which defends itself energetically may finally triumph.

Never was revolution more menacing to the government. After the disasters suffered in the Orient, and the severities of a too oppressive autocratic *régime*, all classes of society, including a portion of the army and the fleet, had revolted. The railways, posts, and telegraph services had struck, so that communications between the various portions of the vast empire were interrupted.

The rural class itself, forming the majority of the nation, began to feel the influence of the revolutionary propaganda. The lot of the peasants was wretched. They were obliged, by the system of the *mir*, to cultivate soil which they could not acquire. The government resolved immediately to conciliate this large class of peasants by turning them into proprietors. Special laws forced the landlords to sell the peasants a portion of their lands, and banks intended to lend the buyers the necessary purchase-money were created. The sums lent were to be repaid by small annuities deducted from the product of the sale of the crops.

Assured of the neutrality of the peasants, the government could contend with the fanatics who were burning the towns, throwing bombs among the crowds, and waging a merciless warfare. All those who could be taken were killed. Such extermination is the only method discovered since the beginning of the world by which a society can be protected against the rebels who wish to destroy it.

The victorious government understood moreover the necessity of satisfying the legitimate claims of the enlightened portion of the nation. It created a parliament instructed to prepare laws and control expenditure.

The history of the Russian Revolution shows us how a government, all of whose natural supports have crumbled in succession, can, with wisdom and firmness, triumph over the most formidable obstacles. It has been very justly said that governments are not overthrown, but that they commit suicide.

3. *Revolutions effected by Governments.—Examples:*
*China, Turkey, &c.*

Governments almost invariably fight revolutions; they hardly ever create them. Representing the needs of the moment and general opinion, they follow the reformers timidly; they do not precede them. Sometimes, however, certain governments have attempted those sudden reforms which we know as revolutions. The stability or instability of the national mind decrees the success or failure of such attempts.

They succeed when the people on whom the government seeks to impose new institutions is composed of semi-barbarous tribes, without fixed laws, without solid traditions; that is to say, without a settled national mind. Such was the condition of Russia in the days of Peter the Great. We know how he sought to Europeanise the semi-Asiatic populations by means of force.

Japan is another example of a revolution effected by a government, but it was her machinery, not her mind that was reformed.

It needs a very powerful autocrat, seconded by a man of genius, to succeed, even partially, in such a task. More often than not the reformer finds that the whole people rises up against him. Then, to the contrary of what befalls in an ordinary revolution, the autocrat is revolutionary and the people is conservative. But an attentive study will soon show you that the peoples are always extremely conservative.

Failure is the rule with these attempts. Whether effected by the upper classes or the lower, revolutions do not change the souls of peoples that have been a long time established. They only change those things that are worn by time and ready to fall.

China is at the present time making a very interesting but impossible experiment, in seeking, by means of the government, suddenly to renew the institutions of the country. The revolution which overturned the dynasty of her ancient sovereigns was the indirect consequence of the discontent provoked by reforms which the government had sought to impose with a view to ameliorating the condition of China. The suppression of opium and gaming, the reform of the army, and the creation of schools, involved an increase of taxation which, as well as the reforms themselves, greatly indisposed the general opinion.

# The Psychology of Revolution

A few cultured Chinese educated in the schools of Europe profited by this discontent to raise the people and proclaim a republic, an institution of which the Chinese could have had no conception.

It surely cannot long survive, for the impulse which has given birth to it is not a movement of progress, but of reaction. The word republic, to the Chinaman intellectualised by his European education, is simply synonymous with the rejection of the yoke of laws, rules, and long-established restraints. Cutting off his pigtail, covering his head with a cap, and calling himself a Republican, the young Chinaman thinks to give the rein to all his instincts. This is more or less the idea of a republic that a large part of the French people entertained at the time of the great Revolution.

China will soon discover the fate that awaits a society deprived of the armour slowly wrought by the past. After a few years of bloody anarchy it will be necessary to establish a power whose tyranny will inevitably be far severer than that which was overthrown. Science has not yet discovered the magic ring capable of saving a society without discipline. There is no need to impose discipline when it has become hereditary, but when the primitive instincts have been allowed to destroy the barriers painfully erected by slow ancestral labours, they cannot be reconstituted save by an energetic tyranny.

As a proof of these assertions we may instance an experiment analogous to that undertaken by China; that recently attempted by Turkey. A few years ago young men instructed in European schools and full of good intentions succeeded, with the aid of a

# The Action of Governments in Revolutions

number of officers, in overthrowing a Sultan whose tyranny seemed insupportable. Having acquired our robust Latin faith in the magic power of formulæ, they thought they could establish the representative system in a country half-civilised, profoundly divided by religious hatred, and peopled by divers races.

The attempt has not prospered hitherto. The authors of the reformation had to learn that despite their liberalism they were forced to govern by methods very like those employed by the government overthrown. They could neither prevent summary executions nor wholesale massacres of Christians, nor could they remedy a single abuse.

It would be unjust to reproach them. What in truth could they have done to change a people whose traditions have been fixed so long, whose religious passions are so intense, and whose Mohammedans, although in the minority, legitimately claim to govern the sacred city of their faith according to their code? How prevent Islam from remaining the State religion in a country where civil law and religious law are not yet plainly separated, and where faith in the Koran is the only tie by which the idea of nationality can be maintained?

It was difficult to destroy such a state of affairs, so that we were bound to see the re-establishment of an autocratic organisation with an appearance of constitutionalism—that is to say, practically the old system once again. Such attempts afford a good example of the fact that a people cannot choose its institutions until it has transformed its mind.

# The Psychology of Revolution

## 4. *Social elements which survive the changes of Government after Revolution.*

What we shall say later on as to the stable foundation of the national soul will enable us to appreciate the force of systems of government that have been long established, such as ancient monarchies. A monarch may easily be overthrown by conspirators, but these latter are powerless against the principles which the monarch represents. Napoleon at his fall was replaced not by his natural heir, but by the heir of kings. The latter incarnated an ancient principle, while the son of the Emperor personified ideas that were as yet imperfectly established in men's minds.

For the same reason a minister, however able, however great the services he has rendered to his country, can very rarely overthrow his Sovereign. Bismarck himself could not have done so. This great minister had single-handed created the unity of Germany, yet his master had only to touch him with his finger and he vanished. A man is as nothing before a principle supported by opinion.

But even when, for various reasons, the principle incarnated by a government is annihilated with that government, as happened at the time of the French Revolution, all the elements of social organisation do not perish at the same time.

If we knew nothing of France but the disturbances of the last hundred years and more we might suppose the country to live in a state of profound anarchy. Now her economic, industrial, and even her political life manifests, on the contrary, a continuity that seems to be independent of all revolutions and governments.

# The Action of Governments in Revolutions

The fact is that beside the great events of which history treats are the little facts of daily life which the books neglect to tell. They are ruled by imperious necessities which halt for no man. Their total mass forms the real framework of the life of the people.

While the study of great events shows us that the nominal government of France has been frequently changed in the space of a century, an examination of the little daily events will prove, on the contrary, that her real government has been little altered.

Who in truth are the real rulers of a people? Kings and ministers, no doubt, in the great crises of national life, but they play no part whatever in the little realities which make up the life of every day. The real directing forces of a country are the administrations, composed of impersonal elements which are never affected by the changes of government. Conservative of traditions, they are anonymous and lasting, and constitute an occult power before which all others must eventually bow. Their action has even increased to such a degree that, as we shall presently show, there is a danger that they may form an anonymous State more powerful than the official State. France has thus come to be governed by heads of departments and government clerks. The more we study the history of revolutions the more we discover that they change practically nothing but the label. To create a revolution is easy, but to change the soul of a people is difficult indeed.

# CHAPTER IV

## THE PART PLAYED BY THE PEOPLE IN REVOLUTIONS

1. *The stability and malleability of the national mind.*
THE knowledge of a people at any given moment of its history involves an understanding of its environment and above all of its past. Theoretically one may deny that past, as did the men of the Revolution, as many men of the present day have done, but its influence remains indestructible.

In the past, built up by slow accumulations cf centuries, was formed the aggregation of thoughts, sentiments, traditions, and prejudices constituting the national mind which makes the strength of a race. Without it no progress is possible. Each generation would necessitate a fresh beginning.

The aggregate composing the soul of a people is solidly established only if it possesses a certain rigidity, but this rigidity must not pass a certain limit, or there would be no such thing as malleability.

Without rigidity the ancestral soul would have no fixity, and without malleability it could not adapt itself to the changes of environment resulting from the progress of civilisation.

Excessive malleability of the national mind impels a people to incessant revolutions. Excess of rigidity leads it to decadence. Living species, like the races of humanity, disappear when, too fixedly established by a long past, they become incapable of adapting themselves to new conditions of existence.

Few peoples have succeeded in effecting a just equilibrium between these two contrary qualities of stability and malleability. The Romans in antiquity and the English in modern times may be cited among those who have best attained it.

The peoples whose mind is most fixed and established often effect the most violent revolutions. Not having succeeded in evolving progressively, in adapting themselves to changes of environment, they are forced to adapt themselves violently when such adaptation becomes indispensable.

Stability is only acquired very slowly. The history of a race is above all the story of its long efforts to establish its mind. So long as it has not succeeded it forms a horde of barbarians without cohesion and strength. After the invasions of the end of the Roman Empire France took several centuries to form a national soul.

She finally achieved one ; but in the course of centuries this soul finally became too rigid. With a little more malleability, the ancient monarchy would have been slowly transformed as it was elsewhere, and we should have avoided, together with the Revolution and its consequences, the heavy task of remaking a national soul.

The preceding considerations show us the part of race in the genesis of revolutions, and explain why the same revolutions will produce such different effects in different countries ; why, for example, the ideas of the

# The Psychology of Revolution

French Revolution, welcomed with such enthusiasm by some peoples, were rejected by others.

Certainly England, although a very stable country, has suffered two revolutions and slain a king ; but the mould of her mental armour was at once stable enough to retain the acquisitions of the past and malleable enough to modify them only within the necessary limits. Never did England dream, as did the men of the French Revolution, of destroying the ancestral heritage in order to erect a new society in the name of reason.

"While the Frenchman," writes M. A. Sorel, " despised his government, detested his clergy, hated the nobility, and revolted against the laws, the Englishman was proud of his religion, his constitution, his aristocracy, his House of Lords. These were like so many towers of the formidable Bastille in which he entrenched himself, under the British standard, to judge Europe and cover her with contempt. He admitted that the command was disputed inside the fort, but no stranger must approach."

The influence of race in the destiny of the peoples appears plainly in the history of the perpetual revolutions of the Spanish republics of South America. Composed of half-castes, that is to say, of individuals whose diverse heredities have dissociated their ancestral characteristics, these populations have no national soul and therefore no stability. A people of half-castes is always ungovernable.

If we would learn more of the differences of political capacity which the racial factor creates we must examine the same nation as governed by two races successively.

# The Part Played by People in Revolutions

The event is not rare in history. It has been manifested in a striking manner of late in Cuba and the Phillipines, which passed suddenly from the rule of Spain to that of the United States.

We know in what anarchy and poverty Cuba existed under Spanish rule ; we know, too, to what a degree of prosperity the island was brought in a few years when it fell into the hands of the United States.

The same experience was repeated in the Phillipines, which for centuries had been governed by Spain. Finally the country was no more than a vast jungle, the home of epidemics of every kind, where a miserable population vegetated without commerce or industry. After a few years of American rule the country was entirely transformed : malaria, yellow fever, plague and cholera had entirely disappeared. The swamps were drained ; the country was covered with railways, factories and schools. In thirteen years the mortality was reduced by two-thirds.

It is to such examples that we must refer the theorist who has not yet grasped the profound significance of the word race, and how far the ancestral soul of a people rules over its destiny.

## 2. *How the people regards Revolution.*

The part of the people has been the same in all revolutions. It is never the people that conceives them nor directs them. Its activity is released by means of leaders.

Only when the direct interests of the people are involved do we see, as recently in Champagne, any fraction of the people rising spontaneously. A movement thus localised constitutes a mere riot.

# The Psychology of Revolution

Revolution is easy when the leaders are very influential. Of this Portugal and Brazil have recently furnished proofs. But new ideas penetrate the people very slowly indeed. Generally it accepts a revolution without knowing why, and when by chance it does succeed in understanding why, the revolution is over long ago.

The people will create a revolution because it is persuaded to do so, but it does not understand very much of the ideas of its leaders; it interprets them in its own fashion, and this fashion is by no means that of the true authors of the revolution. The French Revolution furnished a striking example of this fact.

The Revolution of 1789 had as its real object the substitution of the power of the nobility by that of the *bourgeoisie*; that is, an old *élite* which had become incapable was to be replaced by a new *élite* which did possess capacity.

There was little question of the people in this first phase of the Revolution. The sovereignty of the people was proclaimed, but it amounted only to the right of electing its representatives.

Extremely illiterate, not hoping, like the middle classes, to ascend the social scale, not in any way feeling itself the equal of the nobles, and not aspiring ever to become their equal, the people had views and interests very different to those of the upper classes of society.

The struggles of the assembly with the royal power led it to call for the intervention of the people in these struggles. It intervened more and more, and the bourgeois revolution rapidly became a popular revolution.

# The Part Played by People in Revolutions

An idea having no force of its own, and acting only by virtue of possessing an affective and mystic substratum which supports it, the theoretical ideas of the *bourgeoisie*, before they could act on the people, had to be transformed into a new and very definite faith, springing from obvious practical interests.

This transformation was rapidly effected when the people heard the men envisaged by it as the Government assuring it that it was the equal of its former masters. It began to regard itself as a victim, and proceeded to pillage, burn, and massacre, imagining that in so doing it was exercising a right.

The great strength of the revolutionary principles was that they gave a free course to the instincts of primitive barbarity which had been restrained by the secular and inhibitory action of environment, tradition, and law.

All the social bonds that formerly contained the multitude were day by day dissolving, so that it conceived a notion of unlimited power, and the joy of seeing its ancient masters ferreted out and despoiled. Having become the sovereign people, were not all things permissible to it?

The motto of Liberty, Equality, Fraternity, a true manifestation of hope and faith at the beginning of the Revolution, soon merely served to cover a legal justification of the sentiments of jealousy, cupidity, and hatred of superiors, the true motives of crowds unrestrained by discipline. This is why the Revolution so soon ended in disorder, violence, and anarchy.

From the moment when the Revolution descended from the middle to the lower classes of society, it ceased to be a domination of the instinctive by the

# The Psychology of Revolution

rational, and became, on the contrary, the effort of the instinctive to overpower the rational.

This legal triumph of the atavistic instincts was terrible. The whole effort of societies  an effort indispensable to their continued existence—had always been to restrain, thanks to the power of tradition, customs, and codes, certain natural instincts which man has inherited from his primitive animality. It is possible to dominate them—and the more a people does overcome them the more civilised it is—but they cannot be destroyed. The influence of various exciting causes will readily result in their reappearance.

This is why the liberation of popular passions is so dangerous. The torrent, once escaped from its bed, does not return until it has spread devastation far and wide. "Woe to him who stirs up the dregs of a nation," said Rivarol at the beginning of the Revolution. "There is no age of enlightenment for the populace."

### The supposed Part of the People during Revolution.

The laws of the psychology of crowds show us that the people never acts without leaders, and that although it plays a considerable part in revolutions by following and exaggerating the impulses received, it never directs its own movements.

In all political revolutions we discover the action of leaders. They do not create the ideas which serve as the basis of revolutions, but they utilise them as a means of action. Ideas, leaders, armies, and crowds constitute four elements which all have their part to play in revolutions.

# The Part Played by People in Revolutions

The crowd, roused by the leaders, acts especially by means of its mass. Its action is comparable to that of the shell which perforates an armour-plate by the momentum of a force it did not create. Rarely does the crowd understand anything of the revolutions accomplished with its assistance. It obediently follows its leaders without even trying to find out what they want. It overthrew Charles X. because of his Ordinances without having any idea of the contents of the latter, and would have been greatly embarrassed had it been asked at a later date why it overthrew Louis-Philippe.

Deceived by appearances, many authors, from Michelet to Aulard, have supposed that the people effected our great Revolution.

" The principal actor," said Michelet, "is the people."

" It is an error to say," writes M. Aulard, "that the French Revolution was effected by a few distinguished people or a few heroes. . . . I believe that in the whole history of the period included between 1789 and 1799 not a single person stands out who led or shaped events : neither Louis XVI. nor Mirabeau nor Danton nor Robespierre. Must we say that it was the French people that was the real hero of the French Revolution ? Yes—provided we see the French people not as a multitude but as a number of organised groups."

And in a recent work M. A. Cochin insists on this conception of popular action.

" And here is the wonder: Michelet is right. In proportion as we know them better the facts seem to consecrate the fiction : this crowd, without chiefs and without laws, the very image of chaos, did for five years govern and command, speak and act, with a pre-

# The Psychology of Revolution

cision, a consistency, and an entirety that were marvellous. Anarchy gave lessons in order and discipline to
the defeated party of order . . . twenty-five millions
of men, spread over an area of 30,000 square leagues,
acted as one."

Certainly if this simultaneous conduct of the people
had been spontaneous, as the author supposes, it
would have been marvellous. M. Aulard himself
understands very well the impossibilities of such a
phenomenon, for he is careful, in speaking of the
people, to say that he is speaking of groups, and that
these groups may have been guided by leaders :—

"And what, then, cemented the national unity?
Who saved this nation, attacked by the king and
rent by civil war? Was it Danton? Was it
Robespierre? Was it Carnot? Certainly these
individual men were of service : but unity was in
fact maintained and independence assured by the
grouping of the French into communes and popular
societies—people's clubs. It was the municipal and
Jacobin organisation of France that forced the
coalition of Europe to retreat. But in each group,
if we look more closely, there were two or three
individuals more capable than the rest, who, whether
leaders or led, executed decisions and had the appearance of leaders, but who (if, for instance, we read the
proceedings of the people's clubs) seem to us to have
drawn their strength far more from their group than
from themselves.

M. Aulard's mistake consists in supposing that all
these groups were derived "from a spontaneous
movement of fraternity and reason." France at
that time was covered with thousands of little clubs,

# The Part Played by People in Revolutions

receiving a single impulsion from the great Jacobin Club of Paris, and obeying it with perfect docility. This is what reality teaches us, though the illusions of the Jacobins do not permit them to accept the fact.[1]

### 4. *The Popular Entity and its Constituent Elements.*

In order to answer to certain theoretical conceptions the people was erected into a mystic entity, endowed with all the powers and all the virtues, incessantly praised by the politicians, and overwhelmed with flattery. We shall see what we are to make of this conception of the part played by the people in the French Revolution.

To the Jacobins of this epoch, as to those of our own days, this popular entity constitutes a superior personality possessing the attributes, peculiar to divinities, of never having to answer for its actions and never making a mistake. Its wishes must be

---

[1] In the historical manuals which M. Aulard has prepared for the use of classes in collaboration with M. Debidour the *rôle* attributed to the people as an entity is even more marked. We see it intervening continually and spontaneously; here are a few examples :—

*The " Day " of June the 20th :* " The king dismissed the Girondist members. The people of Paris, indignant, rose spontaneously and invaded the Tuileries."

*The " Day " of August 10th :* " The Legislative Assembly dared not overthrow it ; it was the people of Paris, aided by the Federals of the Departments, who effected this revolution at the price of its blood."

*The conflict of the Girondists and the Mountain :* " This discord in the face of the enemy was dangerous. The people put an end to it on the days of the 31st of May and the 2nd of June, 1793, when it forced the Convention to expel the leaders of the Gironde from its midst and to decree their arrest."

# The Psychology of Revolution

humbly acceded. The people may kill, burn, ravage, commit the most frightful cruelties, glorify its hero to-day and throw him into the gutter to-morrow; it is all one; the politicians will not cease to vaunt its virtues, its high wisdom, and to bow to its every decision.[1]

Now in what does this entity really consist, this mysterious fetich which revolutionists have revered for more than a century?

It may be decomposed into two distinct categories. The first includes the peasants, traders, and workers of all sorts who need tranquillity and order that they may exercise their calling. This people forms the majority, but a majority which never caused a revolution. Living in laborious silence, it is ignored by the historians.

The second category, which plays a capital part in all national disturbances, consists of a subversive social residue dominated by a criminal mentality. Degenerates of alcoholism and poverty, thieves, beggars, destitute "casuals," indifferent workers without employment—these constitute the dangerous bulk of the armies of insurrection.

The fear of punishment prevents many of them from becoming criminals at ordinary times, but they do become criminals as soon as they can exercise their evil instincts without danger.

[1] These pretensions do at least seem to be growing untenable to the more advanced republicans.

"The rage with the socialists" writes M. Clemenceau, "is to endow with all the virtues, as though by a superhuman reason, the crowd whose reason cannot be much to boast of." The famous statesman might say more correctly that reason not only cannot be prominent in the crowd but is practically non-existent.

70

# The Part Played by People in Revolutions

To this sinister substratum are due the massacres which stain all revolutions.

It was this class which, guided by its leaders, continually invaded the great revolutionary Assemblies. These regiments of disorder had no other ideal than that of massacre, pillage, and incendiarism. Their indifference to theories and principles was complete.

To the elements recruited from the lowest dregs of the populace are added, by way of contagion, a host of idle and indifferent persons who are simply drawn into the movement. They shout because there are men shouting, and revolt because there is a revolt, without having the vaguest idea of the cause of shouting or revolution. The suggestive power of their environment absolutely hypnotises them, and impels them to action.

These noisy and maleficent crowds, the kernel of all insurrections, from antiquity to our own times, are the only crowds known to the orator. To the orator they are the sovereign people. As a matter of fact this sovereign people is principally composed of the lower populace of whom Thiers said :—

"Since the time when Tacitus saw it applaud the crimes of the emperors the vile populace has not changed. These barbarians who swarm at the bottom of societies are always ready to stain the people with every crime, at the beck of every power, and to the dishonour of every cause."

At no period of history was the *rôle* of the lowest elements of the population exercised in such a lasting fashion as in the French Revolution.

The massacres began as soon as the beast was unchained—that is, from 1789, long before the

71

# The Psychology of Revolution

Convention. They were carried out with all possible refinements of cruelty. During the killing of September the prisoners were slowly chopped to bits by sabre-cuts in order to prolong their agonies and amuse the spectators, who experienced the greatest delight before the spectacle of the convulsions of the victims and their shrieks of agony.

Similar scenes were observed all over France, even in the early days of the Revolution, although the foreign war did not excuse them then, nor any other pretext.

From March to September a whole series of burnings, killings, and pillagings drenched all France in blood. Taine cites one hundred and twenty such cases. Rouen, Lyons, Strasbourg, &c., fell into the power of the populace.

The Mayor of Troyes, his eyes destroyed by blows of scissors, was murdered after hours of suffering. The Colonel of Dragoons Belzuce was cut to pieces while living. In many places the hearts of the victims were torn out and carried about the cities on the point of a pike.

Such is the behaviour of the base populace so soon as imprudent hands have broken the network of constraints which binds its ancestral savagery. It meets with every indulgence because it is in the interests of the politicians to flatter it. But let us for a moment suppose the thousands of beings who constitute it condensed into one single being. The personality thus formed would appear as a cruel and narrow and abominable monster, more horrible than the bloodiest tyrants of history.

This impulsive and ferocious people has always

# The Part Played by People in Revolutions

been easily dominated so soon as a strong power has opposed it. If its violence is unlimited, so is its servility. All the despotisms have had it for their servant. The Cæsars are certain of being acclaimed by it, whether they are named Caligula, Nero, Marat, Robespierre, or Boulanger.

Beside these destructive hordes whose action during revolution is capital, there exists, as we have already remarked, the mass of the true people, which asks only the right to labour. It sometimes benefits by revolutions, but never causes them. The revolutionary theorists know little of it and distrust it, aware of its traditional and conservative basis. The resistant nucleus of a country, it makes the strength and continuity of the latter. Extremely docile through fear, easily influenced by its leaders, it will momentarily commit every excess while under their influence, but the ancestral inertia of the race will soon take charge again, which is the reason why it so quickly tires of revolution. Its traditional soul quickly incites it to oppose itself to anarchy when the latter goes too far. At such times it seeks the leader who will restore order.

This people, resigned and peaceable, has evidently no very lofty nor complicated political conceptions. Its governmental ideal is always very simple, is something very like dictatorship. This is why, from the times of the Greeks to our own, dictatorship has always followed anarchy. It followed it after the first Revolution, when Bonaparte was acclaimed, and again when, despite opposition, four successive plebiscites raised Louis Napoleon to the head of the republic, ratified his *coup d'État*, re-established the Empire, and in 1870, before the war, approved of his rule.

73

# The Psychology of Revolution

Doubtless in these last instances the people was deceived. But without the revolutionary conspiracies which led to disorder, it would not have been impelled to seek the means of escape therefrom.

The facts recalled in this chapter must not be forgotten if we wish fully to comprehend the various *rôles* of the people during revolution. Its action is considerable, but very unlike that imagined by the legends whose repetition alone constitutes their vitality.

## BOOK II

### THE FORMS OF MENTALITY PREVALENT DURING REVOLUTION

## CHAPTER I

### INDIVIDUAL VARIATIONS OF CHARACTER IN TIME OF REVOLUTION

#### 1. *Transformations of Personality.*

I HAVE dwelt at length elsewhere upon a certain theory of character, without which it is absolutely impossible to understand divers transformations or inconsistencies of conduct which occur at certain moments, notably in time of revolution. Here are the principal points of this theory :

Every individual possesses, besides his habitual mentality, which, when the environment does not alter, is almost constant, various possibilities of character which may be evoked by passing events.

The people who surround us are the creatures of certain circumstances, but not of all circumstances. Our ego consists of the association of innumerable cellular egos, the residues of ancestral personalities. By their combination they form an equilibrium which is fairly permanent when the social environment does not vary. As soon as this environment is consider-

# The Psychology of Revolution

ably modified, as in time of insurrection, this equilibrium is broken, and the dissociated elements constitute, by a fresh aggregation, a new personality, which is manifested by ideas, feelings, and actions very different from those formerly observed in the same individual. Thus it is that during the Terror we see honest *bourgeois* and peaceful magistrates who were noted for their kindness turned into bloodthirsty fanatics.

Under the influence of environment the old personality may therefore give place to one entirely new. For this reason the actors in great religious and political crises often seem of a different essence to ourselves ; yet they do not differ from us ; the repetition of the same events would bring back the same men.

Napoleon perfectly understood these possibilities of character when he said, in Saint Helena :—

" It is because I know just how great a part chance plays in our political decisions, that I have always been without prejudices, and very indulgent as to the part men have taken during our disturbances. . . . In time of revolution one can only say what one has done ; it would not be wise to say that one could not have done otherwise. . . . Men are difficult to understand if we want to be just. . . . Do they know themselves ? Do they account for themselves very clearly ? There are virtues and vices of circumstance."

When the normal personality has been disaggregated under the influence of certain events, how does the new personality form itself ? By several means, the most active of which is the acquisition of a strong belief. This orientates all the elements of the understanding, as the magnet collects into regular curves the filings of a magnetic metal.

Thus were formed the personalities observed in times of great crises : the Crusades, the Reformation, the Revolution notably.

At normal times the environment varies little, so that as a rule we see only a single personality in the individuals that surround us. Sometimes, however, it happens that we observe several, which in certain circumstances may replace one another.

These personalities may be contradictory and even inimical. This phenomenon, exceptional under normal conditions, is considerably accentuated in certain pathological conditions. Morbid psychology has recorded several examples of multiple personality in a single subject, such as the cases cited by Morton Prince and Pierre Janet.

In all these variations of personality it is not the intelligence which is modified, but the feelings, whose association forms the character.

## 2. *Elements of Character Predominant in Time of Revolution.*

During revolution we see several sentiments developed which are commonly repressed, but to which the destruction of social constraints gives a free vent.

These constraints, consisting of the law, morality, and tradition, are not always completely broken. Some survive the upheaval and serve to some extent to damp the explosion of dangerous sentiments.

The most powerful of these restraints is the soul of the race. This determines a manner of seeing, feel-

# The Psychology of Revolution

ing, and willing common to the majority of the individuals of the same people ; it constitutes a hereditary custom, and nothing is more powerful than the ties of custom.

This racial influence limits the variations of a people and determines its destiny within certain limits in spite of all superficial changes.

For example, to take only the instances of history, it would seem that the mentality of France must have varied enormously during a single century. In a few years it passed from the Revolution to Cæsarism, returned to the monarchy, effected another Revolution, and then summoned a new Cæsar. In reality only the outsides of things had changed.

We cannot insist further here on the limits of national variability, but must now consider the influence of certain affective elements, whose development during revolution contributes to modify individual or collective personalities. In particular I will mention hatred, fear, ambition, jealousy or envy, vanity, and enthusiasm. We observe their influence during several of the upheavals of history, notably during the course of the French Revolution, which will furnish us with most of our examples.

*Hatred.*—The hatred of persons, institutions, and things which animated the men of the Revolution is one of these affective phenomena which are the more striking the more one studies their psychology. They detested, not only their enemies, but the members of their own party. " If one were to accept unreservedly," said a recent writer, " the judgments which they expressed of one another, we should have to conclude that they were all traitors and boasters, all incapable and corrupt, all assassins or tyrants." We know with what hatred, scarcely appeased by the death of their enemies, men persecuted the Girondists, Dantonists, Hébertists, Robespierrists, &c.

One of the chief causes of this feeling resided in the fact that these furious sectaries, being apostles in possession of the absolute verity, were unable, like all believers, to tolerate the sight of infidels. A mystic or sentimental certitude is always accompanied by the need of forcing itself on others, is never convinced, and does not shrink from wholesale slaughter when it has the power to commit it.

If the hatreds that divided the men of the Revolution had been of rational origin they would not have lasted long, but, arising from affective and mystic factors, men could neither forget nor forgive. Their sources being identical in the different parties, they manifested themselves on every hand with identical violence. It has been proved, by means of documents, that the Girondists were no less sanguinary than the Montagnards. They were the first to declare, with Pétion, that the vanquished parties should perish. They also, according to M. Aulard, attempted to justify the massacres of September. The Terror must not be considered simply as a means of defence, but as the general process of destruction to which triumphant believers have always treated their detested enemies. Men who can put up with the greatest divergence of ideas cannot tolerate differences of belief.

In religious or political warfare the vanquished can hope for no quarter. From Sulla, who cut the throats of two hundred senators and five or six thousand Romans, to the men who suppressed the Commune, and shot down more than twenty thousand after their victory, this bloody law has never failed. Proved over and over again in the past, it will doubtless be so in the future.

The hatreds of the Revolution did not arise entirely from divergence of belief. Other sentiments—envy, ambition, and self-love—also engendered them. The rivalry of individuals aspiring to power led the chiefs of the various groups in succession to the scaffold.

We must remember, moreover, that the need of division and the hatred resulting therefrom seem to be constituent elements of the Latin mind. They cost our Gaulish ancestors their independence, and had already struck Cæsar.

"No city," he said, "but was divided into two factions ; no canton, no village, no house in which the spirit of party did not breathe. It was very rarely that a year went by without a city taking up arms to attack or repulse its neighbours."

As man has only recently entered upon the age of knowledge, and has always hitherto been guided by sentiments and beliefs, we may conceive the vast importance of hatred as a factor of his history.

Commandant Colin, professor at the College of War, remarks in the following terms on the importance of this feeling during certain wars :—

"In war more than at any other time there is no better inspiring force than hatred ; it was hatred that made Blücher victorious over Napoleon. Analyse the most wonderful manœuvres, the most decisive operations, and if they are not the work of an exceptional man, a Frederick or a Napoleon, you will find they are inspired by passion more than by calculation.

# Variations of Character in Revolution

What would the war of 1870 have been without the hatred which we bore the Germans ? "

The writer might have added that the intense hatred of the Japanese for the Russians, who had so humiliated them, might be classed among the causes of their success. The Russian soldiers, ignorant of the very existence of the Japanese, had no animosity against them, which was one of the reasons of their failure.

There was assuredly a good deal of talk of fraternity at the time of the Revolution, and there is even more to-day. Pacificism, humanitarianism, and solidarity have become catchwords of the advanced parties, but we know how profound are the hatreds concealed beneath these terms, and what dangers overhang our modern society.

*Fear.*—Fear plays almost as large a part in revolutions as hatred. During the French Revolution there were many examples of great individual courage and many exhibitions of collective cowardice.

Facing the scaffold, the men of the Convention were always brave in the extreme ; but before the threats of the rioters who invaded the Assembly they constantly exhibited an excessive pusillanimity, obeying the most absurd injunctions, as we shall see if we re-read the history of the revolutionary Assemblies.

All the forms of fear were observed at this period. One of the most widespread was the fear of appearing moderate. Members of the Assemblies, public prosecutors, representatives "on mission," judges of the revolutionary tribunals, &c., all sought to appear more advanced than their rivals. Fear was one of the principal elements of the crimes committed at this

# The Psychology of Revolution

period. If by some miracle it could have been eliminated from the revolutionary Assemblies, their conduct would have been quite other than it was, and the Revolution itself would have taken a very different direction.

*Ambition, Envy, Vanity,* &c.—In normal times the influence of these various affective elements is forcibly contained by social necessities. Ambition, for instance, is necessarily limited in a hierarchical form of society. Although the soldier does sometimes become a general, it is only after a long term of service. In time of revolution, on the other hand, there is no need to wait. Every one may reach the upper ranks almost immediately, so that all ambitions are violently aroused. The humblest man believes himself fitted for the highest employments, and by this very fact his vanity grows out of all measure.

All the passions being more or less aroused, including ambition and vanity, we see the development of jealousy and envy of those who have succeeded more quickly than others.

The effect of jealousy, always important in times of revolution, was especially so during the great French Revolution. Jealousy of the nobility constituted one of its most important factors. The middle classes had increased in capacity and wealth, to the point of surpassing the nobility. Although they mingled with the nobles more and more, they felt, none the less, that they were held at a distance, and this they keenly resented. This frame of mind had unconsciously made the *bourgeoisie* keen supporters of the philosophic doctrine of equality.

Wounded self-love and jealousy were thus the

causes of hatreds that we can scarcely conceive to-day, when the social influence of the nobility is so small. Many members of the Convention—Carrier, Marat, and others—remembered with anger that they had once occupied subordinate positions in the establishments of great nobles. Mme. Roland was never able to forget that, when she and her mother were invited to the house of a great lady under the *ancien régime*, they had been sent to dine in the servants' quarters.

The philosopher Rivarol has very well described in the following passage, already cited by Taine, the influence of wounded self-love and jealousy upon the revolutionary hatreds :—

"It is not," he writes, "the taxes, nor the *lettres de cachet*, nor any of the other abuses of authority ; it is not the sins of the intendants, nor the long and ruinous delays of justice, that has most angered the nation ; it is the prejudices of the nobility for which it has exhibited the greatest hatred. What proves this clearly is the fact that it is the *bourgeois*, the men of letters, the men of money, in fact all those who are jealous of the nobility, who have raised the poorer inhabitants of the cities against them, and the peasants in the country districts."

This very true statement partly justifies the saying of Napoleon : "Vanity made the Revolution ; liberty was only the pretext."

*Enthusiasm.*—The enthusiasm of the founders of the Revolution equalled that of the apostles of the faith of Mohammed. And it was really a religion that the *bourgeois* of the first Assembly thought to found. They thought to have destroyed an old world,

# The Psychology of Revolution

and to have built a new one upon its ruins. Never did illusion more seductive fire the hearts of men. Equality and fraternity, proclaimed by the new dogmas, were to bring the reign of eternal happiness to all the peoples. Man had broken for ever with a past of barbarity and darkness. The regenerated world would in future be illuminated by the lucid radiance of pure reason. On all hands the most brilliant oratorical formulæ saluted the expected dawn.

That this enthusiasm was so soon replaced by violence was due to the fact that the awakening was speedy and terrible. One can readily conceive the indignant fury with which the apostles of the Revolution attacked the daily obstacles opposed to the realisation of their dreams. They had sought to reject the past, to forget tradition, to make man over again. But the past reappeared incessantly, and men refused to change. The reformers, checked in their onward march, would not give in. They sought to impose by force a dictatorship which speedily made men regret the system abolished, and finally led to its return.

It is to be remarked that although the enthusiasm of the first days did not last in the revolutionary Assemblies, it survived very much longer in the armies, and constituted their chief strength. To tell the truth, the armies of the Revolution were republican long before France became so, and remained republican long after France had ceased to be so.

The variations of character considered in this chapter, being conditioned by certain common aspirations and identical changes of environment, finally

became concrete in a small number of fairly homogeneous mentalities. Speaking only of the more
characteristic, we may refer them to four types:
the Jacobin, mystic, revolutionary, and criminal
mentalities.

# CHAPTER II

## THE MYSTIC MENTALITY AND THE JACOBIN
## MENTALITY

### 1. *Classification of Mentalities predominant in Time of Revolution.*

THE classifications without which the study of the sciences is impossible must necessarily establish the discontinuous in the continuous, and for that reason are to a certain extent artificial. But they are necessary, since the continuous is only accessible in the form of the discontinuous.

To create broad distinctions between the various mentalities observable in time of revolution, as we are about to do, is obviously to separate elements which encroach upon one another, which are fused or superimposed. We must resign ourselves to losing a little in exactitude in order to gain in lucidity. The fundamental types enumerated at the end of the preceding chapter, and which we are about to describe, synthetise groups which would escape analysis were we to attempt to study them in all their complexity.

We have shown that man is influenced by different logics, which under normal conditions exist in juxtaposition, without mutually influencing one another. Under the action of various events they enter into mutual conflict, and the irreducible differences

86

which divide them are visibly manifested, involving considerable individual and social upheavals.

Mystic logic, which we shall presently consider as it appears in the Jacobin mind, plays a very important part. But it is not alone in its action. The other forms of logic—affective logic, collective logic, and rational logic—may predominate according to circumstances.

## 2. *The Mystic Mentality.*

Leaving aside for the moment the influence of affective, rational, and collective logic, we will occupy ourselves solely with the considerable part played by the mystic elements which have prevailed in so many revolutions, and notably in the French Revolution.

The chief characteristic of the mystic temperament consists in the attribution of a mysterious power to superior beings or forces, which are incarnated in the form of idols, fetiches, words, or formulæ.

The mystic spirit is at the bottom of all the religious and most political beliefs. These latter would often vanish could we deprive them of the mystic elements which are their chief support.

Grafted on the sentiments and passionate impulses which it directs, mystic logic constitutes the might of the great popular movements. Men who would be by no means ready to allow themselves to be killed for the best of reasons will readily sacrifice their lives to a mystic ideal which has become an object of adoration.

The principles of the Revolution speedily inspired a wave of mystic enthusiasm analogous to those provoked by the various religious beliefs which had preceded it. All they did was to change the orientation of a mental ancestry which the centuries had solidified.

So there is nothing astonishing in the savage zeal of the men of the Convention. Their mystic mentality was the same as that of the Protestants at the time of the Reformation. The principal heroes of the Terror—Couthon, Saint-Just, Robespierre, &c.—were Apostles. Like Polyeuctes, destroying the altars of the false gods to propagate his faith, they dreamed of converting the globe. Their enthusiasm spilled itself over the earth. Persuaded that their magnificent formulæ were sufficient to overturn thrones, they did not hesitate to declare war upon kings. And as a strong faith is always superior to a doubtful faith, they victoriously faced all Europe.

The mystic spirit of the leaders of the Revolution was betrayed in the least details of their public life. Robespierre, convinced that he was supported by the Almighty, assured his hearers in a speech that the Supreme Being had "decreed the Republic since the beginning of time." In his quality of High Pontiff of a State religion he made the Convention vote a decree declaring that "the French People recognises the existence of the Supreme Being and the immortality of the soul." At the festival of this Supreme Being, seated on a kind of throne, he preached a lengthy sermon.

The Jacobin Club, directed by Robespierre, finally assumed all the functions of a council. There Maximilien proclaimed "the idea of a Great Being who watches over oppressed innocence and who punishes triumphant crime."

All the heretics who criticised the Jacobin orthodoxy were excommunicated—that is, were sent to the Revolutionary Tribunal, which they left only for the scaffold.

The mystic mentality of which Robespierre was the most celebrated representative did not die with him. Men of identical mentality are to be found among the French politicians of to-day. The old religious beliefs no longer rule their minds, but they are the creatures of political creeds which they would very soon force on others, as did Robespierre, if they had the chance of so doing. Always ready to kill if killing would spread their faith, the mystics of all ages have employed the same means of persuasion as soon as they have become the masters.

It is therefore quite natural that Robespierre should still have many admirers. Minds moulded like his are to be met with in their thousands. His conceptions were not guillotined with him. Old as humanity, they will only disappear with the last believer.

This mystic aspect of all revolutions has escaped the majority of the historians. They will persist for a long time yet in trying to explain by means of rational logic a host of phenomena which have nothing to do with reason. I have already cited a passage from the history of MM. Lavisse and Rambaud, in which the Reformation is explained as "the result of the free individual reflections suggested to simple folk by an extremely pious conscience, and a bold and courageous reason."

Such movements are never comprehended by those who imagine that their origin is rational. Political or religious, the beliefs which have moved the world possess a common origin and follow the same laws. They are formed, not by the reason, but more often contrary to reason. Buddhism, Christianity, Islamism, the Reformation, sorcery, Jacobinism, socialism, spiritualism, &c., seem very different forms of belief, but they have, I repeat, identical mystic and affective bases, and obey forms of logic which have no affinity with rational logic. Their might resides precisely in the fact that reason has as little power to create them as to transform them.

The mystic mentality of our modern political apostles is strongly marked in an article dealing with one of our recent ministers, which I cite from a leading journal :

" One may ask into what category does M. A—— fall ? Could we say, for instance, that he belongs to the group of unbelievers ? Far from it ! Certainly M. A—— has not adopted any positive faith ; certainly he curses Rome and Geneva, rejecting all the traditional dogmas and all the known Churches. But if he makes a clean sweep it is in order to found his own Church on the ground so cleared, a Church more dogmatic than all the rest ; and his own inquisition, whose brutal intolerance would have no reason to envy the most notorious of Torquemadas.

" ' We cannot,' he says, ' allow such a thing as scholastic neutrality. We demand lay instruction in all its plenitude, and are consequently the enemies of educational liberty.' If he does not suggest erecting the stake and the pyre, it is only on account of the evolution of manners, which he is forced to take into account to a certain extent, whether he will or no. But, not being able to commit men to the torture, he

90

invokes the secular arm to condemn their doctrines to death. This is exactly the point of view of the great inquisitors. It is the same attack upon thought. This freethinker has so free a spirit that every philosophy he does not accept appears to him, not only ridiculous and grotesque, but criminal. He flatters himself that he alone is in possession of the absolute truth. Of this he is so entirely sure that everyone who contradicts him seems to him an execrable monster and a public enemy. He does not suspect for a moment that after all his personal views are only hypotheses, and that he is all the more laughable for claiming a Divine right for them precisely because they deny divinity. Or, at least, they profess to do so; but they re-establish it in another shape, which immediately makes one regret the old. M. A—— is a sectary of the goddess Reason, of whom he has made a Moloch, an oppressive deity hungry for sacrifice. No more liberty of thought for any one except for himself and his friends; such is the free thought of M. A——. The outlook is truly attractive. But perhaps too many idols have been cast down during the last few centuries for men to bow before this one."

We must hope for the sake of liberty that these gloomy fanatics will never finally become our masters.

Given the silent power of reason over mystic beliefs, it is quite useless to seek to discuss, as is so often done, the rational value of revolutionary or political ideas. Only their influence can interest us. It matters little that the theories of the supposed equality of men, the original goodness of mankind, the possibility of re-making society by means of laws, have been given the lie by observation and experience. These empty illusions must be counted among the most potent motives of action that humanity has known.

### 3. *The Jacobin Mentality.*

Although the term " Jacobin mentality " does not really belong to any true classification, I employ it here because it sums up a clearly defined combination which constitutes a veritable psychological species.

This mentality dominates the men of the French Revolution, but is not peculiar to them, as it still represents one of the most active elements in our politics.

The mystic mentality which we have already considered is an essential factor of the Jacobin mind, but it is not in itself enough to constitute that mind. Other elements, which we shall now examine, must be added.

The Jacobins do not in the least suspect their mysticism. On the contrary, they profess to be guided solely by pure reason. During the Revolution they invoked reason incessantly, and considered it as their only guide to conduct.

The majority of historians have adopted this rationalist conception of the Jacobin mind, and Taine fell into the same error. It is in the abuse of rationalism that he seeks the origin of a great proportion of the acts of the Jacobins. The pages in which he has dealt with the subject contain many truths, however, and as they are in other ways very remarkable, I reproduce the most important passages here :—

" Neither exaggerated self-love nor dogmatic

# Mystic Mentality and Jacobin Mentality

reasoning is rare in the human species. In all countries these two roots of the Jacobin spirit subsist, secret and indestructible. . . . At twenty years of age, when a young man is entering into the world, his reason is stimulated simultaneously with his pride. In the first place, whatever society he may move in, it is contemptible to pure reason, for it has not been constructed by a philosophic legislator according to a principle, but successive generations have arranged it according to their multiple and ever-changing needs. It is not the work of logic, but of history, and the young reasoner shrugs his shoulders at the sight of this old building, whose site is arbitrary, whose architecture is incoherent, and whose inconveniences are obvious. . . . The majority of young people, above all those who have their way to make, are more or less Jacobin on leaving college. . . . Jacobinism is born of social decomposition just as mushrooms are born of a fermenting soil. Consider the authentic monuments of its thought—the speeches of Robespierre and Saint-Just, the debates of the Legislative Assembly and the Convention, the harangues, addresses, and reports of Girondists and Montagnards. Never did men speak so much to say so little; the empty verbiage and swollen emphasis swamp any truth there may be beneath their monotony and their turgidity. The Jacobin is full of respect for the phantoms of his reasoning brain; in his eyes they are more real than living men, and their suffrage is the only suffrage he recognises—he will march onward in all sincerity at the head of a procession of imaginary followers. The millions of metaphysical wills which he has created in the image of his own will sustain

# The Psychology of Revolution

him by their unanimous assent, and he will project outwards, like a chorus of triumph and acclamation, the inward echo of his own voice."

While admiring Taine's description, I think he has not exactly grasped the psychology of the Jacobin.

The mind of the true Jacobin, at the time of the Revolution as now, was composed of elements which we must analyse if we are to understand its function.

This analysis will show in the first place that the Jacobin is not a rationalist, but a believer. Far from building his belief on reason, he moulds reason to his belief, and although his speeches are steeped in rationalism he employs it very little in his thoughts and his conduct.

A Jacobin who reasoned as much as he is accused of reasoning would be sometimes accessible to the voice of reason. Now, observation proves, from the time of the Revolution to our own days, that the Jacobin is never influenced by reasoning, however just, and it is precisely here that his strength resides.

And why is he not accessible to reason? Simply because his vision of things, always extremely limited, does not permit of his resisting the powerful and passionate impulses which guide him.

These two elements, feeble reason and strong passions, would not of themselves constitute the Jacobin mind. There is another.

Passion supports convictions, but hardly ever creates them. Now, the true Jacobin has forcible convictions. What is to sustain them? Here the mystic elements whose action we have already studied come into play. The Jacobin is a mystic who has replaced the old divinities by new gods. Imbued with the power of words and formulæ, he attributes to these a mysterious power. To serve these exigent divinities he does not shrink from the most violent measures. The laws voted by our modern Jacobins furnish a proof of this fact.

The Jacobin mentality is found especially in narrow and passionate characters. It implies, in fact, a narrow and rigid mind, inaccessible to all criticism and to all considerations but those of faith.

The mystic and affective elements which dominate the mind of the Jacobin condemn him to an extreme simplicity. Grasping only the superficial relations of things, nothing prevents him from taking for realities the chimerical images which are born of his imagination. The sequence of phenomena and their results escape him. He never raises his eyes from his dream.

As we may see, it is not by the development of his logical reason that the Jacobin exceeds. He possesses very little logic of this kind, and therefore he often becomes dangerous. Where a superior man would hesitate or halt the Jacobin, who has placed his feeble reason at the service of his impulses, goes forward with certainty.

So that although the Jacobin is a great reasoner, this does not mean that he is in the least guided by reason. When he imagines he is being led by reason it is really his passions and his mysticism that lead him. Like all those who are convinced and hemmed in by the walls of faith, he can never escape therefrom.

A true aggressive theologian, he is astonishingly

like the disciples of Calvin described in a previous chapter. Hypnotised by their faith, nothing could deter them from their object. All those who contradicted their articles of faith were considered worthy of death. They too seemed to be powerful reasoners. Ignorant, like the Jacobins, of the secret forces that led them, they believed that reason was their sole guide, while in reality they were the slaves of mysticism and passion.

The truly rationalistic Jacobin would be incomprehensible, and would merely make reason despair. The passionate and mystical Jacobin is, on the contrary, easily intelligible.

With these three elements—a very weak reasoning power, very strong passions, and an intense mysticism —we have the true psychological components of the mind of the Jacobin.

# CHAPTER III

## THE REVOLUTIONARY AND CRIMINAL
## MENTALITIES

### 1. *The Revolutionary Mentality.*

WE have just seen that the mystic elements are one of the components of the Jacobin mentality. We shall now see that they enter into another form of mentality which is also clearly defined, the revolutionary mentality.

In all ages societies have contained a certain number of restless spirits, unstable and discontented, ready to rebel against any established order of affairs. They are actuated by the mere love of revolt, and if some magic power could realise all their desires they would simply revolt again.

This special mentality often results from a faulty adaptation of the individual to his surroundings, or from an excess of mysticism, but it may also be merely a question of temperament or arise from pathological disturbances.

The need of revolt presents very different degrees of intensity, from simple discontent expressed in words directed against men and things to the need of destroying them. Sometimes the individual turns upon himself the revolutionary frenzy that he cannot otherwise exercise. Russia is full of these madmen, who, not content with committing arson or throwing bombs at hazard into the crowd, finally mutilate themselves, like the Skopzis and other analogous sects.

These perpetual rebels are generally highly suggestible beings, whose mystic mentality is obsessed by fixed ideas. Despite the apparent energy indicated by their actions they are really weak characters, and are incapable of mastering themselves sufficiently to resist the impulses that rule them. The mystic spirit which animates them furnishes pretexts for their violence, and enables them to regard themselves as great reformers.

In normal times the rebels which every society contains are restrained by the laws, by their environment—in short, by all the usual social constraints, and therefore remain undetected. But as soon as a time of disturbance begins these constraints grow weaker, and the rebel can give a free reign to his instincts. He then becomes the accredited leader of a movement. The motive of the revolution matters little to him ; he will give his life indifferently for the red flag or the white, or for the liberation of a country which he has heard vaguely mentioned.

The revolutionary spirit is not always pushed to the extremes which render it dangerous. When, instead of deriving from affective or mystic impulses, it has an intellectual origin, it may become a source of progress. It is thanks to those spirits who are sufficiently independent to be intellectually revolutionary that a civilisation is able to escape from the yoke of tradition and habit when this becomes too heavy. The sciences, arts, and industries especially have progressed by the aid of such men. Galileo, Lavoisier, Darwin, and Pasteur were such revolutionaries.

Although it is not necessary that a nation should possess any large number of such spirits, it is very necessary that it should possess some. Without them men would still be living in caves.

The revolutionary audacity which results in discoveries implies very rare faculties. It necessitates notably an independence of mind sufficient to escape from the influence of current opinions, and a judgement that can grasp, under superficial analogies, the hidden realities. This form of revolutionary spirit is creative, while that examined above is destructive.

The revolutionary mentality may, therefore, be compared to certain physiological states in the life of the individual which are normally useful, but which, when exaggerated, take a pathological form which is always hurtful.

## 2. *The Criminal Mentality.*

All the civilised societies inevitably drag behind them a residue of degenerates, of the unadapted, of persons affected by various taints. Vagabonds, beggars, fugitives from justice, thieves, assassins, and starving creatures that live from day to day, may constitute the criminal population of the great cities. In ordinary times these waste products of civilisation are more or less restrained by the police. During revolution nothing restrains them, and they can easily gratify their instincts to murder and plunder. In the dregs of society the revolutionaries of all times are sure of finding recruits. Eager only to kill and to plunder, little matters to them the cause they are

# The Psychology of Revolution

sworn to defend. If the chances of murder and pillage are better in the party attacked, they will promptly change their colours.

To these criminals, properly so called, the incurable plague of all societies, we must add the class of semi-criminals. Wrongdoers on occasion, they never rebel so long as the fear of the established order restrains them, but as soon as it weakens they enrol themselves in the army of revolution.

These two categories—habitual and occasional criminals—form an army of disorder which is fit for nothing but the creation of disorder. All the revolutionaries, all the founders of religious or political leagues, have constantly counted on their support.

We have already stated that this population, with its criminal mentality, exercised a considerable influence during the French Revolution. It always figured in the front rank of the riots which occurred almost daily. Certain historians have spoken with respect and emotion of the way in which the sovereign people enforced its will upon the Convention, invading the hall armed with pikes, the points of which were sometimes decorated with newly severed heads. If we analyse the elements composing the pretended delegations of the sovereign people, we shall find that, apart from a small number of simple souls who submitted to the impulses of the leaders, the mass was almost entirely formed of the bandits of whom I have been speaking. To them were due the innumerable murders of which the massacres of September and the killing of the Princesse de Lamballe were merely typical.

## Revolutionary and Criminal Mentalities

They terrorised all the great Assemblies, from the Constituent Assembly to the Convention, and for ten years they helped to ravage France. If by some miracle this army of criminals could have been eliminated, the progress of the Revolution would have been very different. They stained it with blood from its dawn to its decline. Reason could do nothing with them but they could do much against reason.

# CHAPTER IV

## THE PSYCHOLOGY OF REVOLUTIONARY CROWDS

### 1. *General Characteristics of the Crowd.*

WHATEVER their origin, revolutions do not produce their full effects until they have penetrated the soul of the multitude. They therefore represent a consequence of the psychology of crowds.

Although I have studied collective psychology at length in another volume, I must here recall its principal laws.

Man, as part of a multitude, is a very different being from the same man as an isolated individual. His conscious individuality vanishes in the unconscious personality of the crowd.

Material contact is not absolutely necessary to produce in the individual the mentality of the crowd. Common passions and sentiments, provoked by certain events, are often sufficient to create it.

The collective mind, momentarily formed, represents a very special kind of aggregate. Its chief peculiarity is that it is entirely dominated by unconscious elements, and is subject to a peculiar collective logic.

Among the other characteristics of crowds, we must note their infinite credulity and exaggerated sensibility, their short-sightedness, and their in-

# The Psychology of Revolutionary Crowds

capacity to respond to the influences of reason. Affirmation, contagion, repetition, and prestige constitute almost the only means of persuading them. Reality and experience have no effect upon them. The multitude will admit anything; nothing is impossible in the eyes of the crowd.

By reason of the extreme sensibility of crowds, their sentiments, good or bad, are always exaggerated. This exaggeration increases still further in times of revolution. The least excitement will then lead the multitude to act with the utmost fury. Their credulity, so great even in the normal state, is still further increased; the most improbable statements are accepted. Arthur Young relates that when he visited the springs near Clermont, at the time of the French Revolution, his guide was stopped by the people, who were persuaded that he had come by order of the Queen to mine and blow up the town. The most horrible tales concerning the Royal Family were circulated, depicting it as a nest of ghouls and vampires.

These various characteristics show that man in the crowd descends to a very low degree in the scale of civilisation. He becomes a savage, with all a savage's faults and qualities, with all his momentary violence, enthusiasm, and heroism. In the intellectual domain a crowd is always inferior to the isolated unit. In the moral and sentimental domain it may be his superior. A crowd will commit a crime as readily as an act of abnegation.

Personal characteristics vanish in the crowd, which exerts an extraordinary influence upon the individuals which form it. The miser becomes generous, the sceptic a believer, the honest man a criminal, the coward a hero. Examples of such transformations abounded during the great Revolution.

As part of a jury or a parliament, the collective man renders verdicts or passes laws of which he would never have dreamed in his isolated condition.

One of the most notable consequences of the influence of a collectivity upon the individuals who compose it is the unification of their sentiments and wills. This psychological unity confers a remarkable force upon crowds.

The formation of such a mental unity results chiefly from the fact that in a crowd gestures and actions are extremely contagious. Acclamations of hatred, fury, or love are immediately approved and repeated.

What is the origin of these common sentiments; this common will? They are propagated by contagion, but a point of departure is necessary before this contagion can take effect. Without a leader the crowd is an amorphous entity incapable of action.

A knowledge of the laws relating to the psychology of crowds is indispensable to the interpretation of the elements of our Revolution, and to a comprehension of the conduct of revolutionary assemblies, and the singular transformations of the individuals who form part of them. Pushed by the unconscious forces of the collective soul, they more often than not say what they did not intend, and vote what they would not have wished to vote.

Although the laws of collective psychology have sometimes been divined instinctively by superior statesmen, the majority of Governments have **not** understood and do not understand them. It is because they do not understand them that so many of them have fallen so easily. When we see the facility with which certain Governments were overthrown by an insignificant riot—as happened in the case of the monarchy of Louis-Philippe—the dangers of an ignorance of collective psychology are evident. The marshal in command of the troops in 1848, which were more than sufficient to defend the king, certainly did not understand that the moment he allowed the crowd to mingle with the troops the latter, paralysed by suggestion and contagion, would cease to do their duty. Neither did he know that as the multitude is extremely sensible to prestige it needs a great display of force to impress it, and that such a display will at once suppress hostile demonstrations. He was equally ignorant of the fact that all gatherings should be dispersed immediately. All these things have been taught by experience, but in 1848 these lessons had not been grasped. At the time of the great Revolution the psychology of crowds was even less understood.

2. *How the Stability of the Racial Mind limits the Oscillations of the Mind of the Crowd.*

A people can in a sense be likened to a crowd. It possesses certain characteristics, but the oscillations of these characteristics are limited by the soul or mind of the race. The mind of the race has a fixity unknown to the transitory mind of the crowd.

When a people possesses an ancestral soul established by a long past the soul of the crowd is always dominated thereby.

# The Psychology of Revolution

A people differs from a crowd also in that it is composed of a collection of groups, each having different interests and passions. In a crowd properly so-called —a popular assembly, for example—there are unities which may belong to very different social categories.

A people sometimes seems as mobile as a crowd, but we must not forget that behind its mobility, its enthusiasms, its violence and destructiveness, the extremely tenacious and conservative instincts of the racial mind persist. The history of the Revolution and the century which has followed shows how the conservative spirit finally overcomes the spirit of destruction. More than one system of government which the people has shattered has been restored by the people.

It is not as easy to work upon the mind of the people—that is, the mind of the race—as on the mind of a crowd. The means of action are indirect and slower (journals, conferences, speeches, books, &c.). The elements of persuasion always come under the headings already given : affirmation, repetition, prestige, and contagion.

Mental contagion may affect a whole people instantaneously, but more often it operates slowly, creeping from group to group. Thus was the Reformation propagated in France.

A people is far less excitable than a crowd ; but certain events—national insults, threats of invasion, &c.—may arouse it instantly. Such a phenomenon was observed on several occasions during the Revolution, notably at the time of the insolent manifesto issued by the Duke of Brunswick. The Duke knew little indeed of the psychology of the French race when he proffered his threats. Not only did he considerably prejudice the cause of Louis XVI.; but he also damaged his own, since his intervention raised from the soil an army eager to fight him.

This sudden explosion of feeling throughout a whole race has been observed in all nations. Napoleon did not understand the power of such explosions when he invaded Spain and Russia. One may easily disaggregate the facile mind of a crowd, but one can do nothing before the permanent soul of a race. Certainly the Russian peasant is a very indifferent being, gross and narrow by nature, yet at the first news of invasion he was transformed. One may judge of this fact on reading a letter written by Elizabeth, wife of the Emperor Alexander I.

" From the moment when Napoleon had crossed our frontiers it was as though an electric spark had spread through all Russia; and if the immensity of its area had made it possible for the news to penetrate simultaneously to every corner of the Empire a cry of indignation would have arisen so terrible that I believe it would have resounded to the ends of the earth. As Napoleon advances this feeling is growing yet stronger. Old men who have lost all or nearly all their goods are saying: 'We shall find a way of living. Anything is preferable to a shameful peace.' Women all of whose kin are in the army regard the dangers they are running as secondary, and fear nothing but peace. Happily this peace, which would be the death-warrant of Russia, will not be negotiated; the Emperor does not conceive of such an idea, and even if he would he could not. This is the heroic side of our position."

# The Psychology of Revolution

The Empress describes to her mother the two following traits, which give some idea of the degree of resistance of which the soul of the Russian is capable :—

"The Frenchmen had caught some unhappy peasants in Moscow, whom they thought to force to serve in their ranks, and in order that they should not be able to escape they branded their hands as one brands horses in the stud. One of them asked what this mark meant; he was told it signified that he was a French soldier. 'What! I am a soldier of the Emperor of the French!' he said. And immediately he took his hatchet, cut off his hand, and threw it at the feet of those present, saying, 'Take it—there's your mark!'

"At Moscow, too, the French had taken a score of peasants of whom they wished to make an example in order to frighten the villagers, who were picking off the French foraging parties and were making war as well as the detachments of regular troops. They ranged them against a wall and read their sentence in Russian. They waited for them to beg for mercy : instead of that they took farewell of one another and made their sign of the cross. The French fired on the first of them ; they waited for the rest to beg for pardon in their terror, and to promise to change their conduct. They fired on the second, and on the third, and so on all the twenty, without a single one having attempted to implore the *clemency* of the enemy. Napoleon has not once had the pleasure of profaning this word in Russia."

Among the characteristics of the popular mind we must mention that in all peoples and all ages it has

108

been saturated with mysticism. The people will always be convinced that superior beings—divinities, Governments, or great men—have the power to change things at will. This mystic side produces an intense need of adoration. The people must have a fetich, either a man or a doctrine. This is why, when threatened with anarchy, it calls for a Messiah to save it.

Like the crowd, but more slowly, the people readily passes from adoration to hatred. A man may be the hero of the people at one period, and finally earn its curses. These variations of popular opinion concerning political personalities may be observed in all times. The history of Cromwell furnishes us with a very curious example.[1]

### 3. *The Rôle of the Leader in Revolutionary Movements.*

All the varieties of crowds—homogeneous and heterogeneous, assemblies, peoples, clubs, &c.—are, as we have often repeated, aggregates incapable of unity and action so long as they find no master to lead them.

I have shown elsewhere, making use of certain physiological experiments, that the unconscious collective mind of the crowd seems bound up with the mind of the leader. The latter gives it a single will and imposes absolute obedience.

---

[1] After having overthrown a dynasty and refused a crown he was buried like a king among kings. Two years later his body was torn from the tomb, and his head, cut off by the executioner, was exposed above the gate of the House of Parliament. A little while ago a statue was raised to him. The old anarchist turned autocrat now figures in the gallery of demigods.

# The Psychology of Revolution

The leader acts especially through suggestion. His success depends on his fashion of provoking this suggestion. Many experiments have shown to what point a collectivity may be subjected to suggestion.[1]

According to the suggestions of the leaders, the multitude will be calm, furious, criminal, or heroic. These various suggestions may sometimes appear to present a rational aspect, but they will only appear to be reasonable. A crowd is in reality inaccessible to reason; the only ideas capable of influencing it will always be sentiments evoked in the form of images.

The history of the Revolution shows on every page how easily the multitude follows the most

[1] Among the numerous experiments made to prove this fact one of the most remarkable was performed on the pupils of his class by Professor Glosson and published in the *Revue Scientifique* for October 28, 1899.

"I prepared a bottle filled with distilled water carefully wrapped in cotton and packed in a box. After several other experiments I stated that I wished to measure the rapidity with which an odour would diffuse itself through the air, and asked those present to raise their hands the moment they perceived the odour. . . . I took out the bottle and poured the water on the cotton, turning my head away during the operation, then took up a stop-watch and awaited the result. . . . I explained that I was absolutely sure that no one present had ever smelt the odour of the chemical composition I had spilt. . . . At the end of fifteen seconds the majority of those in front had held up their hands, and in forty seconds the odour had reached the back of the hall by fairly regular waves. About three-quarters of those present declared that they perceived the odour. A larger number would doubtless have succumbed to suggestion, if at the end of a minute I had not been forced to stop the experiment, some of those in the front rows being unpleasantly affected by the odour, and wishing to leave the hall."

contradictory impulses given by its different leaders. We see it applaud just as vigorously at the triumph of the Girondists, the Hébertists, the Dantonists, and the Terrorists as at their successive downfalls. One may be quite sure, also, that the crowd understood nothing of these events.

At a distance one can only confusedly perceive the part played by the leaders, for they commonly work in the shade. To grasp this clearly we must study them in contemporary events. We shall then see how readily the leader can provoke the most violent popular movements. We are not thinking here of the strikes of the postmen or railway men, in which the discontent of the employees might intervene, but of events in which the crowd was not in the least interested. Such, for example, was the popular rising provoked by a few Socialist leaders amidst the Parisian populace on the morrow of the execution of Ferrer, in Spain. The French crowd had never heard of Ferrer. In Spain his execution was almost unnoticed. In Paris the incitements of a few leaders sufficed to hurl a regular popular army upon the Spanish Embassy, with the intention of burning it. Part of the garrison had to be employed to protect it. Energetically repulsed, the assailants contented themselves with sacking a few shops and building some barricades.

At the same time, the leaders gave another proof of their influence. Finally understanding that the burning of a foreign embassy might be extremely dangerous, they ordered a pacific demonstration for the following day, and were as faithfully obeyed as if they had ordered the most violent riot. No example could better show the importance of leaders and the submission of the crowd.

The historians who, from Michelet to M. Aulard, have represented the revolutionary crowd as having acted on its own initiative, without leaders, do not comprehend its psychology.

# CHAPTER V

## THE PSYCHOLOGY OF THE REVOLUTIONARY ASSEMBLIES

### 1. *Psychological Characteristics of the great Revolutionary Assemblies.*

A GREAT political assembly, a parliament for example, is a crowd, but a crowd which sometimes fails in effectual action on account of the contrary sentiments of the hostile groups composing it.

The presence of these groups, actuated by different interests, must make us consider an assembly as formed of superimposed and heterogeneous crowds, each obeying its particular leaders. The law of the mental unity of crowds is manifested only in each group, and it is only as a result of exceptional circumstances that the different groups act with a single intention.

Each group in an assembly represents a single being. The individuals contributing to the formation of this being are no longer themselves, and will unhesitatingly vote against their convictions and their wishes. On the eve of the day when Louis XVI. was to be condemned Vergniaud protested with indignation against the suggestion that he should vote for his death; but he did so vote on the following day.

# The Psychology of Revolution

The action of a group consists chiefly in fortifying hesitating opinions. All feeble individual convictions become confirmed upon becoming collective.

Leaders of great repute or unusual violence can sometimes, by acting on all the groups of an assembly, make them a single crowd. The majority of the members of the Convention enacted measures entirely contrary to their opinions under the influence of a very small number of such leaders.

Collectivities have always given way before active sectaries. The history of the revolutionary Assemblies shows how pusillanimous they were, despite the boldness of their language respecting kings, before the leaders of the popular riots. The invasion of a band of energumens commanded by an imperious leader was enough to make them vote then and there the most absurd and contradictory measures.

An assembly, having the characteristics of a crowd, will, like a crowd, be extreme in its sentiments. Excessive in its violence, it will be excessive in its cowardice. In general it will be insolent to the weak and servile before the strong.

We remember the fearful humility of the Parliament when the youthful Louis XIV. entered, whip in hand, to pronounce his brief speech. We know with what increasing impertinence the Constituent Assembly treated Louis XVI. as it felt that he was becoming defenceless. Finally, we recall the terror of the Convention under the reign of Robespierre.

This characteristic of assemblies being a general law, the convocation of an assembly by a sovereign when his power is failing must be regarded as a gross error in psychology. The assembling of the States

# Psychology of Revolutionary Assemblies

General cost the life of Louis XVI. It all but lost Henry III. his throne, when, obliged to leave Paris, he had the unhappy idea of assembling the Estates at Blois. Conscious of the weakness of the king, the Estates at once spoke as masters of the situation, modifying taxes, dismissing officials, and claiming that their decisions should have the force of law.

This progressive exaggeration of sentiments was plainly demonstrated in all the assemblies of the Revolution. The Constituent Assembly, at first extremely respectful toward the royal authority and its prerogatives, finally proclaimed itself a sovereign Assembly, and treated Louis XVI as a mere official. The Convention, after relatively moderate beginnings, ended with a preliminary form of the Terror, when judgments were still surrounded by certain legal guarantees : then, quickly increasing its powers, it enacted a law depriving all accused persons of the right of defence, permitting their condemnation upon the mere suspicion of being suspect. Yielding more and more to its sanguinary frenzy, it finally decimated itself. Girondists, Hébertists, Dantonists, and Robespierrists successively ended their careers at the hands of the executioner.

This exaggeration of the sentiments of assemblies explains why they were always so little able to control their own destinies and why they so often arrived at conclusions exactly contrary to the ends proposed. Catholic and royalist, the Constituent Assembly, instead of the constitutional monarchy it wished to establish and the religion it wished to defend, rapidly led France to a violent republic and the persecution of the clergy.

# The Psychology of Revolution

Political assemblies are composed, as we have seen, of heterogeneous groups, but they have sometimes been formed of homogeneous groups, as, for instance, certain of the clubs, which played so enormous a part during the Revolution, and whose psychology deserves a special examination.

## 2. *The Psychology of the Revolutionary Clubs.*

Small assemblies of men possessing the same opinions, the same beliefs, and the same interests, which eliminate all dissentient voices, differ from the great assemblies by the unity of their sentiments and therefore their wills. Such were the communes, the religious congregations, the corporations, and the clubs during the Revolution, the secret societies during the first half of the nineteenth century, and the Freemasons and syndicalists of to-day.

The points of difference between a heterogeneous assembly and a homogeneous club must be thoroughly grasped if we are to comprehend the progress of the French Revolution. Until the Directory and especially during the Convention the Revolution was directed by the clubs.

Despite the unity of will due to the absence of dissident parties the clubs obey the laws of the psychology of crowds. They are consequently subjugated by leaders. This we see especially in the Jacobin Club, which was dominated by Robespierre.

The function of the leader of a club, a homogeneous crowd, is far more difficult than that of a leader of a heterogeneous crowd. The latter may easily be led by harping on a small number of strings, but in a homogeneous group like a club, whose senti-

116

ments and interests are identical, the leader must know how to humour them and is often himself led.

Part of the strength of homogeneous agglomerations resides in their anonymity. We know that during the Commune of 1871 a few anonymous orders sufficed to effect the burning of the finest monuments of Paris : the Hôtel de Ville, the Tuileries, the Cour des Comptes, the buildings of the Legion of Honour, &c. A brief order from the anonymous committees, " Burn Finances, burn Tuileries," &c., was immediately executed. An unlooked-for chance only saved the Louvre and its collections. We know too what religious attention is in our days accorded to the most absurd injunctions of the anonymous leaders of the trades unions. The clubs of Paris and the insurrectionary Commune were not less scrupulously obeyed at the time of the Revolution. An order emanating from these was sufficient to hurl upon the Assembly a popular army which dictated its wishes.

Summing up the history of the Convention in another chapter, we shall see how frequent were these irruptions, and with what servility the Assembly, which according to the legends was so powerful bowed itself before the most imperative injunctions of a handful of rioters. Instructed by experience, the Directory closed the clubs and put an end to the invasion of the populace by energetically shooting them down.

The Convention had early grasped the superiority of homogeneous groups over heterogeneous assemblies in matters of government, which is why it subdivided itself into committees composed each of a limited number of individuals. These committees—

of Public Safety, of Finance, &c.—formed small sovereign assemblies in the midst of the larger Assembly. Their power was held in check only by that of the clubs.

The preceding considerations show the power of groups over the wills of the members composing them. If the group is homogeneous, this action is considerable ; if it is heterogeneous, it is less considerable but may still become important, either because the more powerful groups of an assembly will dominate those whose cohesion is weaker or because certain contagious sentiments will often extend themselves to all the members of an assembly.

A memorable example of this influence of groups occurred at the time of the Revolution, when, on the night of the 4th of August, the nobles voted, on the proposition of one of their members, the abandonment of feudal privileges. Yet we know that the Revolution resulted in part from the refusal of the clergy and the nobles to renounce their privileges. Why did they refuse to renounce them at first? Simply because men in a crowd do not act as the same men singly. Individually no member of the nobility would ever have abandoned his rights.

Of this influence of assemblies upon their members Napoleon at St. Helena cited some curious examples : "Nothing was more common than to meet with men at this period quite unlike the reputation that their acts and words would seem to justify. For instance, one might have supposed Monge to be a terrible fellow ; when war was decided upon he mounted the tribune of the Jacobins and declared that he would give his two daughters to the two first soldiers to be

wounded by the enemy. He wanted the nobles
to be killed, &c. Now, Monge was the most gentle
and feeble of men, and wouldn't have had a chicken
killed if he had had to do it with his own hands, or
even to have it done in his presence."

### 3. *A Suggested Explanation of the Progressive Exaggeration of Sentiments in Assemblies.*

If collective sentiments were susceptible of exact
quantitative measurement, we might translate them
by a curve which, after a first gradual ascent, runs
upward with extreme rapidity and then falls almost
vertically. The equation of this curve might be called
the equation of the variations of collective sentiments
subjected to a constant excitation.

It is not always easy to explain the acceleration of
certain sentiments under the influence of a constant
exciting cause. Perhaps, however, one may say that
if the laws of psychology are comparable to those of
mechanics, a cause of invariable dimensions acting in
a continuous fashion will rapidly increase the intensity
of a sentiment. We know, for example, that a force
which is constant in dimension and direction, such as
gravity acting upon a mass, will cause an accelerated
movement. The speed of a free object falling in
space under the influence of gravity will be about
32 feet during the first second, 64 feet during the
next, 96 feet during the next, &c. It would be easy,
were the moving body allowed to fall from a sufficient
height, to give it a velocity sufficient to perforate a
plate of steel.

But although this explanation is applicable to the
acceleration of a sentiment subjected to a constant

exciting cause, it does not tell us why the effects of acceleration finally and suddenly cease. Such a fall is only comprehensible if we bring in physiological factors—that is, if we remember that pleasure, like pain, cannot exceed certain limits, and that all sensations, when too violent, result in the paralysis of sensation. Our organism can only support a certain maximum of joy, pain, or effort, and it cannot support that maximum for long together. The hand which grasps a dynamometer soon exhausts its effort, and is obliged suddenly to let go.

The study of the causes of the rapid disappearance of certain groups of sentiments in assemblies will remind us of the fact that beside the party which is predominant by means of its strength or prestige there are others whose sentiments, restrained by this force or prestige, have not reached their full development. Some chance circumstance may somewhat weaken the prevailing party, when immediately the suppressed sentiments of the adverse parties may become preponderant. The Mountain learned this lesson after Thermidor.

All analogies that we may seek to establish between the laws of material phenomena and those which condition the evolution of affective and mystic factors are evidently extremely rough. They must be so until the mechanism of the cerebral functions is better understood than it is to-day.

# PART II

## THE FRENCH REVOLUTION

# BOOK I

*THE ORIGINS OF THE FRENCH REVOLUTION*

## CHAPTER I

### THE OPINIONS OF HISTORIANS CONCERNING THE FRENCH REVOLUTION

#### 1. *The Historians of the Revolution.*

THE most contradictory opinions have been expressed respecting the French Revolution, and although only a century separates us from the period in question it seems impossible as yet to judge it calmly. For de Maistre it was " a satanic piece of work," and " never was the action of the spirit of darkness so evidently manifested." For the modern Jacobins it has regenerated the human race.

Foreigners who live in France still regard it as a subject to be avoided in conversation.

" Everywhere," writes Barrett Wendell, " this memory and these traditions are still endowed with such vitality that few persons are capable of considering them dispassionately. They still excite both enthusiasm and resentment ; they are still regarded with a loyal and ardent spirit of partisanship. The better you come to understand France the more clearly you see that even to-day no study of the

# The Psychology of Revolution

Revolution strikes any Frenchman as having been impartial."

This observation is perfectly correct. To be interpretable with equity, the events of the past must no longer be productive of results and must not touch the religious or political beliefs whose inevitable intolerance I have denoted.

We must not therefore be surprised that historians express very different ideas respecting the Revolution. For a long time to come some will still see in it one of the most sinister events of history, while to others it will remain one of the most glorious. All writers on the subject have believed that they have related its course with impartiality, but in general they have merely supported contradictory theories of peculiar simplicity. The documents being innumerable and contradictory, their conscious or unconscious choice has readily enabled them to justify their respective theories.

The older historians of the Revolution—Thiers, Quinet, and, despite his talent, Michelet himself, are somewhat eclipsed to-day. Their doctrines were by no means complicated; a historic fatalism prevails generally in their work. Thiers regarded the Revolution as the result of several centuries of absolute monarchy, and the Terror as the necessary consequence of foreign invasion. Quinet described the excesses of 1793 as the result of a long-continued despotism, but declared that the tyranny of the Convention was unnecessary, and hampered the work of the Revolution. Michelet saw in this last merely the work of the people, whom he blindly admired, and commenced the glorification continued by other historians.

The former reputation of all these historians has

been to a great extent effaced by that of Taine. Although equally impassioned, he threw a brilliant light upon the revolutionary period, and it will doubtless be long before his work is superseded.

Work so important is bound to show faults. Taine is admirable in the representation of facts and persons, but he attempts to judge by the standard of rational logic events which were not dictated by reason, and which, therefore, he cannot interpret. His psychology, excellent when it is merely descriptive, is very weak as soon as it becomes explanatory. To affirm that Robespierre was a pedantic "swotter" is not to reveal the causes of his absolute power over the Convention, at a time when he had spent several months in decimating it with perfect impunity. It has very justly been said of Taine that he saw well and understood little.

Despite these restrictions his work is highly remarkable and has not been equalled. We may judge of his immense influence by the exasperation which he causes among the faithful defenders of Jacobin orthodoxy, of which M. Aulard, professor at the Sorbonne, is to-day the high priest. The latter has devoted two years to writing a pamphlet against Taine, every line of which is steeped in passion. All this time spent in rectifying a few material errors which are not really significant has only resulted in the perpetration of the very same errors.

Reviewing his work, M. A. Cochin shows that M. Aulard has at least on every other occasion been deceived by his quotations, whereas Taine erred far more rarely. The same historian shows also that we must not trust M. Aulard's sources.

"These sources—proceedings, pamphlets, journals,

and the speeches and writings of patriots—are precisely the authentic publications of patriotism, edited by patriots, and edited, as a rule, for the benefit of the public. He ought to have seen in all this simply the special pleading of the defendant : he had, before his eyes, a ready-made history of the Revolution, which presents, side by side with each of the acts of the 'People,' from the massacres of September to the law of Prairial, a ready-made explanation according to the republican system of defence."

Perhaps the fairest criticism that one can make of the work of Taine is that it was left incomplete. He studied more especially the *rôle* of the populace and its leaders during the revolutionary period. This inspired him with pages vibrating with an indignation which we can still admire, but several important aspects of the Revolution escaped him.

Whatever one may think of the Revolution, an irreducible difference will always exist between historians of the school of Taine and those of the school of M. Aulard. The latter regards the sovereign people as admirable, while the former shows us that when abandoned to its instincts and liberated from all social restraint it relapses into primitive savagery. The conception of M. Aulard, entirely contrary to the lessons of the psychology of crowds, is none the less a religious dogma in the eyes of modern Jacobins. They write of the Revolution according to the methods of believers, and take for learned works the arguments of virtual theologians.

2. *The Theory of Fatalism in respect of the Revolution.* Advocates and detractors of the Revolution often

admit the fatality of revolutionary events. This theory is well synthetised in the following passage from the *History of the Revolution*, by Emile Olivier :—

"No man could oppose it. The blame belongs neither to those who perished nor to those who survived; there was no individual force capable of changing the elements and of foreseeing the events which were born of the nature of things and circumstances."

Taine himself inclines to this idea :—

"At the moment when the States General were opened the course of ideas and events was not only determined but even visible. Each generation unwittingly bears within itself its future and its past; from the latter its destinies might have been foretold long before the issue."

Other modern authors, who profess no more indulgence for the violence of the revolutionaries than did Taine, are equally convinced of this fatality. M. Sorel, after recalling the saying of Bossuet concerning the revolutions of antiquity : " Everything is surprising if we only consider particular causes, and yet everything goes forward in regular sequence," expresses an intention which he very imperfectly realises : " to show in the Revolution, which seems to some the subversion and to others the regeneration of the old European world, the natural and necessary result of the history of Europe, and to show, moreover, that this revolution had no result—not even the most unexpected—that did not ensue from this history, and was not explained by the precedents of the *ancien régime*."

Guizot also had formerly attempted to prove that our Revolution, which he quite wrongly compared to that of England, was perfectly natural and effected no innovations :—

# The Psychology of Revolution

"Far from having broken with the natural course of events in Europe, neither the English revolution nor our own did, intended, or said anything that had not been said, intended, and done a hundred years before its outbreak.

" . . . Whether we regard the general doctrines of the two revolutions or the application made of them —whether we deal with the government of the State or with the civil legislation, with property or with persons, with liberty or with power, we shall find nothing of which the invention can be attributed to them, nothing that will not be encountered elsewhere, or that was not at least originated in times which we qualify as normal."

All these assertions merely recall the banal law that a phenomenon is simply the consequence of previous phenomena. Such very general propositions do not teach us much.

We must not try to explain too many events by the principle of fatality adopted by so many historians. I have elsewhere discussed the significance of such fatalities, and have shown that the whole effort of civilisation consists in trying to escape therefrom. Certainly history is full of necessities, but it is also full of contingent facts which were, and might not have been. Napoleon himself, on St. Helena, enumerated six circumstances which might have checked his prodigious career. He related, notably, that on taking a bath at Auxonne, in 1786, he only escaped death by the fortuitous presence of a sandbank. If Bonaparte had died, then we may admit that another general would have arisen, and might have become dictator. But what would have become of the Imperial epic and its consequences without the man of genius who led our victorious armies into all the capitals of Europe?

It is permissible to consider the Revolution as being partly a necessity, but it was above all—which is what the fatalistic writers already cited do not show us—a permanent struggle between theorists who were imbued with a new ideal, and the economic, social, and political laws which ruled mankind, and which they did not understand. Not understanding them, they sought in vain to direct the course of events, were exasperated at their failure, and finally committed every species of violence. They decreed that the paper money known as *assignats* should be accepted as the equivalent of gold, and all their threats could not prevent the fictitious value of such money falling almost to nothing. They decreed the law of the maximum, and it merely increased the evils it was intended to remedy. Robespierre declared before the Convention "that all the *sans-culottes* will be paid at the expense of the public treasury, which will be fed by the rich," and in spite of requisitions and the guillotine the treasury remained empty.

Having broken all human restraints, the men of the Revolution finally discovered that a society cannot live without them; but when they sought to create them anew they saw that even the strongest society, though supported by the fear of the guillotine, could not replace the discipline which the past had slowly built up in the minds of men. As for understanding the evolution of society, or judging men's hearts and minds, or foreseeing the consequences of the laws they enacted, they scarcely attempted to do so.

The events of the Revolution did not ensue from

irreducible necessities. They were far more the consequence of Jacobin principles than of circumstances, and might have been quite other than they were. Would the Revolution have followed the same path if Louis XVI. had been better advised, or if the Constituent Assembly had been less cowardly in times of popular insurrection? The theory of revolutionary fatality is only useful to justify violence by presenting it as inevitable.

Whether we are dealing with science or with history we must beware of the ignorance which takes shelter under the shibboleth of fatalism. Nature was formerly full of a host of fatalities which science is slowly contriving to avoid. The function of the superior man is, as I have shown elsewhere, to avert such fatalities.

### 3. *The Hesitations of recent Historians of the Revolution.*

The historians whose ideas we have examined in the preceding chapter were extremely positive in their special pleading. Confined within the limits of belief, they did not attempt to penetrate the domain of knowledge. A monarchical writer was violently hostile to the Revolution, and a liberal writer was its violent apologist.

At the present time we can see the commencement of a movement which will surely lead to the study of the Revolution as one of those scientific phenomena into which the opinions and beliefs of a writer enter so little that the reader does not even suspect them.

This period has not yet come into being; we are still in the period of doubt. The liberal writers who used to be so positive are now so no longer. One may judge of this new state of mind by the following extracts from recent authors :—

M. Hanotaux, having vaunted the utility of the Revolution, asks whether its results were not bought too dearly, and adds :—

" History hesitates, and will, for a long time yet, hesitate to answer."

M. Madelin is equally dubious in the book he has recently published :—

" I have never felt sufficient authority to form, even in my inmost conscience, a categorical judgment on so complex a phenomenon as the French Revolution. To-day I find it even more difficult to form a brief judgement. Causes, facts, and consequences seem to me to be still extremely debatable subjects."

One may obtain a still better idea of the transformation of the old ideas concerning the Revolution by perusing the latest writings of its official defenders. While they professed formerly to justify every act of violence by representing it as a simple act of defence, they now confine themselves to pleading extenuating circumstances. I find a striking proof of this new frame of mind in the history of France for the use of schools, published by MM. Aulard and Debidour. Concerning the Terror we read the following lines :—

" Blood flowed in waves ; there were acts of injustice and crimes which were useless from the point of view of national defence, and odious. But men had lost their heads in the tempest, and, harassed by a thousand dangers, the patriots struck out in their rage."

We shall see in another part of this work that the first of the two authors whom I have cited is, in spite of his uncompromising Jacobinism, by no means indulgent toward the men formerly qualified as the "Giants of the Convention."

The judgments of foreigners upon our Revolution are usually distinctly severe, and we cannot be surprised when we remember how Europe suffered during the twenty years of upheaval in France.

The Germans in particular have been most severe. Their opinion is summed up in the following lines by M. Faguet :—

"Let us say it courageously and patriotically, for patriotism consists above all in telling the truth to one's own country : Germany sees in France, with regard to the past, a people who, with the great words 'liberty' and 'fraternity' in its mouth, oppressed, trampled, murdered, pillaged, and fleeced her for fifteen years ; and with regard to the present, a people who, with the same words on its banners, is organising a despotic, oppressive, mischievous, and ruinous demo-cracy, which none would seek to imitate. This is what Germany may well see in France ; and this, according to her books and journals, is, we may assure ourselves, what she does see."

For the rest, whatever the worth of the verdicts pronounced upon the French Revolution, we may be certain that the writers of the future will consider it as an event as passionately interesting as it is instructive.

A Government bloodthirsty enough to guillotine old men of eighty years, young girls, and little children : which covered France with ruins, and yet succeeded in repulsing Europe in arms ; an archduchess of Austria, Queen of France, dying on the scaffold, and a few years later another archduchess, her relative, replacing her on the same throne and marrying a sub-lieutenant, turned Emperor—here are tragedies unique in human history. The psychologists, above all, will derive lessons from a history hitherto so little studied by them. No doubt they will finally discover that psychology can make no progress until it renounces chimerical theories and laboratory experiments in order to study the events and the men who surround us.[1]

### 4. *Impartiality in History.*

Impartiality has always been considered as the most essential quality of the historian. All historians since Tacitus have assured us that they are impartial.

---

[1] This advice is far from being banal. The psychologists of the day pay very little attention to the world about them, and are even surprised that any one should study it. I have come across an interesting proof of this indifferent frame of mind in a review of one of my books which appeared in the *Revue philosophique* and was inspired by the editor of the review. The author reproaches me with "exploring the world and the newspapers rather than books."

I most gladly accept this reproach. The manifold facts of the journals and the realities of the world are far more instructive than philosophical lucubrations such as the *Revue* is stuffed with.

Philosophers are beginning to see the puerility of such reproaches. It was certainly of the forty volumes of this fastidious publication that Mr. William James was thinking when he wrote that all these dissertations simply represented "a string of facts clumsily observed and a few quarrelsome discussions." Although he is the author of the best known treatise on psychology extant, the eminent thinker realises "the fragility of a science that oozes metaphysical criticism at every joint." For more than twenty years I have tried to interest psychologists in the study of realities, but the stream of university metaphysics is hardly yet turned aside, although it has lost its former force

# The Psychology of Revolution

In reality the writer sees events as the painter sees a landscape—that is, through his own temperament ; through his character and the mind of the race.

A number of artists, placed before the same landscape, would necessarily interpret it in as many different fashions. Some would lay stress upon details neglected by others. Each reproduction would thus be a personal work—that is to say, would be interpreted by a certain form of sensibility.

It is the same with the writer. We can no more speak of the impartiality of the historian than we can speak of the impartiality of the painter.

Certainly the historian may confine himself to the reproduction of documents, and this is the present tendency. But these documents, for periods as near us as the Revolution, are so abundant that a man's whole life would not suffice to go through them. Therefore the historian must make a choice.

Consciously sometimes, but more often unconsciously, the author will select the material which best corresponds with his political, moral, and social opinions.

It is therefore impossible, unless he contents himself with simple chronologies summing up each event with a few words and a date, to produce a truly impartial volume of history. No author could be impartial ; and it is not to be regretted. The claim to impartiality, so common to-day, results in those flat, gloomy, and prodigiously wearisome works which render the comprehension of a period completely impossible.

Should the historian, under a pretext of impartiality, abstain from judging men—that is, from speaking in tones of admiration or reprobation ?

# Opinions Concerning French Revolution

This question, I admit, allows of two very different solutions, each of which is perfectly correct, according to the point of view assumed—that of the moralist or that of the psychologist.

The moralist must think exclusively of the interest of society, and must judge men only according to that interest. By the very fact that it exists and wishes to continue to exist a society is obliged to admit a certain number of rules, to have an indestructible standard of good and evil, and consequently to create very definite distinctions between vice and virtue. It thus finally creates average types, to which the man of the period approaches more or less closely, and from which he cannot depart very widely without peril to society.

It is by such similar types and the rules derived from social necessities that the moralist must judge the men of the past. Praising those which were useful and blaming the rest, he thus helps to form the moral types which are indispensable to the progress of civilisation and which may serve others as models. Poets such as Corneille, for example, create heroes superior to the majority of men, and possibly inimitable ; but they thereby help greatly to stimulate our efforts. The example of heroes must always be set before a people in order to ennoble its mind.

Such is the moralist's point of view. That of the psychologist would be quite different. While a society has no right to be tolerant, because its first duty is to live, the psychologist may remain indifferent. Considering things as a scientist, he no longer asks their utilitarian value, but seeks merely to explain them.

His situation is that of the observer before any phenomenon. It is obviously difficult to read in cold blood that Carrier ordered his victims to be buried up to the neck so that they might then be blinded and subjected to horrible torments. Yet if we wish to comprehend such acts we must be no more indignant than the naturalist before the spider slowly devouring a fly. As soon as the reason is moved it is no longer reason, and can explain nothing.

The functions of the historian and the psychologist are not, as we see, identical, but of both we may demand the endeavour, by a wise interpretation of the facts, to discover, under the visible evidences, the invisible forces which determine them.

# CHAPTER II

## THE PSYCHOLOGICAL FOUNDATIONS OF THE
### *ANCIEN RÉGIME*

### 1. *The Absolute Monarchy and the Bases of the Ancien Régime.*

MANY historians assure us that the Revolution was directed against the autocracy of the monarchy. In reality the kings of France had ceased to be absolute monarchs long before its outbreak.

Only very late in history—not until the reign of Louis XIV.—did they finally obtain incontestable power. All the preceding sovereigns, even the most powerful, such as Francis I., for example, had to sustain a constant struggle either against the seigneurs, or the clergy, or the parliaments, and they did not always win. Francis himself had not sufficient power to protect his most intimate friends against the Sorbonne and the Parliament. His friend and councillor Berquin, having offended the Sorbonne, was arrested upon the order of the latter body. The king ordered his release, which was refused. He was obliged to send archers to remove him from the Conciergerie, and could find no other means of protecting him than that of keeping him beside him in the Louvre. The Sorbonne by no means considered itself beaten. Profiting by the king's absence, it arrested

Berquin again and had him tried by Parliament. Condemned at ten in the morning, he was burned alive at noon.

Built up very gradually, the power of the kings of France was not absolute until the time of Louis XIV. It then rapidly declined, and it would be truly difficult to speak of the absolutism of Louis XVI.

This pretended master was the slave of his court, his ministers, the clergy, and the nobles. He did what they forced him to do and rarely what he wished. Perhaps no Frenchman was so little free as the king.

The great power of the monarchy resided originally in the Divine origin which was attributed to it, and in the traditions which had accumulated during the ages. These formed the real social framework of the country.

The true cause of the disappearance of the *ancien régime* was simply the weakening of the traditions which served as its foundations. When after repeated criticism it could find no more defenders, the *ancien régime* crumbled like a building whose foundations have been destroyed.

## 2. *The Inconveniences of the Ancien Régime*

A long-established system of government will always finally seem acceptable to the people governed. Habit masks its inconveniences, which appear only when men begin to think. Then they ask how they could ever have supported them. The truly unhappy man is the man who believes himself miserable.

It was precisely this belief which was gaining ground at the time of the Revolution, under the influence of the writers whose work we shall presently study.

# The Foundations of the *Ancien Régime*

Then the imperfections of the *ancien régime* stared all men in the face. They were numerous; it is enough to mention a few.

Despite the apparent authority of the central power, the kingdom, formed by the successive conquest of independent provinces, was divided into territories each of which had its own laws and customs, and each of which paid different imposts. Internal customs-houses separated them. The unity of France was thus somewhat artificial. It represented an aggregate of various countries which the repeated efforts of the kings, including Louis XIV., had not succeeded in wholly unifying. The most useful effect of the Revolution was this very unification.

To such material divisions were added social divisions constituted by different classes—nobles, clergy, and the Third Estate, whose rigid barriers could only with the utmost difficulty be crossed.

Regarding the division of the classes as one of its sources of power, the *ancien régime* had rigorously maintained that division. This became the principal cause of the hatreds which the system inspired. Much of the violence of the triumphant *bourgeoisie* represented vengeance for a long past of disdain and oppression. The wounds of self-love are the most difficult of all to forget. The Third Estate had suffered many such wounds. At a meeting of the States General in 1614, at which its representatives were obliged to remain bareheaded on their knees, one member of the Third Estate having dared to say that the three orders were like three brothers, the spokes-man of the nobles replied "that there was no frater-nity between it and the Third; that the nobles did not wish the children of cobblers and tanners to call them their brothers."

Despite the march of enlightenment the nobles and the clergy obstinately preserved their privileges and their demands, no longer justifiable now that these classes had ceased to render services.

Kept from the exercise of public functions by the royal power, which distrusted them, and progressively replaced by a *bourgeoisie* which was more and more learned and capable, the social *rôle* of nobility and clergy was only an empty show. This point has been luminously expounded by Taine :—

" Since the nobility, having lost its special capacity, and the Third Estate, having acquired general capacity, were now on a level in respect of education and aptitudes, the inequality which divided them had become hurtful and useless. Instituted by custom, it was no longer ratified by the consciousness, and the Third Estate was with reason angered by privileges which nothing justified, neither the capacity of the nobles nor the incapacity of the *bourgeoisie*."

By reason of the rigidity of castes established by a long past we cannot see what could have persuaded the nobles and the clergy to renounce their privileges. Certainly they did finally abandon them one memorable evening, when events forced them to do so ; but then it was too late, and the Revolution, unchained, was pursuing its course.

It is certain that modern progress would successively have established all that the Revolution effected—the equality of citizens before the law, the suppression of the privileges of birth, &c. Despite the conservative spirit of the Latins, these things would have been won, as they were by the majority of the peoples. We might in this manner have been saved twenty years of warfare and devastation ; but we must have had a different mental constitution, and, above all, different statesmen.

The profound hostility of the *bourgeoisie* against the classes maintained above it by tradition was one of the great factors of the Revolution, and perfectly explains why, after its triumph, the first class despoiled the vanquished of their wealth. They behaved as conquerors—like William the Conqueror, who, after the conquest of England, distributed the soil among his soldiers.

But although the *bourgeoisie* detested the nobility they had no hatred for royalty, and did not regard it as revocable. The maladdress of the king and his appeals to foreign powers only very gradually made him unpopular.

The first Assembly never dreamed of founding a republic. Extremely royalist, in fact, it thought simply to substitute a constitutional for an absolute monarchy. Only the consciousness of its increasing power exasperated it against the resistance of the king ; but it dared not overthrow him.

### 3. *Life under the Ancien Régime.*

It is difficult to form a very clear idea of life under the *ancien régime*, and, above all, of the real situation of the peasants.

The writers who defend the Revolution as theologians defend religious dogmas draw such gloomy pictures of the existence of the peasants under the *ancien régime* that we ask ourselves how it was that

# The Psychology of Revolution

all these unhappy creatures had not died of hunger long before. A good example of this style of writing may be found in a book by M. A. Rambaud, formerly professor at the Sorbonne, published under the title *History of the French Revolution*. One notices especially an engraving bearing the legend, *Poverty of Peasants under Louis XIV*. In the foreground a man is fighting some dogs for some bones, which for that matter are already quite fleshless. Beside him a wretched fellow is twisting himself and compressing his stomach. Farther back a woman lying on the ground is eating grass. At the back of the landscape figures of which one cannot say whether they are corpses or persons starving are also stretched on the soil. As an example of the administration of the *ancien régime* the same author assures us that "a place in the police cost 300 livres and brought in 400,000." Such figures surely indicate a great disinterestedness on the part of those who sold such productive employment! He also informs us "that it cost only 120 livres to get people arrested," and that "under Louis XV. more than 150,000 *lettres de cachet* were distributed."

The majority of books dealing with the Revolution are conceived with as little impartiality and critical spirit, which is one reason why this period is really so little known to us.

Certainly there is no lack of documents, but they are absolutely contradictory. To the celebrated description of La Bruyère we may oppose the enthusiastic picture drawn by the English traveller Young of the prosperous condition of the peasants of some of the French provinces.

# The Foundations of the *Ancien Régime*

Were they really crushed by taxation, and did they, as has been stated, pay four-fifths of their revenue instead of a fifth as to-day? Impossible to say with certainty. One capital fact, however, seems to prove that under the *ancien régime* the situation of the inhabitants of the rural districts could not have been so very wretched, since it seems established that more than a third of the soil had been bought by peasants.

We are better informed as to the financial system. It was very oppressive and extremely complicated. The budgets usually showed deficits, and the imposts of all kinds were raised by tyrannical farmers-general. At the very moment of the Revolution this condition of the finances became the cause of universal discontent, which is expressed in the *cahiers* of the States General. Let us remark that these *cahiers* did not represent a previous state of affairs, but an actual condition due to a crisis of poverty produced by the bad harvest of 1788 and the hard winter of 1789. What would these *cahiers* have told us had they been written ten years earlier?

Despite these unfavourable circumstances the *cahiers* contained no revolutionary ideas. The most advanced merely asked that taxes should be imposed only with the consent of the States General and paid by all alike. The same *cahiers* sometimes expressed a wish that the power of the king should be limited by a Constitution defining his rights and those of the nation. If these wishes had been granted a constitutional monarchy could very easily have been substituted for the absolute monarchy, and the Revolution would probably have been avoided.

# The Psychology of Revolution

Unhappily, the nobility and the clergy were too strong and Louis XVI. too weak for such a solution to be possible.

Moreover, it would have been rendered extremely difficult by the demands of the *bourgeoisie*, who claimed to substitute themselves for the nobles, and were the real authors of the Revolution. The movement started by the middle classes rapidly exceeded their hopes, needs, and aspirations. They had claimed equality for their own profit, but the people also demanded equality. The Revolution thus finally became the popular government which it was not and had no intention of becoming at the outset.

### 4. *Evolution of Monarchical Feeling during the Revolution.*

Despite the slow evolution of the affective elements, it is certain that during the Revolution the sentiments, not of the people only, but also of the revolutionary Assemblies with regard to the monarchy, underwent a very rapid change. Between the moment when the legislators of the first Assembly surrounded Louis XVI. with respect and the moment when his head was cut off a very few years had elapsed.

These changes, superficial rather than profound, were in reality a mere transposition of sentiments of the same order. The love which the men of this period professed for the king was transferred to the new Government which had inherited his power. The mechanism of such a transfer may easily be demonstrated.

Under the *ancien régime*, the sovereign, holding his power by Divine right, was for this reason invested with a kind of supernatural power. His people looked up to him from every corner of the country.

This mystic belief in the absolute power of royalty was shattered only when repeated experience proved that the power attributed to the adored being was fictitious. He then lost his prestige. Now, when prestige is lost the crowd will not forgive the fallen idol for deluding them, and seek anew the idol without which they cannot exist.

From the outset of the Revolution numerous facts, which were daily repeated, revealed to the most fervent believers the fact that royalty no longer possessed any power, and that there were other powers capable, not only of contending with royalty, but possessed of superior force.

What, for instance, was thought of the royal power by the multitudes who saw the king held in check by the Assembly, and incapable, in the heart of Paris, of defending his strongest fortress against the attacks of armed bands?

The royal weakness thus being obvious, the power of the Assembly was increasing. Now, in the eyes of the crowd weakness has no prestige; it turns always to force.

In the Assemblies feeling was very fluid, but did not evolve very rapidly, for which reason the monarchical faith survived the taking of the Bastille the flight of the king, and his understanding with foreign sovereigns.

The royalist faith was still so powerful that the Parisian riots and the events which led to the execution of Louis XVI. were not enough finally to destroy, in the provinces, the species of secular piety which enveloped the old monarchy.[1]

It persisted in a great part of France during the whole of the Revolution, and was the origin of the royalist conspiracies and insurrections in various departments which the Convention had such trouble to suppress. The royalist faith had disappeared in Paris, where the weakness of the king was too plainly visible; but in the provinces the royal power, representing God on earth, still retained its prestige.

The royalist sentiments of the people must have been deeply rooted to survive the guillotine. The royalist movements persisted, indeed, during the whole of the Revolution, and were accentuated under the Directory, when forty-nine departments sent royalist deputies to Paris, which provoked the Directory to the *coup d'État* of Fructidor.

This monarchical feeling, with difficulty repressed by the Revolution, contributed to the success of Bonaparte when he came to occupy the throne of the ancient kings, and in great measure to re-establish the *ancien régime*.

---

[1] As an instance of the depth of this hereditary love of the people for its kings, Michelet relates the following fact, which occurred in the reign of Louis XV.: "When it was known in Paris that Louis XV., who had left for the army, was detained ill at Metz, it was night. People got up and ran tumultuously hither and thither without knowing where they were going; the churches were opened in the middle of the night . . . people assembled at every cross-road, jostling and questioning one another without knowing what they were after. In several churches the priest who was reciting the prayer for the king's health was stopped by his tears, and the people replied by sobs and cries. . . . The courier who brought the news of his convalescence was embraced and almost stifled; people kissed his horse, and led him in triumph. . . . Every street resounded with a cry of joy: 'The king is healed.'"

146

# CHAPTER III

MENTAL ANARCHY AT THE TIME OF THE REVOLU‚
TION AND THE INFLUENCE ATTRIBUTED TO
THE PHILOSOPHERS

1. *Origin and Propagation of Revolutionary Ideas.*
THE outward life of men in every age is moulded
upon an inward life consisting of a framework of
traditions, sentiments, and moral influences which
direct their conduct and maintain certain fundamental
notions which they accept without discussion.

Let the resistance of this social framework weaken,
and ideas which could have had no force before will
germinate and develop. Certain theories whose
success was enormous at the time of the Revolution
would have encountered an impregnable wall two
centuries earlier.

The aim of these considerations is to recall to the
reader the fact that the outward events of revolutions
are always a consequence of invisible transformations
which have slowly gone forward in men's minds. Any
profound study of a revolution necessitates a study
of the mental soil upon which the ideas that direct its
course have to germinate.

Generally slow in the extreme, the evolution of ideas
is often invisible for a whole generation. Its extent
can only be grasped by comparing the mental condition

of the same social classes at the two extremities of the curve which the mind has followed. To realise the different conceptions of royalty entertained by educated men under Louis XIV. and Louis XVI., we must compare the political theories of Bossuet and Turgot.

Bossuet expressed the general conceptions of his time concerning the absolute monarchy when he based the authority of a Government upon the will of God, "sole judge of the actions of kings, always irresponsible before men." Religious faith was then as strong as the monarchical faith from which it seemed inseparable, and no philosopher could have shaken it.

The writings of the reforming ministers of Louis XVI., those of Turgot, for instance, are animated by quite another spirit. Of the Divine right of kings there is hardly a word, and the rights of the peoples begin to be clearly defined.

Many events had contributed to prepare for such an evolution—unfortunate wars, famines, imposts, general poverty at the end of the reign of Louis XV., &c. Slowly destroyed, respect for monarchical authority was replaced by a mental revolt which was ready to manifest itself as soon as occasion should arise.

When once the mental framework commences to crumble the end comes rapidly. This is why at the time of the Revolution ideas were so quickly propagated which were by no means new, but which until then had exerted no influence, as they had not fallen on fruitful ground.

Yet the ideas which were then so attractive and effectual had often been expressed. For a long time they had inspired the politics of England. Two thousand years earlier the Greek and Latin authors had written in defence of liberty, had cursed tyrants, and proclaimed the rights of popular sovereignty.

The middle classes who effected the Revolution, although, like their fathers, they had learned all these things in text-books, were not in any degree moved by them, because the moment when such ideas could move them had not arrived. How should the people have been impressed by them at a time when all men were accustomed to regard all hierarchies as natural necessities ?

The actual influence of the philosophers in the genesis of the Revolution was not that which was attributed to them. They revealed nothing new, but they developed the critical spirit which no dogma can resist once the way is prepared for its downfall.

Under the influence of this developing critical spirit things which were no longer very greatly respected came to be respected less and less. When tradition and prestige had disappeared the social edifice suddenly fell.

This progressive disaggregation finally descended to the people, but was not commenced by the people. The people follows examples, but never sets them.

The philosophers, who could not have exerted any influence over the people, did exert a great influence over the enlightened portion of the nation. The unemployed nobility, who had long been ousted from their old functions, and who were consequently inclined to be censorious, followed their leadership. Incapable of foresight, the nobles were the first to break with the traditions that were their only *raison d'être*. As steeped in humanitarianism and rationalism as the *bourgeoisie* of to-day, they continually sapped their

149

own privileges by their criticisms. As to-day, the most ardent reformers were found among the favourites of fortune. The aristocracy encouraged dissertations on the social contract, the rights of man, and the equality of citizens. At the theatre it applauded plays which criticised privileges, the arbitrariness and the incapacity of men in high places, and abuses of all kinds.

As soon as men lose confidence in the foundations of the mental framework which guides their conduct they feel at first uneasy and then discontented. All classes felt their old motives of action gradually disappearing. Things that had seemed sacred for centuries were now sacred no longer.

The censorious spirit of the nobility and of the writers of the day would not have sufficed to move the heavy load of tradition, but that its action was added to that of other powerful influences. We have already stated, in citing Bossuet, that under the *ancien régime* the religious and civil governments, widely separated in our days, were intimately connected. To injure one was inevitably to injure the other. Now, even before the monarchical idea was shaken the force of religious tradition was greatly diminished among cultivated men. The constant progress of knowledge had sent an increasing number of minds from theology to science by opposing the truth observed to the truth revealed.

This mental evolution, although as yet very vague, was sufficient to show that the traditions which for so many centuries had guided men had not the value which had been attributed to them, and that it would soon be necessary to replace them.

# Mental Anarchy at Time of Revolution

But where discover the new elements which might take the place of tradition? Where seek the magic ring which would raise a new social edifice on the remains of that which no longer contented men?

Men were agreed in attributing to reason the power that tradition and the gods seemed to have lost. How could its force be doubted? Its discoveries having been innumerable, was it not legitimate to suppose that by applying it to the construction of societies it would entirely transform them? Its possible function increased very rapidly in the thoughts of the more enlightened, in proportion as tradition seemed more and more to be distrusted.

The sovereign power attributed to reason must be regarded as the culminating idea which not only engendered the Revolution but governed it throughout. During the whole Revolution men gave themselves up to the most persevering efforts to break with the past, and to erect society upon a new plan dictated by logic.

Slowly filtering downward, the rationalistic theories of the philosophers meant to the people simply that all the things which had been regarded as worthy of respect were now no longer worthy. Men being declared equal, the old masters need no longer be obeyed.

The multitude easily succeeded in ceasing to respect what the upper classes themselves no longer respected. When the barrier of respect was down the Revolution was accomplished.

The first result of this new mentality was a general insubordination. Mme. Vigée Lebrun relates that on the promenade at Longchamps men of the people leaped on the footboards of the carriages, saying, "Next year you will be behind and we shall be inside."

The populace was not alone in manifesting insubordination and discontent. These sentiments were general on the eve of the Revolution. "The lesser clergy," says Taine, "are hostile to the prelates; the provincial gentry to the nobility of the court; the vassals to the seigneurs; the peasants to the townsmen," &c.

This state of mind, which had been communicated from the nobles and clergy to the people, also invaded the army. At the moment the States General were opened Necker said: "We are not sure of the troops." The officers were becoming humanitarian and philosophical. The soldiers, recruited from the lowest class of the population, did not philosophise, but they no longer obeyed.

In their feeble minds the ideas of equality meant simply the suppression of all leaders and masters, and therefore of all obedience. In 1790 more than twenty regiments threatened their officers, and sometimes, as at Nancy, threw them into prison.

The mental anarchy which, after spreading through all the classes of society, finally invaded the army was the principal cause of the disappearance of the *ancien régime*. "It was the defection of the army affected by the ideas of the Third Estate," wrote Rivarol, "that destroyed royalty."

2. *The supposed Influence of the Philosophers of the Eighteenth Century upon the Genesis of the Revolution—Their dislike of Democracy.*

Although the philosophers who have been supposed the inspirers of the French Revolution did attack certain privileges and abuses, we must not for that reason regard them as partisans of popular government. Democracy, whose *rôle* in Greek history was familiar to them, was generally highly antipathetic to them. They were not ignorant of the destruction and violence which are its invariable accompaniments, and knew that in the time of Aristotle it was already defined as "a State in which everything, even the law, depends on the multitude set up as a tyrant and governed by a few declamatory speakers."

Pierre Bayle, the true forerunner of Voltaire, recalled in the following terms the consequences of popular government in Athens :—

"If one considers this history, which displays at great length the tumult of the assemblies, the factions dividing the city, the seditious disturbing it, the most illustrious subjects persecuted, exiled, and punished by death at the will of a violent windbag, one would conclude that this people, which so prided itself on its liberty, was really the slave of a small number of caballers, whom they called demagogues, and who made it turn now in this direction, now in that, as their passions changed, almost as the sea heaps the waves now one way, now another, according to the winds which trouble it. You will seek in vain in Macedonia, which was a monarchy, for as many examples of tyranny as Athenian history will afford."

Montesquieu had no greater admiration for the democracy. Having described the three forms of government—republican, monarchical, and despotic— he shows very clearly what popular government may lead to :—

"Men were free with laws ; men would fain be free

without them ; what was a maxim is called severity ;
what was order is called hindrance.    Formerly the
welfare of individuals constituted the public wealth,
but now the public wealth becomes the patrimony of
individuals.    The republic is spoil, and its strength is
merely the power of a few citizens and the licence
of all."

". . . Little petty tyrants spring up who have all
the vices of a single tyrant.    Very soon what is left of
liberty becomes untenable ; a single tyrant arises, and
the people loses all, even the advantages of corruption.

" Democracy has therefore two extremes to avoid ;
the extreme of the spirit of equality leads to the
despotism of a single person, as the despotism of a
single person leads to conquest."

The ideal of Montesquieu was the English constitutional government, which prevented the monarchy
from degenerating into despotism.    Otherwise the
influence of this philosopher at the moment of the
Revolution was very slight.

As for the Encyclopædists, to whom such a considerable *rôle* is attributed, they hardly dealt with
politics, excepting d'Holbach, a liberal monarchist like
Voltaire and Diderot.    They wrote chiefly in defence
of individual liberty, opposing the encroachments of
the Church, at that time extremely intolerant and
inimical to philosophers.    Being neither Socialists nor
democrats, the Revolution could not utilise any of
their principles.

Voltaire himself was by no means a partisan of
democracy.

" Democracy," he said, " seems only to suit a very
small country, and even then it must be fortunately

situated. Little as it may be, it will make many mistakes, because it will be composed of men. Discord will prevail there as in a convent full of monks ; but there will be no St. Bartholomew's day, no Irish massacres, no Sicilian Vespers, no Inquisition, no condemnation to the galleys for having taken water from the sea without paying for it ; unless we suppose this republic to be composed of devils in a corner of hell."

All these men who are supposed to have inspired the Revolution had opinions which were far from subversive, and it is really difficult to see that they had any real influence on the development of the revolutionary movement. Rousseau was one of the very few democratic philosophers of his age, which is why his *Contrat Social* became the Bible of the men of the Terror. It seemed to furnish the rational justification necessary to excuse the acts deriving from unconscious mystic and affective impulses which no philosophy had inspired.

To be quite truthful, the democratic instincts of Rousseau were by no means above suspicion. He himself considered that his projects for social reorganisation, based upon popular sovereignty, could be applied only to a very small State ; and when the Poles asked him for a draft democratic Constitution he advised them to choose a hereditary monarch.

Among the theories of Rousseau that relating to the perfection of the primitive social state had a great success. He asserted, together with various writers of his time, that primitive mankind was perfect ; it was corrupted only by society. By modifying society by means of good laws one might bring back the happiness of the early world. Ignorant of all psychology, he believed that men were the same throughout time and space and that they could all be ruled by the same laws and institutions. This was then the general belief. "The vices and virtues of the people," wrote Helvetius, "are always a necessary effect of its legislation. . . . How can we doubt that virtue is in the case of all peoples the result of the wisdom, more or less perfect, of the administration?"

There could be no greater mistake.

### 3. The Philosophical Ideas of the Bourgeoisie at the Time of the Revolution.

It is by no means easy to say just what were the social and political conceptions of a Frenchman of the middle classes at the moment of the Revolution. They might be reduced to a few formulæ concerning fraternity, equality, and popular government, summed up in the celebrated Declaration of the Rights of Man, of which we shall have occasion to quote a few passages.

The philosophers of the eighteenth century do not seem to have been very highly rated by the men of the Revolution. Rarely are they quoted in the speeches of the time. Hypnotised by their classical memories of Greece and Rome, the new legislators re-read their Plato and their Plutarch. They wished to revive the constitution of Sparta, with its manners, its frugal habits, and its laws.

Lycurgus, Solon, Miltiades, Manlius Torquatus, Brutus, Mucius Scævola, even the fabulous Minos himself, became as familiar in the tribune as in the theatre, and the public went crazy over them. The shades of the heroes of antiquity hovered over the revolutionary assemblies. Posterity alone has replaced them by the shades of the philosophers of the eighteenth century.

We shall see that in reality the men of this period, generally represented as bold innovators guided by subtle philosophers, professed to effect no innovations whatever, but to return to a past long buried in the mists of history, and which, moreover, they scarcely ever in the least understood.

The more reasonable, who did not go so far back for their models, aimed merely at adopting the English constitutional system, of which Montesquieu and Voltaire had sung the praises, and which all nations were finally to imitate without violent crises.

Their ambitions were confined to a desire to perfect the existing monarchy, not to overthrow it. But in time of revolution men often take a very different path from that they propose to take. At the time of the convocation of the States General no one would ever have supposed that a revolution of peaceful *bourgeoisie* and men of letters would rapidly be transformed into one of the most sanguinary dictatorships of history.

# CHAPTER IV

## PSYCHOLOGICAL ILLUSIONS RESPECTING THE FRENCH REVOLUTION

1. *Illusions respecting Primitive Man, the Return to a State of Nature, and the Psychology of the People.*

WE have already repeated, and shall again repeat, that the errors of a doctrine do not hinder its propagation, so that all we have to consider here is its influence upon men's minds.

But although the criticism of erroneous doctrines is seldom of practical utility, it is extremely interesting from a psychological point of view. The philosopher who wishes to understand the working of men's minds should always carefully consider the illusions which they live with. Never, perhaps, in the course of history have these illusions appeared so profound and so numerous as during the Revolution.

One of the most prominent was the singular conception of the nature of our first ancestors and primitive societies. Anthropology not having as yet revealed the conditions of our remoter forbears, men supposed, being influenced by the legends of the Bible, that man had issued perfect from the hands of the Creator. The first societies were models which were afterwards ruined by civilisation, but to which mankind must

158

return. The return to the state of nature was very soon the general cry. " The fundamental principle of all morality, of which I have treated in my writings," said Rousseau, " is that man is a being naturally good, loving justice and order."

Modern science, by determining, from the surviving remnants, the conditions of life of our first ancestors, has long ago shown the error of this doctrine. Primitive man has become an ignorant and ferocious brute, as ignorant as the modern savage of goodness, morality, and pity. Governed only by his instinctive impulses, he throws himself on his prey when hunger drives him from his cave, and falls upon his enemy the moment he is aroused by hatred. Reason, not being born, could have no hold over his instincts.

The aim of civilisation, contrary to all revolutionary beliefs, has been not to return to the state of nature but to escape from it. It was precisely because the Jacobins led mankind back to the primitive condition by destroying all the social restraints without which no civilisation can exist that they transformed a political society into a barbarian horde.

The ideas of these theorists concerning the nature of man were about as valuable as those of a Roman general concerning the power of omens. Yet their influence as motives of action was considerable. The Convention was always inspired by such ideas.

The errors concerning our primitive ancestors were excusable enough, since before modern discoveries had shown us the real conditions of their existence these were absolutely unknown. But the absolute ignorance of human psychology displayed by the men of the Revolution is far less easy to understand.

# The Psychology of Revolution

It would really seem as though the philosophers and writers of the eighteenth century must have been totally deficient in the smallest faculty of observation. They lived amidst their contemporaries without seeing them and without understanding them. Above all, they had not a suspicion of the true nature of the popular mind. The man of the people always appeared to them in the likeness of the chimerical model created by their dreams. As ignorant of psychology as of the teachings of history, they considered the plebeian man as naturally good, affectionate, grateful, and always ready to listen to reason.

The speeches delivered by members of the Assembly show how profound were these illusions. When the peasants began to burn the *châteaux* they were greatly astonished, and addressed them in sentimental harangues, praying them to cease, in order not to "give pain to their good king," and adjured them "to surprise him by their virtues."

2. *Illusions respecting the Possibility of separating Man from his Past and the Power of Transformation attributed to the Law.*

One of the principles which served as a foundation for the revolutionary institutions was that man may readily be cut off from his past, and that a society may be re-made in all its parts by means of institutions. Persuaded in the light of reason that, except for the primitive ages which were to serve as models, the past represented an inheritance of errors and superstitions, the legislators of the day resolved to break entirely with that past. The better to emphasise their intention, they founded a new era, transformed the calendar, and changed the names of the months and seasons.

Supposing all men to be alike, they thought they could legislate for the human race. Condorcet imagined that he was expressing an evident truth when he said: "A good law must be good for all men, just as a geometrical proposition is true for all."

The theorists of the Revolution never perceived, behind the world of visible things, the secret springs which moved them. A century of biological progress was needed to show how grievous were their mistakes, and how wholly a being of whatever species depends on its past.

With the influence of the past, the reformers of the Revolution were always clashing, without ever understanding it. They wanted to annihilate it, but were annihilated by it instead.

The faith of law-makers in the absolute power of laws and institutions, rudely shaken by the end of the Revolution, was absolute at its outbreak. Grégoire said from the tribune of the Constituent Assembly, without provoking the least astonishment: "We could if we would change religion, but we do not want to." We know that they did want to later, and we know how miserably their attempt failed.

Yet the Jacobins had in their hands all the elements of success. Thanks to the completest of tyrannies, all obstacles were removed, and the laws which it pleased them to impose were always accepted. After ten years of violence, of destruction and burning and pillage and massacre and general upheaval, their impotence was revealed so startlingly that they fell into universal reprobation. The dictator then invoked by the whole of France was obliged to re-establish the greater part of that which had been destroyed.

The attempt of the Jacobins to re-fashion society in the name of pure reason constitutes an experiment of the highest interest. Probably mankind will never have occasion to repeat it on so vast a scale.

Although the lesson was a terrible one, it does not seem to have been sufficient for a considerable class of minds, since even in our days we hear Socialists propose to rebuild society from top to bottom according to their chimerical plans.

3. *Illusions respecting the Theoretical Value of the great Revolutionary Principles.*

The fundamental principles on which the Revolution was based in order to create a new dispensation are contained in the Declarations of Rights which were formulated successively in 1789, 1793, and 1795. All three Declarations agree in proclaiming that "the principle of sovereignty resides in the nation."

For the rest, the three Declarations differ on several points, notably in the matter of equality. That of 1789 simply states (Article 1): "Men are born and remain free and having equal rights." That of 1793 goes farther, and assures us (Article 3): "All men are equal by nature." That of 1795 is more modest and says (Article 3): "Equality consists in the law being the same for all." Besides this, having mentioned rights, the third Declaration considers it useful to speak of duties. Its morality is simply that of the Gospel. Article 2 says : " All the duties of a man and a citizen derive from these two principles engraved on all hearts by nature : do not do unto others that which you would not they should do unto you ; do constantly unto others the good you would wish to receive from them."

The essential portions of these proclamations, the only portions which have really survived, were those relating to equality and popular sovereignty.

Despite the weakness of its rational meaning, the part played by the Republican device, *Liberty*, *Equality*, *Fraternity*, was considerable.

This magic formula, which is still left engraven on many of our walls until it shall be engraven on our hearts, has really possessed the supernatural power attributed to certain words by the old sorcerers.

Thanks to the new hopes excited by its promises, its power of expansion was considerable. Thousands of men lost their lives for it. Even in our days, when a revolution breaks out in any part of the world, the same formula is always invoked.

Its choice was happy in the extreme. It belongs to the category of indefinite dream-evoking sentences, which every one is free to interpret according to his own desires, hatreds, and hopes. In matters of faith the real sense of words matters very little ; it is the meaning attached to them that makes their importance.

Of the three principles of the revolutionary device, equality was most fruitful of consequences. We shall see in another part of this book that it is almost the only one which still survives, and is still productive of effects.

It was certainly not the Revolution that introduced the idea of equality into the world. Without going back even to the Greek republics, we may remark that the theory of equality was taught in the clearest fashion by Christianity and Islamism. All men, subjects of the one God, were equal before Him, and judged solely according to their merits. The dogma of the equality of souls before God was an essential dogma with Mohammedans as well as with Christians.

But to proclaim a principle is not enough to secure its observation. The Christian Church soon renounced its theoretical equality, and the men of the Revolution only remembered it in their speeches.

The sense of the term "equality" varies according to the persons using it. It often conceals sentiments very contrary to its real sense, and then represents the imperious need of having no one above one, joined to the no less lively desire to feel above others. With the Jacobins of the Revolution, as with those of our days, the word "equality" simply involves a jealous hatred of all superiority. To efface superiority, such men pretend to unify manners, customs, and situations. All despotisms but that exercised by themselves seem odious.

Not being able to avoid the natural inequalities, they deny them. The second Declaration of Rights, that of 1793, affirms, contrary to the evidence, that "all men are equal by nature."

It would seem that in many of the men of the

# Illusions Respecting the French Revolution

Revolution the ardent desire for equality merely concealed an intense need of inequalities. Napoleon was obliged to re-establish titles of nobility and decorations for their benefit. Having shown that it was among the most rabid revolutionists that he found the most docile instruments of domination, Taine continues :—

" Suddenly, through all their preaching of liberty and equality, appeared their authoritative instincts, their need of commanding, even as subordinates, and also, in most cases, an appetite for money or for pleasure. Between the delegate of the Committee of Public Safety and the minister, prefect, or sub-prefect of the Empire the difference is small : it is the same man under the two costumes, first *en carmagnole*, then in the braided coat."

The dogma of equality had as its first consequence the proclamation of popular sovereignty by the *bourgeoisie*. This sovereignty remained otherwise highly theoretical during the whole Revolution.

The principle of authority was the lasting legacy of the Revolution. The two terms " liberty " and " fraternity " which accompany it in the republican device had never much influence. We may even say that they had none during the Revolution and the Empire, but merely served to decorate men's speeches.

Their influence was hardly more considerable later. Fraternity was never practised and the peoples have never cared much for liberty. To-day our working-men have completely surrendered it to their unions.

To sum up: although the Republican motto has

been little applied it has exerted a very great influence. Of the French Revolution practically nothing has remained in the popular mind but the three celebrated words which sum up its gospel, and which its armies spread over Europe.

## BOOK II

### *THE RATIONAL, AFFECTIVE, MYSTIC, AND COLLECTIVE INFLUENCES ACTIVE DURING THE REVOLUTION*

## CHAPTER I

### THE PSYCHOLOGY OF THE CONSTITUENT ASSEMBLY

1. *Psychological Influences active during the French Revolution.*

THE genesis of the French Revolution, as well as its duration, was conditioned by elements of a rational, affective, mystic, and collective nature, each category of which was ruled by a different logic. It is, as I have said, because they have not been able to dissociate the respective influences of these factors that so many historians have interpreted this period so indifferently.

The rational element usually invoked as an explanation exerted in reality but a very slight influence. It prepared the way for the Revolution, but maintained it only at the outset, while it was still exclusively middle-class. Its action was manifested by many measures of the time, such as the proposals to reform the taxes, the suppression of the privileges of a useless nobility, &c.

As soon as the Revolution reached the people, the

167

# The Psychology of Revolution

influence of the rational elements speedily vanished before that of the affective and collective elements. As for the mystic elements, the foundation of the revolutionary faith, they made the army fanatical and propagated the new belief throughout the world.

We shall see these various elements as they appeared in events and in the psychology of individuals. Perhaps the most important was the mystic element. The Revolution cannot be clearly comprehended—we cannot repeat it too often—unless it is considered as the formation of a religious belief. What I have said elsewhere of all beliefs applies equally to the Revolution. Referring, for instance, to the chapter on the Reformation, the reader will see that it presents more than one analogy with the Revolution.

Having wasted so much time in demonstrating the slight rational value of beliefs, the philosophers are to-day beginning to understand their function better. They have been forced to admit that these are the only factors which possess an influence sufficient to transform all the elements of a civilisation.

They impose themselves on men apart from reason and have the power to polarise men's thoughts and feelings in one direction. Pure reason had never such a power, for men were never impassioned by reason.

The religious form rapidly assumed by the Revolution explains its power of expansion and the prestige which it possessed and has retained.

Few historians have understood that this great monument ought to be regarded as the foundation of a new religion. The penetrating mind of Tocqueville, I believe, was the first to perceive as much.

# Psychology of the Constituent Assembly

" The French Revolution," he wrote, "was a political revolution which operated in the manner of and assumed something of the aspect of a religious revolution. See by what regular and characteristic traits it finally resembled the latter : not only did it spread itself far and wide like a religious revolution, but, like the latter, it spread itself by means of preaching and propaganda. A political revolution which inspires proselytes, which is preached as passionately to foreigners as it is accomplished at home : consider what a novel spectacle was this."

The religious side of the Revolution being granted, the accompanying fury and devastation are easily explained. History shows us that such are always the accompaniments of the birth of religions. The Revolution was therefore certain to provoke the violence and intolerance the triumphant deities demand from their adepts. It overturned all Europe for twenty years, ruined France, caused the death of millions of men, and cost the country several invasions : but it is as a rule only at the cost of such catastrophes that a people can change its beliefs.

Although the mystic element is always the foundation of beliefs, certain affective and rational elements are quickly added thereto. A belief thus serves to group sentiments and passions and interests which belong to the affective domain. Reason then envelops the whole, seeking to justify events in which, however, it played no part whatever.

At the moment of the Revolution every one, according to his aspirations, dressed the new belief in a different rational vesture. The peoples saw in it only the suppression of the religious and political despotisms

# The Psychology of Revolution

and hierarchies under which they had so often suffered. Writers like Goethe and thinkers like Kant imagined that they saw in it the triumph of reason. Foreigners like Humboldt came to France "to breathe the air of liberty and to assist at the obsequies of despotism."

These intellectual illusions did not last long. The evolution of the drama soon revealed the true foundations of the dream.

## 2. *Dissolution of the Ancien Régime. The assembling of the States General.*

Before they are realised in action, revolutions are sketched out in men's thoughts. Prepared by the causes already studied, the French Revolution commenced in reality with the reign of Louis XVI. More discontented and censorious every day, the middle classes added claim to claim. Everybody was calling for reform.

Louis XVI. thoroughly understood the utility of reform, but he was too weak to impose it on the clergy and the nobility. He could not even retain his reforming ministers, Malesherbes and Turgot. What with famines and increased taxation, the poverty of all classes increased, and the huge pensions drawn by the Court formed a shocking contrast to the general distress.

The notables convoked to attempt to remedy the financial situation refused a system of equal taxation, and granted only insignificant reforms which the Parliament did not even consent to register. It had to be dissolved. The provincial Parliaments made common cause with that of Paris, and were also dissolved. But they led

# Psychology of the Constituent Assembly

opinion, and in all parts of France promoted the demand for a meeting of the States General, which had not been convoked for nearly two hundred years.

The decision was taken : 5,000,000 Frenchmen, of whom 100,000 were ecclesiastics and 150,000 nobles, sent their representatives. There were in all 1,200 deputies, of whom 578 were of the Third Estate, consisting chiefly of magistrates, advocates, and physicians. Of the 300 deputies of the clergy, 200, of plebeian origin, threw in their lot with the Third Estate against the nobility and clergy.

From the first sessions a psychological conflict broke out between the deputies of different social conditions and (therefore) different mentalities. The magnificent costumes of the privileged deputies contrasted in a humiliating fashion with the sombre fashions of the Third Estate.

At the first session the members of the nobility and the clergy were covered, according to the prerogatives of their class, before the king. Those of the Third Estate wished to imitate them, but the privileged members protested. On the following day more protests of wounded self-love were heard. The deputies of the Third Estate invited those of the nobility and the clergy who were sitting in separate halls to join them for the verification of their powers. The nobles refused. The negotiations lasted more than a month. Finally, the deputies of the Third Estate, on the proposition of the Abbé Siéyès, considering that they represented 95 per cent. of the nation, declared themselves constituted as a National Assembly. From that moment the Revolution pursued its course.

# The Psychology of Revolution

### 3. *The Constituent Assembly.*

The power of a political assembly resides, above all, in the weakness of its adversaries. Astonished by the slight resistance encountered, and carried away by the ascendancy of a handful of orators, the Constituent Assembly, from its earliest sessions, spoke and acted as a sovereign body. Notably it arrogated to itself the power of decreeing imposts, a serious encroachment upon the prerogatives of the royal power.

The resistance of Louis XVI. was feeble enough. He simply had the hall in which the States assembled closed. The deputies then met in the hall of the tennis-court, and took the oath that they would not separate until the Constitution of the kingdom was an established fact.

The majority of the deputies of the clergy went with them. The king revoked the decision of the Assembly, and ordered the deputies to retire. The Marquis de Dreux-Brézé, the Grand Master of Ceremonies, having invited them to obey the order of the sovereign, the President of the Assembly declared " that the nation assembled cannot receive orders," and Mirabeau replied to the envoy of the sovereign that, being united by the will of the people, the Assembly would only withdraw at the point of the bayonet. Again the king gave way.

On the 9th of June the meeting of deputies took the title of the Constituent Assembly. For the first time in centuries the king was forced to recognise the existence of a new power, formerly ignored—that of the people, represented by its elected representatives. The absolute monarchy was no more.

# Psychology of the Constituent Assembly

Feeling himself more and more seriously threatened, Louis XVI. summoned to Versailles a number of regiments composed of foreign mercenaries. The Assembly demanded the withdrawal of the troops. The king refused, and dismissed Necker, replacing him by the Marshal de Broglie, reputed to be an extremely authoritative person.

But the Assembly had able supporters. Camille Desmoulins and others harangued the crowd in all directions, calling it to the defence of liberty. They sounded the tocsin, organised a militia of 12,000 men, took muskets and cannon from the Invalides, and on the 14th of July the armed bands marched upon the Bastille. The fortress, barely defended, capitulated in a few hours. Seven prisoners were found within it, of whom one was an idiot and four were accused of forgery.

The Bastille, the prison of many victims of arbitrary power, symbolised the royal power to many minds; but the people who demolished it had not suffered by it. Scarcely any but members of the nobility were imprisoned there.

The influence exercised by the taking of this fortress has continued to our days. Serious historians like M. Rambaud assure us that "the taking of the Bastille is a culminating fact in the history, not of France only but of all Europe, and inaugurates a new epoch in the history of the world."

Such credulity is a little excessive. The importance of the event lay simply in the psychological fact that for the first time the people received an obvious proof of the weakness of an authority which had lately been formidable.

# The Psychology of Revolution

When the principle of authority is injured in the public mind it dissolves very rapidly. What might not one demand of a king who could not defend his principal fortress against popular attacks? The master regarded as all-powerful had ceased to be so.

The taking of the Bastille was the beginning of one of those phenomena of mental contagion which abound in the history of the Revolution. The foreign mercenary troops, although they could scarcely be interested in the movement, began to show symptoms of mutiny. Louis XVI. was reduced to accepting their disbandment. He recalled Necker, went to the Hôtel de Ville, sanctioned by his presence the accomplished facts, and accepted from La Fayette, commandant of the National Guard, the new cockade of red, white, and blue which allied the colours of Paris to those of the king.

Although the riot which ended in the taking of the Bastille can by no means be regarded as " a culminating fact in history," it does mark the precise moment of the commencement of popular government. The armed people thenceforth intervened daily in the deliberations of the revolutionary Assemblies, and seriously influenced their conduct.

This intervention of the people in conformity with the dogma of its sovereignty has provoked the respectful admiration of many historians of the Revolution. Even a superficial study of the psychology of crowds would speedily have shown them that the mystic entity which they call the people was merely translating the will of a few leaders. It is not correct to say that the people took the Bastille, attacked the Tuileries, invaded the Convention, &c., but that

certain leaders—generally by means of the clubs—
united armed bands of the populace, which they led
against the Bastille, the Tuileries, &c. During the
Revolution the same crowds attacked or defended the
most contrary parties, according to the leaders who
happened to be at their heads. A crowd never has
any opinion but that of its leaders.

Example constituting one of the most potent forms
of suggestion, the taking of the Bastille was inevitably
followed by the destruction of other fortresses. Many
*châteaux* were regarded as so many little Bastilles,
and in order to imitate the Parisians who had
destroyed theirs the peasants began to burn them.
They did so with the greater fury because the seigneurial homes contained the titles of feudal dues. It
was a species of Jacquerie.

The Constituent Assembly, so proud and haughty
towards the king, was, like all the revolutionary assemblies which followed it, extremely pusillanimous before
the people.

Hoping to put an end to the disorders of the night
of August 4th, it voted, on the proposition of a member of the nobility, the Comte de Noailles, the abolition of seigneurial rights. Although this measure
suppressed at one stroke the privileges of the nobles,
it was voted with tears and embracings. Such accesses
of sentimental enthusiasm are readily explained when
we recall how contagious emotion is in a crowd, above
all in an assembly oppressed by fear.

If the renunciation of their rights had been effected
by the nobility a few years earlier, the Revolution
would doubtless have been avoided, but it was now
too late. To give way only when one is forced to do

# The Psychology of Revolution

so merely increases the demands of those to whom one yields. In politics one should always look ahead and give way long before one is forced to do so.

Louis XVI. hesitated for two months to ratify the decisions voted by the Assembly on the night of the 4th of August. He had retired to Versailles. The leaders sent thither a band of 7,000 or 8,000 men and women of the people, assuring them that the royal residence contained great stores of bread. The railings of the palace were forced, some of the bodyguard were killed, and the king and all his family were led back to Paris in the midst of a shrieking crowd, many of whom bore on the ends of their pikes the heads of the soldiers massacred. The dreadful journey lasted six hours. These events constituted what are known as the "days" of October.

The popular power increased, and in reality the king, like the whole assembly, was henceforth in the hands of the people—that is, at the mercy of the clubs and their leaders. This popular power was to prevail for nearly ten years, and the Revolution was to be almost entirely its work.

While proclaiming that the people constituted the only sovereign, the Assembly was greatly embarrassed by riots which went far beyond its theoretical expectations. It had supposed that order would be restored while it fabricated a Constitution destined to assure the eternal happiness of mankind.

We know that during the whole duration of the Revolution one of the chief occupations of the assemblies was to make, unmake, and remake Constitutions. The theorists attributed to them then, as they do to-day, the power of transforming society ; the

# Psychology of the Constituent Assembly

Assembly, therefore, could not neglect its task. In the meantime it published a solemn Declaration of the Rights of Man which summarised its principles.

The Constitution, proclamations, declarations, and speeches had not the slightest effect on the popular movements, nor on the dissentients who daily increased in number in the heart of the Assembly. The latter became more and more subjected to the ascendancy of the advanced party, which was supported by the clubs. Danton, Camille Desmoulins, and later Marat and Hébert, violently excited the populace by their harangues and their journals. The Assembly was rapidly going down the slope that leads to extremes.

During all these disorders the finances of the country were not improving. Finally convinced that philanthropic speeches would not alter their lamentable condition, and seeing that bankruptcy threatened, the Assembly decreed, on the 2nd of November, 1789, the confiscation of the goods of the Church. Their revenues, consisting of the tithes collected from the faithful, amounted to some £8,000,000, and their value was estimated at about £120,000,000. They were divided among some hundreds of prelates, Court abbés, &c., who owned a quarter of all France. These goods, henceforth entitled "national domains," formed the guarantee of the *assignats*, the first issue of which was for 400,000,000 francs (£16,000,000 sterling). The public accepted them at the outset, but they multiplied so under the Directory and the Convention, which issued 45,000,000,000 francs in this form (£1,800,000,000 sterling), that an assignat of 100 livres was finally worth only a few halfpence.

Stimulated by his advisers, the feeble Louis

# The Psychology of Revolution

attempted in vain to struggle against the decrees of the Assembly by refusing to sanction them.

Under the influence of the daily suggestions of the leaders and the power of mental contagion the revolutionary movement was spreading everywhere independently of the Assembly and often even against it.

In the towns and villages revolutionary municipalities were instituted, protected by the local National Guards. Those of neighbouring towns commenced to make mutual arrangements to defend themselves should need arise. Thus federations were formed, which were soon rolled into one; this sent 14,000 National Guards to Paris, who assembled on the Champ-de-Mars on the 14th of July, 1790. There the king swore to maintain the Constitution decreed by the National Assembly.

Despite this vain oath it became more evident every day that no agreement was possible between the hereditary principles of the monarchy and those proclaimed by the Assembly.

Feeling himself completely powerless, the king thought only of flight. Arrested at Varennes and brought back a prisoner to Paris, he was shut up in the Tuileries. The Assembly, although still extremely royalist, suspended him from power, and decided to assume the sole charge of the government.

Never did sovereign find himself in a position so difficult as that of Louis at the time of his flight. The genius of a Richelieu would hardly have extricated him. The only element of defence on which he could have relied had from the beginning absolutely failed him.

During the whole duration of the Constituent

# Psychology of the Constituent Assembly

Assembly the immense majority of Frenchmen and of the Assembly remained royalist, so that had the sovereign accepted a liberal monarchy he could perhaps have remained in power. It would seem that Louis had little to promise in order to come to an agreement with the Assembly.

Little, perhaps, but with his structure of mind that little was strictly impossible. All the shades of his forbears would have risen up in front of him had he consented to modify the mechanism of the monarchy inherited from so many ancestors. And even had he attempted to do so, the opposition of his family, the clergy, the nobles, and the Court could never have been surmounted. The ancient castes on which the monarchy rested, the nobility and the clergy, were then almost as powerful as the monarch himself. Every time it seemed as though he might yield to the injunctions of the Assembly it was because he was constrained to do so by force, and to attempt to gain time. His appeals to alien Powers represented the resolution of a desperate man who had seen all his natural defences fail him.

He, and especially the queen, entertained the strangest illusions as to the possible assistance of Austria, for centuries the rival of France. If Austria indolently consented to come to his aid, it was only in the hope of receiving a great reward. Mercy gave him to understand that the payment expected consisted of Alsace, the Alps, and Navarre.

The leaders of the clubs, finding the Assembly too royalist, sent the people against it. A petition was signed, inviting the Assembly to convoke a new constituent power to proceed to the trial of Louis XVI.

# The Psychology of Revolution

Monarchical in spite of all, and finding that the Revolution was assuming a character far too demagogic, the Assembly resolved to defend itself against the actions of the people. A battalion of the National Guard, commanded by La Fayette, was sent to the Champ-de-Mars, where the crowd was assembled, to disperse it. Fifty of those present were killed.

The Assembly did not long persist in its feeble resistance. Extremely fearful of the people, it increased its arrogance towards the king, depriving him every day of some part of his prerogatives and authority. He was now scarcely more than a mere official obliged to execute the wishes of others.

The Assembly had imagined that it would be able to exercise the authority of which it had deprived the king, but such a task was infinitely above its resources. A power so divided is always weak. "I know nothing more terrible," said Mirabeau, "than the sovereign authority of six hundred persons."

Having flattered itself that it could combine in itself all the powers of the State, and exercise them as Louis XVI. had done, the Assembly very soon exercised none whatever.

As its authority failed anarchy increased. The popular leaders continually stirred up the people. Riot and insurrection became the sole power. Every day the Assembly was invaded by rowdy and imperious delegations which operated by means of threats and demands.

All these popular movements, which the Assembly, under the stress of fear, invariably obeyed, had nothing spontaneous about them. They simply represented the manifestations of new powers—the clubs and the

# Psychology of the Constituent Assembly

Commune—which had been set up beside the Assembly.

The most powerful of these clubs was the Jacobin, which had quickly created more than five hundred branches in the country, all of which were under the orders of the central body. Its influence remained preponderant during the whole duration of the Revolution. It was the master of the Assembly, and then of France, its only rival the insurrectionary Commune, whose power was exercised only in Paris.

The weakness of the national Assembly and all its failures had made it extremely unpopular. It became conscious of this, and, feeling that it was every day more powerless, decided to hasten the creation of the new Constitution in order that it might dissolve. Its last action, which was tactless enough, was to decree that no member of the Constituent Assembly should be elected to the Legislative Assembly. The members of the latter were thus deprived of the experience acquired by their predecessors.

The Constitution was completed on the 3rd of September, 1791, and accepted on the 13th by the king, to whom the Assembly had restored his powers.

This Constitution organised a representative Government, delegating the legislative power to deputies elected by the people, and the executive power to the king, whose right of veto over the decrees of the Assembly was recognised. New departmental divisions were substituted for the old provinces. The imposts were abolished, and replaced by direct and indirect taxes, which are still in force.

The Assembly, which had just altered the territorial divisions and overthrown all the old social organisation, thought itself powerful enough to transform the religious organisation of the country also. It claimed notably that the members of the clergy should be elected by the people, and should be thus withdrawn from the influence of their supreme head, the Pope.

This civil constitution of the clergy was the origin of religious struggles and persecutions which lasted until the days of the Consulate. Two-thirds of the priests refused the oath demanded of them.

During the three years which represented the life of the Constituent Assembly the Revolution had produced considerable results. The principal result was perhaps the beginning of the transference to the Third Estate of the riches of the privileged classes. In this way while interests were created to be defended fervent adherents were raised up to the new *régime*. A Revolution supported by the gratification of acquired appetites is bound to be powerful. The Third Estate, which had supplanted the nobles, and the peasants, who had bought the national domains, would readily understand that the restoration of the *ancien régime* would despoil them of all their advantages. The energetic defence of the Revolution was merely the defence of their own fortunes.

This is why we see, during part of the Revolution, nearly half the departments vainly rising against the despotism that crushed them. The Republicans triumphed over all opposition. They were extremely powerful in that they had to defend, not only a new ideal, but new material interests. We shall see that the influence of these two factors lasted during the whole of the Revolution, and contributed powerfully to the establishment of the Empire.

# CHAPTER II

## THE PSYCHOLOGY OF THE LEGISLATIVE ASSEMBLY

### 1. *Political Events during the Life of the Legislative Assembly.*

BEFORE examining the mental characteristics of the Legislative Assembly let us briefly sum up the considerable political events which marked its short year's life. They naturally played an important part in respect of its psychological manifestations.

Extremely monarchical, the Legislative Assembly had no more idea than its predecessor of destroying the monarchy. The king appeared to it to be slightly suspect, but it still hoped to be able to retain him on the throne.

Unhappily for him, Louis was incessantly begging for intervention from abroad. Shut up in the Tuileries, defended only by his Swiss Guards, the timid sovereign was drifting among contrary influences. He subsidised journals intended to modify public opinion, but the obscure " penny-a-liners " who edited them knew nothing of acting on the mind of the crowd. Their only means of persuasion was to menace with the gallows all the partisans of the Revolution, and to predict the invasion of France by an army which would rescue the king.

Royalty no longer counted on anything but the

183

foreign Courts. The nobles were emigrating. Prussia, Austria, and Russia were threatening France with a war of invasion. The Court favoured their lead. To the coalition of the three kings against France the Jacobin Club proposed to oppose a league of peoples. The Girondists were then, with the Jacobins, at the head of the revolutionary movement. They incited the masses to arm themselves—600,000 volunteers were equipped. The Court accepted a Girondist minister. Dominated by him, Louis XVI. was obliged to propose to the Assembly a war against Austria. It was immediately agreed to.

In declaring war the king was not sincere. The queen revealed the French plans of campaign and the secret deliberations of the Council to the Austrians.

The beginnings of the struggle were disastrous. Several columns of troops, attacked by panic, disbanded. Stimulated by the clubs, and persuaded— justly, for that matter—that the king was conspiring with the enemies of France, the population of the *faubourgs* rose in insurrection. Its leaders, the Jacobins, and above all Danton, sent to the Tuileries on the 20th of June a petition threatening the king with revocation. It then invaded the Tuileries, heaping invectives on the sovereign.

Fatality impelled Louis toward his tragic destiny. While the threats of the Jacobins against royalty had roused many of the departments to indignation, it was learned that a Prussian army had arrived on the frontiers of Lorraine.

The hope of the king and queen respecting the help to be obtained from abroad was highly chimerical. Marie-Antoinette suffered from an absolute illusion as to the psychology of the Austrian and the French peoples. Seeing France terrorised by a few energumens, she supposed that it would be equally easy to terrify the Parisians, and by means of threats to lead them back under the king's authority. Inspired by her, Fersen undertook to publish the manifesto of the Duke of Brunswick, threatening Paris with "total subversion if the royal family were molested."

The effect produced was diametrically opposite to that intended. The manifesto aroused indignation against the monarch, who was regarded as an accomplice, and increased his unpopularity. From that day he was marked for the scaffold.

Carried away by Danton, the delegates of the sections installed themselves at the Hôtel de Ville as an insurrectionary Commune, which arrested the commandant of the National Guard, who was devoted to the king, sounded the tocsin, equipped the National Guard, and on the 10th of August hurled them, with the populace, against the Tuileries. The regiments called in by Louis disbanded themselves. Soon none were left to defend him but his Swiss and a few gentlemen. Nearly all were killed. Left alone, the king took refuge with the Assembly. The crowds demanded his denouncement. The Legislative Assembly decreed his suspension and left a future Assembly, the Convention, to decide upon his fate.

2. *Mental Characteristics of the Legislative Assembly.*

The Legislative Assembly, formed of new men, presented quite a special interest from the psychological point of view. Few assemblies have offered in such a degree the characteristics of the political collectivity.

It comprised seven hundred and fifty deputies, divided into pure royalists, constitutional royalists, republicans, Girondists, and Montagnards. Advocates and men of letters formed the majority. It also contained, but in smaller numbers, superior officers, priests, and a very few scientists.

The philosophical conceptions of the members of this Assembly seem rudimentary enough. Many were imbued with Rousseau's idea of a return to a state of nature. But all, like their predecessors, were dominated more especially by recollections of Greek and Latin antiquity. Cato, Brutus, Gracchus, Plutarch, Marcus Aurelius, and Plato, continually evoked, furnished the images of their speech. When the orator wished to insult Louis XVI. he called him Caligula.

In hoping to destroy tradition they were revolutionaries, but in claiming to return to a remote past they showed themselves extremely reactionary.

For the rest, all these theories had very little influence on their conduct. Reason was continually figuring in their speeches, but never in their actions. These were always dominated by those affective and mystic elements whose potency we have so often demonstrated.

The psychological characteristics of the Legislative Assembly were those of the Constituent Assembly, but were greatly accentuated. They may be summed up in four words: impressionability, mobility, timidity, and weakness.

# Psychology of the Legislative Assembly

This mobility and impressionability are revealed in the constant variability of their conduct. One day they exchange noisy invective and blows. On the following day we see them " throwing themselves into one another's arms with torrents of tears." They eagerly applaud an address demanding the punishment of those who have petitioned for the king's dethronement, and the same day accord the honours of the session to a delegation which has come to demand his downfall.

The pusillanimity and weakness of the Assembly in the face of threats was extreme. Although royalist it voted the suspension of the king, and on the demand of the Commune delivered him, with his family, to be imprisoned in the Temple,

Thanks to its weakness, it was as incapable as the Constituent Assembly of exercising any power, and allowed itself to be dominated by the Commune and the clubs, which were directed by such influential leaders as Hébert, Tallien, Rossignol, Marat, Robespierre, &c.

Until Thermidor, 1794, the insurrectionary Commune constituted the chief power in the State, and behaved precisely as if it had been charged with the government of Paris.

It was the Commune that demanded the imprisonment of Louis XVI. in the tower of the Temple, when the Assembly wished to imprison him in the palace of the Luxembourg. It was the Commune again that filled the prisons with suspects, and then ordered them to be killed.

We know with what refinements of cruelty a handful of some 150 bandits, paid at the rate of 24 livres a day,

# The Psychology of Revolution

and directed by a few members of the Commune, exterminated some 1,200 persons in four days. This crime was known as the massacre of September. The mayor of Paris, Pétion, received the band of assassins with respect, and gave them drink. A few Girondists protested somewhat, but the Jacobins were silent.

The terrorised Assembly affected at first to ignore the massacres, which were encouraged by several of its more influential deputies, notably Couthon and Billaud-Varenne. When at last it decided to condemn them it was without attempting to prevent their continuation.

Conscious of its impotence, the Legislative Assembly dissolved itself a fortnight later in order to give way to the Convention.

Its work was obviously disastrous, not in intention but in fact. Royalist, it abandoned the monarchy; humanitarian, it allowed the massacres of September; pacific, it pushed France into a formidable war, thus showing that a weak Government always ends by bringing ruin upon its country.

The history of the two previous revolutionary Assemblies proves once more to what point events carry within them their inevitable consequences. They constitute a train of necessities of which we can sometimes choose the first, but which then evolve without consulting us. We are free to make a decision, but powerless to avert its consequences.

The first measures of the Constituent Assembly were rational and voluntary, but the results which followed were beyond all will or reason or foresight.

Which of the men of 1789 would have ventured to desire or predict the death of Louis XVI., the wars

# Psychology of the Legislative Assembly

of La Vendée, the Terror, the permanent guillotine and the final anarchy, or the ensuing return to tradition and order, guided by the iron hand of a soldier?

In the development of events which ensued from the early actions of the revolutionary Assemblies the most striking, perhaps, was the rise and development of the government of the crowd—of mob rule.

Behind the facts which we have been considering—the taking of the Bastille, the invasion of Versailles, the massacres of September, the attack on the Tuileries, the murder of the Swiss Guards, and the downfall and imprisonment of the king—we can readily perceive the laws affecting the psychology of crowds and their leaders.

We shall now see that the power of the multitude will progressively increase, overcome all other powers, and finally replace them.

# CHAPTER III

## THE PSYCHOLOGY OF THE CONVENTION

### 1. *The Legend of the Convention.*

THE history of the Convention is not merely fertile in psychological documents. It also shows how powerless the witnesses of any period and even their immediate successors are to form an exact idea of the events which they have witnessed, and the men who have surrounded them.

More than a century has elapsed since the Revolution, and men are only just beginning to form judgments concerning this period which, if still often doubtful enough, are slightly more accurate than of old.

This happens, not only because new documents are being drawn from the archives, but because the legends which enveloped that sanguinary period in a magical cloud are gradually vanishing with the passage of time.

Perhaps the most tenacious legend of all was that which until formerly used to surround the personages to whom our fathers applied the glorious epithet, "the Giants of the Convention."

The struggles of the Convention against France in insurrection and Europe in arms produced such an impression that the heroes of this formidable struggle seemed to belong to a race of supermen or Titans.

# The Psychology of the Convention

The epithet "giant" seemed justified so long as the events of the period were confused and massed together. Regarded as connected when it was simply simultaneous, the work of the armies was confounded with that of the Convention. The glory of the first recoiled upon the second, and served as an excuse for the hecatombs of the Terror, the ferocity of the civil war, and the devastation of France.

Under the penetrating scrutiny of modern criticism, the heterogeneous mass of events has been slowly disentangled. The armies of the Republic have retained their old prestige, but we have been forced to recognise that the men of the Convention, absorbed entirely by their intestine conflicts, had very little to do with their victories. At the most two or three members of the committees of the Assembly were concerned with the armies, and the fact that they were victorious was due, apart from their numbers and the talents of their young generals, to the enthusiasm with which a new faith had inspired them.

In a later chapter, devoted to the revolutionary armies, we shall see how they conquered Europe in arms. They set out inspired by the ideas of liberty and equality which constituted the new gospel, and once on the frontiers, which were to keep them so long, they retained a special mentality, very different from that of the Government, which they first knew nothing of and afterwards despised.

Having no part whatever in their victories, the men of the Convention contented themselves with legislating at hazard according to the injunctions of the leaders who directed them, and who claimed to be regenerating France by means of the guillotine.

191

# The Psychology of Revolution

But it was thanks to these valiant armies that the history of the Convention was transformed into an apotheosis which affected several generations with a religious respect which even to-day is hardly extinct.

Studying in detail the psychology of the "Giants" of the Convention, we find their magnitude shrink very rapidly. They were in general extremely mediocre. Their most fervent defenders, such as M. Aulard, are obliged to admit as much.

This is how M. Aulard puts it in his *History of the French Revolution :—*

"It has been said that the generation which from 1789 to 1799 did such great and terrible things was a generation of giants, or, to put it more plainly, that it was a generation more distinguished than that which preceded it or that which followed. This is a retrospective illusion. The citizens who formed the municipal and Jacobin or nationalist groups by which the Revolution was effected do not seem to have been superior, either in enlightenment or in talents, to the Frenchmen of the time of Louis XV. or of Louis Philippe. Were those exceptionally gifted whose names history has retained because they appeared on the stage of Paris, or because they were the most brilliant orators of the various revolutionary Assemblies ? Mirabeau, up to a certain point, deserved the title of genius ; but as to the rest— Robespierre, Danton, Vergniaud—had they truly more talent, for example, than our modern orators? In 1793, in the time of the supposed 'giants,' Mme. Roland wrote in her memoirs : 'France was as though drained of men ; their dearth during this revolution is truly surprising ; there have scarcely been any but pigmies.' "

If after considering the men of the Convention individually we consider them in a body, we may say that they did not shine either by intelligence or by virtue or by courage. Never did a body of men manifest such pusillanimity. They had no courage save in their speeches or in respect of remote dangers. This Assembly, so proud and threatening in its speech when addressing royalty, was perhaps the most timid and docile political collectivity that the world has ever known. We see it slavishly obedient to the orders of the clubs and the Commune, trembling before the popular delegations which invaded it daily, and obeying the injunctions of the rioters to the point of handing over to them its most brilliant members. The Convention affords the world a melancholy spectacle, voting, at the popular behest, laws so absurd that it is obliged to annul them as soon as the rioters have quitted the hall.

Few Assemblies have given proof of such weakness. When we wish to show how low a popular Government can fall we have only to point to the Convention.

## 2. *Results of the Triumph of the Jacobin Religion*

Among the causes that gave the Convention its special physiognomy, one of the most important was the definite establishment of a revolutionary religion. A dogma which was at first in process of formation was at last finally erected.

This dogma was composed of an aggregate of somewhat inconsistent elements. Nature, the rights

193

of man, liberty, equality, the social contract, hatred of tyrants, and popular sovereignty formed the articles of a gospel which, to its disciples, was above discussion. The new truths had found apostles who were certain of their power, and who finally, like believers all the world over, sought to impose them by force. No heed should be taken of the opinion of unbelievers; they all deserved to be exterminated.

The hatred of heretics having been always, as we have seen, in respect of the Reformation, an irreducible characteristic of great beliefs, we can readily comprehend the intolerance of the Jacobin religion.

The history of the Reformation proves also that the conflict between two allied beliefs is very bitter. We must not, therefore, be astonished that in the Convention the Jacobins fought furiously against the other republicans, whose faith hardly differed from their own.

The propaganda of the new apostles was very energetic. To convert the provinces they sent thither zealous disciples escorted by guillotines. The inquisitors of the new faith would have no paltering with error. As Robespierre said, " The republic is the destruction of everything that is opposed to it." What matter that the country refused to be regenerated? It should be regenerated despite itself. " We will make a cemetery of France," said Carrier, " rather than fail to regenerate it in our own way."

The Jacobin policy derived from the new faith was very simple. It consisted in a sort of equalitarian Socialism, directed by a dictatorship which would brook no opposition.

Of practical ideas consistent with the economic

# The Psychology of the Convention

necessities and the true nature of man, the theorists who ruled France would have nothing to say. Speech and the guillotine sufficed them. Their speeches were childish. "Never a fact," says Taine, "nothing but abstractions, strings of sentences about Nature, reason, the people, tyrants, liberty: like so many puffed-out balloons uselessly jostling in space. If we did not know that it all ended in practical and dreadful results, we should think they were games of logic, school exercises, academical demonstrations, ideological combinations."

The theories of the Jacobins amounted practically to an absolute tyranny. To them it seemed evident that a sovereign State must be obeyed without discussion by citizens rendered equal as to conditions and fortune.

The power with which they invested themselves was far greater than that of the monarchs who had preceded them. They fixed the prices of merchandise and arrogated the right to dispose of the life and property of citizens.

Their confidence in the regenerative virtues of the revolutionary faith was such that after having declared war upon kings they declared war upon the gods. A calendar was established from which the saints were banished. They created a new divinity, Reason, whose worship was celebrated in Notre-Dame, with ceremonies which were in many ways identical with those of the Catholic faith, upon the altar of the "late Holy Virgin." This cult lasted until Robespierre substituted a personal religion of which he constituted himself the high priest.

The sole masters of France, the Jacobins and their

disciples were able to plunder the country with impunity, although they were never in the majority
anywhere.

Their numbers are not easy to determine exactly.
We know only that they were very small. Taine
valued them at 5,000 in Paris, among 700,000 inhabitants; in Besançon 300 among 300,000; and in all
France about 300,000.

"A small feudality of brigands, set over a
conquered France," according to the words of the
same author, they were able, in spite of their small
numbers, to dominate the country, and this for several
reasons. In the first place, their faith gave them a
considerable strength. Then, because they represented the Government, and for centuries the French
had obeyed those who were in command. Finally,
because it was believed that to overthrow them would
be to bring back the *ancien régime*, which was greatly
dreaded by the numerous purchasers of the national
domains. Their tyranny must have grown frightful
indeed to force so many departments to rise against
them.

The first factor of their power was very important.
In the conflict between powerful faiths and weak
faiths victory never falls to the latter. A powerful
faith creates strong wills, which will always overpower
weak wills. That the Jacobins themselves did finally
perish was because their accumulated violence had
bound together thousands of weak wills whose united
weight overbalanced their own strong wills.

It is true that the Girondists, whom the Jacobins
persecuted with so much hatred, had also well-estab-
lished beliefs, but in the struggle which ensued their

education told against them, together with their respect for certain traditions and the rights of others, scruples which did not in the least trouble their adversaries.

"The majority of the sentiments of the Girondists," writes Emile Ollivier, "were delicate and generous ; those of the Jacobin mob were low, gross, and brutal. The name of Vergniaud, compared with that of the 'divine' Marat, measures a gulf which nothing could span."

Dominating the Convention at the outset by the superiority of their talents and their eloquence, the Girondists soon fell under the domination of the Montagnards—worthless energumens, who carried little weight, but were always active, and who knew how to excite the passions of the populace. It was violence and not talent that impressed the Assemblies.

### 3. *Mental Characteristics of the Convention.*

Beside the characteristics common to all assemblies there are some created by influences of environment and circumstances, which give any particular assembly of men a special physiognomy. Most of the characteristics observable in the Constituent and Legislative Assemblies reappeared, in an exaggerated form, in the Convention.

This Assembly comprised about seven hundred and fifty deputies, of whom rather more than a third had sat in the Constituent or the Legislative Assembly. By terrorising the population the Jacobins contrived to triumph at the elections. The majority of the electors, six millions out of seven, preferred to abstain from voting.

# The Psychology of Revolution

As to the professions, the Assembly contained a large number of lawyers, advocates, notaries, bailiffs, ex-magistrates, and a few literary men.

The mentality of the Convention was not homogeneous. Now, an assembly composed of individuals of widely different characters soon splits up into a number of groups. The Convention very early contained three—the Gironde, the Mountain, and the Plain. The constitutional monarchists had almost disappeared.

The Gironde and the Mountain, extreme parties, consisted of about a hundred members apiece, who successively became leaders. In the Mountain were the most advanced members : Couthon, Hérault de Séchelles, Danton, Camille Desmoulins, Marat, Collot d'Herbois, Billaud - Varennes, Barras, Saint - Just, Fouché, Tallien, Carrier, Robespierre, &c. In the Gironde were Brissot, Pétion, Condorcet, Vergniaud, &c.

The five hundred other members of the Assembly— that is, the great majority—constituted what was known as the Plain.

This latter formed a floating mass, silent, undecided, and timid ; ready to follow every impulse and to be carried away by the excitement of the moment. It gave ear indifferently to the stronger of the two preceding groups. After obeying the Gironde for some time it allowed itself to be led away by the Mountain, when the latter triumphed over its enemy. This was a natural consequence of the law already stated, by which the weak invariably fall under the dominion of the stronger wills.

The influence of great manipulators of men was

# The Psychology of the Convention

displayed in a high degree during the Convention. It was constantly led by a violent minority of narrow minds, whose intense convictions lent them great strength.

A brutal and audacious minority will always lead a fearful and irresolute majority. This explains the constant tendency toward extremes to be observed in all revolutionary assemblies. The history of the Convention verifies once more the law of acceleration studied in another chapter.

The men of the Convention were thus bound to pass from moderation to greater and greater violence. Finally they decimated themselves. Of the 180 Girondists who at the outset led the Convention 140 were killed or fled, and finally the most fanatical of the Terrorists, Robespierre, reigned alone over a terrified crowd of servile representatives.

Yet it was among the five hundred members of the majority, uncertain and floating as it was, that the intelligence and experience were to be found. The technical committees to whom the useful work of the Convention was due were recruited from the Plain.

More or less indifferent to politics, the members of the Plain were chiefly anxious that no one should pay particular attention to them. Shut up in their committees, they showed themselves as little as possible in the Assembly, which explains why the sessions of the Convention contained barely a third of the deputies.

Unhappily, as often happens, these intelligent and honest men were completely devoid of character, and the fear which always dominated them made them

# The Psychology of Revolution

vote for the worst of the measures introduced by their dreaded masters.

The men of the Plain voted for everything they were ordered to vote for—the creation of the Revolutionary Tribunal, the Terror, &c. It was with their assistance that the Mountain crushed the Gironde, and Robespierre destroyed the Hébertists and Dantonists. Like all weak people, they followed the strong. The gentle philanthropists who composed the Plain, and constituted the majority of the Assembly, contributed, by their pusillanimity, to bring about the frightful excesses of the Convention.

The psychological note always prevailing in the Convention was a horrible fear. It was more especially through fear that men cut off one another's heads, in the doubtful hope of keeping their own on their shoulders.

Such a fear was, of course, very comprehensible. The unhappy deputies deliberated amid the hootings and vociferations of the tribunes. At every moment veritable savages, armed with pikes, invaded the Assembly, and the majority of the members no longer dared to attend the sessions. When by chance they did go it was only to vote in silence according to the orders of the Mountain, which was only a third as numerous.

The fear which dominated the latter, although less visible, was just as profound. Men destroyed their enemies, not only because they were shallow fanatics, but because they were convinced that their own existence was threatened. The judges of the revolutionary Tribunals trembled no less. They would have willingly acquitted Danton, and the widow

# The Psychology of the Convention

of Camille Desmoulins, and many others. They dared not.

But it was above all when Robespierre became the sole master that the phantom of fear oppressed the Assembly. It has truly been said that a glance from the master made his colleagues shrink with fear. On their faces one read "the pallor of fear and the abandon of despair."

All feared Robespierre and Robespierre feared all. It was because he feared conspiracies against him that he cut off men's heads, and it was also through fear that others allowed him to do so.

The memoirs of members of the Convention show plainly what a horrible memory they retained of this gloomy period. Questioned twenty years later, says Taine, on the true aim and the intimate thoughts of the Committee of Public Safety, Barrère replied :—

" We had only one feeling, that of self-preservation ; only one desire, that of preserving our lives, which each of us believed to be threatened. You had your neighbour's head cut off so that your neighbour should not have you yourself guillotined."

The history of the Convention constitutes one of the most striking examples that could be given of the influence of leaders and of fear upon an assembly.

# CHAPTER IV

## THE GOVERNMENT OF THE CONVENTION

### 1. *The activity of the Clubs and the Commune during the Convention.*

DURING the whole of its existence the Convention was governed by the leaders of the clubs and of the Commune.

We have already seen what was their influence on the preceding Assemblies. It became overwhelming during the Convention. The history of this latter is in reality that of the clubs and the Commune which dominated it. They enslaved, not only the Convention, but also all France. Numerous little provincial clubs, directed by that of the capital, supervised magistrates, denounced suspects, and undertook the execution of all the revolutionary orders.

When the clubs or the Commune had decided upon certain measures they had them voted by the Assembly then and there. If the Assembly resisted, they sent their armed delegations thither—that is, armed bands recruited from the scum of the populace. They conveyed injunctions which were always slavishly obeyed. The Commune was so sure of its strength that it even demanded of the Convention the immediate expulsion of deputies who displeased it.

While the Convention was composed generally of

educated men, the members of the Commune and the clubs comprised a majority of small shopkeepers, labourers, and artisans, incapable of personal opinions, and always guided by their leaders—Danton, Camille Desmoulins, Robespierre, &c.

Of the two powers, clubs and insurrectionary Commune, the latter exercised the greater influence in Paris, because it had made for itself a revolutionary army. It held under its orders forty-eight committees of National Guards, who asked nothing more than to kill, sack, and, above all, plunder.

The tyranny with which the Commune crushed Paris was frightful. For example, it delegated to a certain cobbler, Chalandon by name, the right of surveillance over a portion of the capital—a right implying the power to send to the Revolutionary Tribunal, and therefore to the guillotine, all those whom he suspected. Certain streets were thus almost depopulated by him.

The Convention struggled feebly against the Commune at the outset, but did not prolong its resistance. The culminating point of the conflict occurred when the Convention wished to arrest Hébert, the friend of the Commune, and the latter sent armed bands who threatened the Assembly and demanded the expulsion of the Girondists who had provoked the measure. Upon the Convention refusing the Commune besieged it on June 2, 1798, by means of its revolutionary army, which was under the orders of Hanriot. Terrified, the Assembly gave up twenty-seven of its members. The Commune immediately sent a delegation ironically to felicitate it upon its obedience.

# The Psychology of Revolution

After the fall of the Girondists the Convention submitted itself completely to the injunctions of the omnipotent Commune. The latter decreed the levy of a revolutionary army, to be accompanied by a tribunal and a guillotine, which was to traverse the whole of France in order to execute suspects.

Only towards the end of its existence, after the fall of Robespierre, did the Convention contrive to escape from the yoke of the Jacobins and the Commune. It closed the Jacobin club and guillotined its leading members.

Despite such sanctions the leaders still continued to excite the populace and hurl it against the Convention. In Germinal and Prairial it underwent regular sieges. Armed delegations even succeeded in forcing the Convention to vote the re-establishment of the Commune and the convocation of a new Assembly, a measure which the Convention hastened to annul the moment the insurgents had withdrawn. Ashamed of its fear, it sent for regiments which disarmed the *faubourgs* and made nearly ten thousand arrests. Twenty-six leaders of the movement were put to death, and six deputies who were concerned in the riot were guillotined.

But the Convention did not resist to any purpose. When it was no longer led by the clubs and the Commune it obeyed the Committee of Public Safety and voted its decrees without discussion.

"The Convention," writes H. Williams, "which spoke of nothing less than having all the princes and kings of Europe brought to its feet loaded with chains, was made prisoner in its own sanctuary by a handful of mercenaries."

# The Government of the Convention

## 2. *The Government of France during the Convention—The Terror.*

As soon as it assembled in 1792 the Convention began by decreeing the abolition of royalty, and in spite of the hesitation of a great number of its members, who knew that the provinces were royalist, it proclaimed the Republic.

Intimately persuaded that such a proclamation would transform the civilised world, it instituted a new era and a new calendar. The year I. of this era marked the dawn of a world in which reason alone was to reign. It was inaugurated by the trial of Louis XVI., a measure which was ordered by the Commune, but which the majority of the Convention did not desire.

At its outset, in fact, the Convention was governed by its relatively moderate elements, the Girondists. The president and the secretaries had been chosen among the best known of this party. Robespierre, who was later to become the absolute master of the Convention, possessed so little influence at this time that he obtained only six votes for the presidency, while Pétion received two hundred and thirty-five.

The Montagnards had at first only a very slight influence. Their power was of later growth. When they were in power there was no longer room in the Convention for moderate members.

Despite their minority the Montagnards found a way to force the Assembly to bring Louis to trial. This was at once a victory over the Girondists, the condemnation of all kings, and a final divorce between the old order and the new.

# The Psychology of Revolution

To bring about the trial they manœuvred very skilfully, bombarding the Convention with petitions from the provinces, and sending a deputation from the insurrectional Commune of Paris, which demanded a trial.

According to a characteristic common to the Assemblies of the Revolution, that of yielding to threats and always doing the contrary of what they wished, the men of the Convention dared not resist. The trial was decided upon.

The Girondists, who individually would not have wished for the death of the king, voted for it out of fear once they were assembled. Hoping to save his own head, the Duc d'Orleans, Louis cousin, voted with them. If, on mounting the scaffold on January 21, 1793, Louis had had that vision of the future which we attribute to the gods, he would have seen following him, one by one, the greater number of the Girondists whose weakness had been unable to defend him.

Regarded only from the purely utilitarian point of view, the execution of the king was one of the mistakes of the Revolution. It engendered civil war and armed Europe against France. In the Convention itself his death gave rise to intestine struggles, which finally led to the triumph of the Montagnards and the expulsion of the Girondists.

The measures passed under the influence of the Montagnards finally became so despotic that sixty departments, comprising the West and the South, revolted. The insurrection, which was headed by many of the expelled deputies, would perhaps have succeeded had not the compromising assistance of the royalists caused men to fear the return of the *ancien*

# The Government of the Convention

*régime.* At Toulon, in fact, the insurgents acclaimed Louis XVII.

The civil war thus begun lasted during the greater part of the life of the Revolution. It was fought with the utmost savagery. Old men, women, children, all were massacred, and villages and crops were burned. In the Vendée alone the number of the killed was reckoned at something between half a million and a million.

Civil war was soon followed by foreign war. The Jacobins thought to remedy all these ills by creating a new Constitution. It was always a tradition with all the revolutionary assemblies to believe in the magic virtues of formulæ. In France this conviction has never been affected by the failure of experiments.

"A robust faith," writes one of the great admirers of the Revolution, M. Rambaud, "sustained the Convention in this labour; it believed firmly that when it had formulated in a law the principles of the Revolution its enemies would be confounded, or, still better, converted, and that the advent of justice would disarm the insurgents."

During its lifetime the Convention drafted two Constitutions—that of 1793, or the year I., and that of 1795, or the year III. The first was never applied, an absolute dictatorship very soon replacing it; the second created the Directory.

The Convention contained a large number of lawyers and men of affairs, who promptly comprehended the impossibility of government by means of a large Assembly. They soon divided the Convention into small committees, each of which had an independent existence — business committees,

committees of legislation, finance, agriculture, **arts,** &c. These committees prepared the laws which the Assembly usually voted with its eyes closed.

Thanks to them, the work of the Convention was not purely destructive. They drafted many very useful measures, creating important colleges, establishing the metric system, &c. The majority of the members of the Assembly, as we have already seen, took refuge in these committees in order to evade the political conflict which would have endangered their heads.

Above the business committees, which had nothing to do with politics, was the Committee of Public Safety, instituted in April, 1793, and composed of nine members. Directed at first by Danton, and in the July of the same year by Robespierre, it gradually absorbed all the powers of government, including that of giving orders to ministers and generals. Carnot directed the operations of the war, Cambon the finances, and Saint-Just and Collot-d'Herbois the general policy.

Although the laws voted by the technical committees were often very wise, and constituted the lasting work of the Convention, those which the Assembly voted in a body under the threats of the delegations which invaded it were manifestly ridiculous.

Among these laws, which were not greatly in the interests of the public or of the Convention itself, were the law of the maximum, voted in September, 1793, which pretended to fix the price of provisions, and which merely established a continual dearth; the destruction of the royal tombs at Saint-Denis; the

# The Government of the Convention

trial of the queen, the systematic devastation of the Vendée by fire, the establishment of the Revolutionary Tribunal, &c.

The Terror was the chief means of government during the Convention. Commencing in September, 1793, it reigned for six months—that is, until the death of Robespierre. Vainly did certain Jacobins—Danton, Camille Desmoulins, Hérault de Séchelles, &c.—propose that clemency should be given a trial. The only result of this proposition was that its authors were sent to the scaffold. It was merely the lassitude of the public that finally put an end to this shameful period.

The successive struggles of the various parties in the Convention and its tendency towards extremes eliminated one by one the men of importance who had once played their part therein. Finally it fell under the exclusive domination of Robespierre. While the Convention was disorganising and ravaging France, the armies were winning brilliant victories. They had seized the left bank of the Rhine, Belgium, and Holland. The treaty of Basle ratified these conquests.

We have already mentioned, and we shall return to the matter again, that the work of the armies must be considered absolutely apart from that of the Convention. Contemporaries understood this perfectly, but to-day it is often forgotten.

When the Convention was dissolved, in 1795, after lasting for three years, it was regarded with universal distrust. The perpetual plaything of popular caprice, it had not succeeded in pacifying France, but had plunged her into anarchy. The general opinion respecting the Convention is well summed up in a letter written in July, 1799, by the Swedish *chargé d'affaires*, Baron Drinkmann : " I venture to hope that no people will ever be governed by the will of more cruel and imbecile scoundrels than those that have ruled France since the beginning of her new liberty."

### 3. *The End of the Convention. The Beginnings of the Directory.*

At the end of its existence, the Convention, always trusting to the power of formulæ, drafted a new Constitution, that of the year III., intended to replace that of 1793, which had never been put into execution. The legislative power was to be shared by a so-called Council of Ancients composed of 150 members, and a council of deputies numbering 500. The executive power was confided to a Directory of five members, who were appointed by the Ancients upon nomination by the Five Hundred, and renewed every year by the election of one of their number. It was specified that two-thirds of the members of the new Assembly should be chosen from among the deputies of the Convention. This prudent measure was not very efficacious, as only ten departments remained faithful to the Jacobins.

To avoid the election of royalists, the Convention had decided to banish all *emigrés* in perpetuity.

The announcement of this Constitution did not produce the anticipated effect upon the public. It had no effect upon the popular riots, which continued. One of the most important was that which threatened the Convention on the 5th of October, 1795. The

# The Government of the Convention

leaders hurled a veritable army upon the Assembly. Before such provocation, the Convention finally decided to defend itself, and sent for troops, entrusting the command to Barras.

Bonaparte, who was then beginning to emerge from obscurity, was entrusted with the task of repression. With such a leader action was swift and energetic. Vigorously pounded with ball near the church at St. Roch, the insurgents fled, leaving some hundreds of dead on the spot.

This action, which displayed a firmness to which the Convention was little habituated, was only due to the celerity of the military operations, for while these were being carried out the insurgents had sent delegates to the Assembly, which, as usual, showed itself quite ready to yield to them.

The repression of this riot constituted the last important act of the Convention. On the 26th of October, 1795, it declared its mission terminated, and gave way to the Directory.

We have already laid stress upon some of the psychological lessons furnished by the government of the Convention. One of the most striking of these is the impotence of violence to dominate men's minds in permanence.

Never did any Government possess such formidable means of action, yet in spite of the permanent guillotine, despite the delegates sent with the guillotine into the provinces, despite its Draconian laws, the Convention had to struggle perpetually against riots, insurrections, and conspiracies. The cities, the departments, and the *faubourgs* of Paris were continually rising in revolt, although heads were falling by the thousand.

# The Psychology of Revolution

This Assembly, which thought itself sovereign, fought against the invincible forces which were fixed in men's minds, and which material constraint was powerless to overcome. Of these hidden motive forces it never understood the power, and it struggled against them in vain. In the end the invisible forces triumphed.

# CHAPTER V

## INSTANCES OF REVOLUTIONARY VIOLENCE

1. *Psychological Causes of Revolutionary Violence.*
WE have shown in the course of the preceding chapters that the revolutionary theories constituted a new faith.

Humanitarian and sentimental, they exalted liberty and fraternity. But, as in many religions, we can observe a complete contradiction between doctrine and action. In practice no liberty was tolerated, and fraternity was quickly replaced by frenzied massacres.

This opposition between principles and conduct results from the intolerance which accompanies all beliefs. A religion may be steeped in humanitarianism and forbearance, but its sectaries will always want to impose it on others by force, so that violence is the inevitable result.

The cruelties of the Revolution were thus the inherent results of the propagation of the new dogmas. The Inquisition, the religious wars of France, St. Bartholomew's Day, the revocation of the Edict of Nantes, the " Dragonnades," the persecution of the Jansenists, &c., belonged to the same family as the Terror and derived from the same psychological sources.

Louis XIV. was not a cruel king, yet under the

213

impulse of his faith he drove hundreds of thousands of Protestants out of France, after first shooting down a considerable number and sending others to the galleys.

The methods of persuasion adopted by all believers are by no means a consequence of their fear of the dissentient opposition. Protestants and Jansenists were anything but dangerous under Louis XIV. Intolerance arises above all from the indignation experienced by a mind which is convinced that it possesses the most dazzling verities against the men who deny those truths, and who are surely not acting in good faith. How can one support error when one has the necessary strength to wipe it out?

Thus have reasoned the believers of all ages. Thus reasoned Louis XIV. and the men of the Terror. These latter also were convinced that they were in possession of absolute truths, which they believed to be obvious, and whose triumph was certain to regenerate humanity. Could they be more tolerant toward their adversaries than the Church and the kings of France had been toward heretics?

We are forced to believe that terror is a method which all believers regard as a necessity, since from the beginning of the ages religious codes have always been based upon terror. To force men to observe their prescriptions, believers have sought to terrify them with threats of an eternal hell of torments.

The apostles of the Jacobin belief behaved as their fathers had done, and employed the same methods. If similar events occurred again we should see identical actions repeated. If a new belief—Socialism, for example—were to triumph to-morrow, it would be led to employ methods of propaganda like those of the Inquisition and the Terror.

But were we to regard the Jacobin Terror solely as the result of a religious movement, we should not completely apprehend it. Around a triumphant religious belief, as we saw in the case of the Reformation, gather a host of individual interests which are dependent on that belief. The Terror was directed by a few fanatical apostles, but beside this small number of ardent proselytes, whose narrow minds dreamed of regenerating the world, were great numbers of men who lived only to enrich themselves. They rallied readily around the first victorious leader who promised to enable them to enjoy the results of their pillage.

" The Terrorists of the Revolution," writes Albert Sorel, " resorted to the Terror because they wished to remain in power, and were incapable of doing so by other means. They employed it for their own salvation, and after the event they stated that their motive was the salvation of the State. Before it became a system it was a means of government, and the system was only invented to justify the means."

We may thus fully agree with the following verdict on the Terror, written by Emile Ollivier in his work on the Revolution: "The Terror was above all a Jacquerie, a regularised pillage, the vastest enterprise of theft that any association of criminals has ever organised."

## 2. *The Revolutionary Tribunals.*

The Revolutionary Tribunals constituted the principal means of action of the Terror. Besides that of Paris, created at the instigation of Danton, and which

215

# The Psychology of Revolution

a year afterwards sent its founder to the guillotine, France was covered with such tribunals.

"One hundred and seventy-eight tribunals," says Taine, "of which 40 were perambulant, pronounced death sentences in all parts of the country, which were carried out instantly on the spot. Between the 16th of April, 1793, and the 9th of Thermidor in the year II. that of Paris guillotined 2,625 persons, and the provincial judges worked as hard as those of Paris. In the little town of Orange alone 331 persons were guillotined. In the city of Arras 299 men and 93 women were guillotined. . . . In the city of Lyons alone the revolutionary commissioner admitted to 1,684 executions. . . . The total number of these murders has been put at 17,000, among whom were 1,200 women, of whom a number were octogenarians."

Although the Revolutionary Tribunal of Paris claimed only 2,625 victims, it must not be forgotten that all the suspects had already been summarily massacred during the "days" of September.

The Revolutionary Tribunal of Paris, a mere instrument of the Committee of Public Safety, limited itself in reality, as Fouquier-Tinville justly remarked during his trial, to executing its orders. It surrounded itself at first with a few legal forms which did not long survive. Interrogatory, defence, witnesses—all were finally suppressed. Moral proof—that is, mere suspicion—sufficed to procure condemnation. The president usually contented himself with putting a vague question to the accused. To work more rapidly still, Fouquier-Tinville proposed to have the guillotine installed on the same premises as the Tribunal.

This Tribunal sent indiscriminately to the scaffold

# Instances of Revolutionary Violence

all the accused persons arrested by reason of party hatred, and very soon, in the hands of Robespierre, it constituted an instrument of the bloodiest tyranny. When Danton, one of its founders, became its victim, he justly asked pardon of God and men, before mounting the scaffold for having assisted to create such a Tribunal.

Nothing found mercy before it : neither the genius of Lavoisier, nor the gentleness of Lucile Desmoulins, nor the merit of Malesherbes. "So much talent," said Benjamin Constant, "massacred by the most cowardly and brutish of men!"

To find any excuse for the Revolutionary Tribunal, we must return to our conception of the religious mentality of the Jacobins, who founded and directed it. It was a piece of work comparable in its spirit and its aim to the Inquisition. The men who furnished its victims—Robespierre, Saint-Just, and Couthon—believed themselves the benefactors of the human race in suppressing all infidels, the enemies of the faith that was to regenerate the earth.

The executions during the Terror did not affect the members of the aristocracy only, since 4,000 peasants and 3,000 working-men were guillotined.

Given the emotion produced in Paris in our days by a capital execution, one might suppose that the execution of so many persons at one time would produce a very great emotion. But habit had so dulled sensibility that people paid but little attention to the matter at last. Mothers would take their children to see people guillotined as to-day they take them to the marionette theatre.

The daily spectacle of executions made the men of

217

the time very indifferent to death. All mounted the scaffold with perfect tranquillity, the Girondists singing the Marseillaise as they climbed the steps.

This resignation resulted from the law of habitude, which very rapidly dulls emotion. To judge by the fact that royalist risings were taking place daily, the prospect of the guillotine no longer terrified men. Things happened as though the Terror terrorised no one. Terror is an efficacious psychological process so long as it does not last. The real terror resides far more in threats than in their realisation.

### 3. *The Terror in the Provinces.*

The executions of the Revolutionary Tribunals in the provinces represented only a portion of the massacres effected in the departments during the Terror. The revolutionary army, composed of vagabonds and brigands, marched through France killing and pillaging. Its method of procedure is well indicated by the following passage from Taine :—

" At Bedouin, a town of 2,000 inhabitants, where unknown hands had cut down the tree of liberty, 433 houses were demolished or fired, 16 persons were guillotined, and 47 shot down ; all the other inhabitants were expelled and reduced to living as vagabonds in the mountains, and to taking shelter in caverns which they hollowed out of the earth."

The fate of the wretches sent before the Revolutionary Tribunals was no better. The first mockery of trial was quickly suppressed. At Nantes, Carrier drowned and shot down according to his fancy nearly 5,000 persons—men, women, and children.

The details of these massacres figured in the

# Instances of Revolutionary Violence

*Moniteur* after the reaction of Thermidor. I cite a few lines :—

" I saw," says Thomas, " after the taking of Noirmoutier, men and women and old people burned alive . . . women violated, girls of fourteen and fifteen, and massacred afterward, and tender babes thrown from bayonet to bayonet ; children who were taken from beside their mothers stretched out on the ground."

In the same number we read a deposition by one Julien, relating how Carrier forced his victims to dig their graves and to allow themselves to be buried alive. The issue of October 15, 1794, contained a report by Merlin de Thionville proving that the captain of the vessel *le Destin* had received orders to embark forty-one victims to be drowned—" among them a blind man of 78, twelve women, twelve girls, and fourteen children, of whom ten were from 10 to 6 and five at the breast."

In the course of Carrier's trial (*Moniteur*, December 30, 1794) it was proved that he "had given orders to drown and shoot women and children, and had ordered General Haxo to exterminate all the inhabitants of La Vendée and to burn down their dwellings."

Carrier, like all wholesale murderers, took an intense joy in seeing his victims suffer. " In the department in which I hunted the priests," he said, " I have never laughed so much or experienced such pleasure as in watching their dying grimaces" (*Moniteur*, December 22, 1794).

Carrier was tried to satisfy the reaction of Thermidor. But the massacres of Nantes were

# The Psychology of Revolution

repeated in many other towns. Fouché slew more than 2,000 persons at Lyons, and so many were killed at Toulon that the population fell from 29,000 to 7,000 in a few months.

We must say in defence of Carrier, Fréron, Fouché, and all these sinister persons, that they were incessantly stimulated by the Committee of Public Safety. Carrier gave proof of this during his trial.

" I admit," said he (*Moniteur*, December 24, 1794), "that 150 or 200 prisoners were shot every day, but it was by order of the commission. I informed the Convention that the brigands were being shot down by hundreds, and it applauded this letter, and ordered its insertion in the *Bulletin*. What were these deputies doing then who are so furious against me now? They were applauding. Why did they still keep me 'on mission'? Because I was then the saviour of the country, and now I am a bloodthirsty man."

Unhappily for him, Carrier did not know, as he remarked in the same speech, that only seven or eight persons led the Convention. But the terrorised Assembly approved of all that these seven or eight ordered, so that they could say nothing in reply to Carrier's argument. He certainly deserved to be guillotined, but the whole Convention deserved to be guillotined with him, since it had approved of the massacres.

The defence of Carrier, justified by the letters of the Committee, by which the representatives " on mission" were incessantly stimulated, shows that the violence of the Terror resulted from a system, and not, as has sometimes been claimed, from the initiative of a few individuals.

# Instances of Revolutionary Violence

The thirst for destruction during the Terror was by no means assuaged by the destruction of human beings only; there was an even greater destruction of inanimate things. The true believer is always an iconoclast. Once in power, he destroys with equal zeal the enemies of his faith and the images, temples, and symbols which recall the faith attacked.

We know that the first action of the Emperor Theodosius when converted to the Christian religion was to break down the majority of the temples which for six thousand years had been built beside the Nile. We must not, therefore, be surprised to see the leaders of the Revolution attacking the monuments and works of art which for them were the vestiges of an abhorred past.

Statues, manuscripts, stained glass windows, and plate were frenziedly broken. When Fouché, the future Duke of Otranto under Napoleon, and minister under Louis XVIII., was sent as commissary of the Convention to the Nièvre, he ordered the demolition of all the towers of the *châteaux* and the belfries of the churches "because they wounded equality."

Revolutionary vandalism expended itself even on the tomb. Following a report read by Barrère to the Convention, the magnificent royal tombs at Saint-Denis, among which was the admirable mausoleum of Henri II., by Germain Pilon, were smashed to pieces, the coffins emptied, and the body of Turenne sent to the Museum as a curiosity, after one of the keepers had extracted the teeth in order to sell them as curiosities. The moustache and beard of Henri IV. were also torn out.

It is impossible to witness such comparatively

# The Psychology of Revolution

enlightened men consenting to the destruction of the artistic patriotism of France without a feeling of sadness. To excuse them, we must remember that intense beliefs give rise to the worst excesses, and also that the Convention, almost daily invaded by rioters, always yielded to the popular will.

This glowing record of devastation proves, not only the power of fanaticism : it shows us what becomes of men who are liberated from all social restraints, and of the country which falls into their hands.

# CHAPTER VI

## THE ARMIES OF THE REVOLUTION

1. *The Revolutionary Assemblies and the Armies.*

IF nothing were known of the revolutionary Assemblies, and notably of the Convention, beyond their internal dissensions, their weakness, and their acts of violence, their memory would indeed be a gloomy one.

But even for its enemies this bloodstained epoch must always retain an undeniable glory, thanks to the success of its armies. When the Convention dissolved France was already the greater by Belgium and the territories on the left bank of the Rhine.

Regarding the Convention as a whole, it seems equitable to credit it with the victories of the armies of France, but if we analyse this whole in order to study each of its elements separately their independence will at once be obvious. It is at once apparent that the Convention had a very small share in the military events of the time. The armies on the frontier and the revolutionary Assemblies in Paris formed two separate worlds, which had very little influence over one another, and which regarded matters in a very different light.

We have seen that the Convention was a weak Government, which changed its ideas daily, according to popular impulse; it was really an example of the profoundest anarchy. It directed nothing, but was itself continually directed; how, then, could it have commanded armies?

Completely absorbed in its intestine quarrels, the Assembly had abandoned all military questions to a special committee, which was directed almost single-handed by Carnot, and whose real function was to furnish the troops with provisions and ammunition. The merit of Carnot consisted in the fact that besides directing over 752,000 men at the disposal of France, upon points which were strategically valuable, he also advised the generals of the armies to take the offensive, and to preserve a strict discipline.

The sole share of the Assembly in the defence of the country was the decree of the general levy. In the face of the numerous enemies then threatening France, no Government could have avoided such a measure. For some little time, too, the Assembly had sent representatives to the armies instructed to decapitate certain generals, but this policy was soon abandoned.

As a matter of fact the military activities of the Assembly were always extremely slight. The armies, thanks to their numbers, their enthusiasm, and the tactics devised by their youthful generals, achieved their victories unaided. They fought and conquered independently of the Convention.

2. *The Struggle of Europe against the Revolution.*

Before enumerating the various psychological factors which contributed to the successes of the revolutionary armies, it will be useful briefly to recall the origin and the development of the war against Europe.

# The Armies of the Revolution

At the commencement of the Revolution the foreign sovereigns regarded with satisfaction the difficulties of the French monarchy, which they had long regarded as a rival power. The King of Prussia, believing France to be greatly enfeebled, thought to enrich himself at her expense, so he proposed to the Emperor of Austria to help Louis on condition of receiving Flanders and Alsace as an indemnity. The two sovereigns signed an alliance against France in February, 1792. The French anticipated attack by declaring war upon Austria, under the influence of the Girondists. The French army was at the outset subjected to several checks. The allies penetrated into Champagne, and came within 130 miles of Paris. Dumouriez' victory at Valmy forced them to retire.

Although 300 French and 200 Prussians only were killed in this battle, it had very significant results. The fact that an army reputed invincible had been forced to retreat gave boldness to the young revolutionary troops, and everywhere they took the offensive. In a few weeks the soldiers of Valmy had chased the Austrians out of Belgium, where they were welcomed as liberators.

But it was under the Convention that the war assumed such importance. At the beginning of 1793 the Assembly declared that Belgium was united to France. From this resulted a conflict with England which lasted for twenty-two years.

Assembled at Antwerp in April, 1793, the representatives of England, Prussia, and Austria resolved to dismember France. The Prussians were to seize Alsace and Lorraine; the Austrians, Flanders and Artois; the English, Dunkirk. The Austrian ambassador proposed to crush the Revolution by terror, " by exterminating practically the whole of the party directing the nation." In the face of such declarations France had perforce to conquer or to perish.

During this first coalition, between 1793 and 1797, France had to fight on all her frontiers, from the Pyrenees to the north.

At the outset she lost her former conquests, and suffered several reverses. The Spaniards took Perpignan and Bayonne ; the English, Toulon ; and the Austrians, Valenciennes. It was then that the Convention, towards the end of 1793, ordered a general levy of all Frenchmen between the ages of eighteen and forty, and succeeded in sending to the frontiers a total of some 750,000 men. The old regiments of the royal army were combined with battalions of volunteers and conscripts.

The allies were repulsed, and Maubeuge was relieved after the victory of Wattigny, which was gained by Jourdan. Hoche rescued Lorraine. France took the offensive, reconquering Belgium and the left bank of the Rhine. Jourdan defeated the Austrians at Fleurus, drove them back upon the Rhine, and occupied Cologne and Coblentz. Holland was invaded. The allied sovereigns resigned themselves to suing for peace, and recognised the French conquests.

The successes of the French were favoured by the fact that the enemy never put their whole heart into the affair, as they were preoccupied by the partition of Poland, which they effected in 1793–5. Each Power wished to be on the spot in order to obtain more territory. This motive had already caused the

# The Armies of the Revolution

King of Prussia to retire after the battle of Valmy in 1792.

The hesitations of the allies and their mutual distrust were extremely advantageous to the French. Had the Austrians marched upon Paris in the summer of 1793, " we should," said General Thiébault, " have lost a hundred times for one. They alone saved us, by giving us time to make soldiers, officers, and generals."

After the treaty of Basle, France had no important adversaries on the Continent, save the Austrians. It was then that the Directory attacked Austria in Italy. Bonaparte was entrusted with the charge of this campaign. After a year of fighting, from April, 1796, to April, 1797, he forced the last enemies of France to demand peace.

3. *Psychological and Military Factors which determined the Success of the Revolutionary Armies.*

To realise the causes of the success of the revolutionary armies we must remember the prodigious enthusiasm, endurance, and abnegation of these ragged and often barefoot troops. Thoroughly steeped in revolutionary principles, they felt that they were the apostles of a new religion, which was destined to regenerate the world.

The history of the armies of the Revolution recalls that of the nomads of Arabia, who, excited to fanaticism by the ideals of Mohammed, were transformed into formidable armies which rapidly conquered a portion of the old Roman world. An analogous faith endowed the Republican soldiers with a heroism and intrepidity which never failed them, and which no reverse could shake. When the Convention gave place to the Directory they had liberated the country, and had carried a war of invasion into the enemy's territory. At this period the soldiers were the only true Republicans left in France.

Faith is contagious, and the Revolution was regarded as a new era, so that several of the nations invaded, oppressed by the absolutism of their monarchs, welcomed the invaders as liberators. The inhabitants of Savoy ran out to meet the troops. At Mayence the crowd welcomed them with enthusiasm, planted trees of liberty, and formed a Convention in imitation of that of Paris.

So long as the armies of the Revolution had to deal with peoples bent under the yoke of absolute monarchy, and having no personal ideal to defend, their success was relatively easy. But when they entered into conflict with peoples who had an ideal as strong as their own victory became far more difficult.

The new ideal of liberty and equality was capable of seducing peoples who had no precise convictions, and were suffering from the despotism of their masters, but it was naturally powerless against those who possessed a potent ideal of their own which had been long established in their minds. For this reason Bretons and Vendéeans, whose religious and monarchical sentiments were extremely powerful, successfully struggled for years against the armies of the Republic.

In March, 1793, the insurrections of the Vendée and Brittany had spread to ten departments. The

# The Armies of the Revolution

Vendéeans in Poitou and the Chouans in Brittany put 80,000 men in the field.

The conflicts between contrary ideals—that is, between beliefs in which reason can play no part—are always pitiless, and the struggle with the Vendée immediately assumed the ferocious savagery always observable in religious wars. It lasted until the end of 1795, when Hoche finally "pacified" the country. This pacification was the simple result of the practical extermination of its defenders.

"After two years of civil war," writes Molinari, "the Vendée was no more than a hideous heap of ruins. About 900,000 individuals—men, women, children, and aged people—had perished, and the small number of those who had escaped massacre could scarcely find food or shelter. The fields were devastated, the hedges and walls destroyed, and the houses burned."

Besides their faith, which so often rendered them invincible, the soldiers of the Revolution had usually the advantage of being led by remarkable generals, full of ardour and formed on the battle-field.

The majority of the former leaders of the army, being nobles, had emigrated so that a new body of officers had to be organised. The result was that those gifted with innate military aptitudes had a chance of showing them, and passed through all the grades of rank in a few months. Hoche, for instance, a corporal in 1789, was a general of division and commander of an army at the age of twenty-five. The extreme youth of these leaders resulted in a spirit of aggression to which the armies opposed to them were not accustomed. Selected only according to merit, and hampered by no traditions, no routine, they quickly succeeded in working out a tactics suited to the new necessities.

Of soldiers without experience opposed to seasoned professional troops, drilled and trained according to the methods in use everywhere since the Seven Years' War, one could not expect complicated manœuvres.

Attacks were delivered simply by great masses of troops. Thanks to the numbers of the men at the disposal of their generals, the considerable gaps provoked by this efficacious but barbarous procedure could be rapidly filled.

Deep masses of men attacked the enemy with the bayonet, and quickly routed men accustomed to methods which were more careful of the lives of soldiers. The slow rate of fire in those days rendered the French tactics relatively easy of employment. It triumphed, but at the cost of enormous losses. It has been calculated that between 1792 and 1800 the French army left more than a third of its effective force on the battle-field (700,000 men out of 2,000,000).

Examining events from a psychological point of view, we shall continue to elicit- the consequences from the facts on which they are consequent.

A study of the revolutionary crowds in Paris and in the armies presents very different but readily interpreted pictures.

We have proved that crowds, unable to reason, obey simply their impulses, which are always changing, but we have also seen that they are readily capable of heroism, that their altruism is often highly

# The Armies of the Revolution

developed, and that it is easy to find thousands of men ready to give their lives for a belief.

Psychological characteristics so diverse must naturally, according to the circumstances, lead to dissimilar and even absolutely contradictory actions. The history of the Convention and its armies proves as much. It shows us crowds composed of similar elements acting so differently in Paris and on the frontiers that one can hardly believe the same people can be in question.

In Paris the crowds were disorderly, violent, murderous, and so changeable in their demands as to make all government impossible.

In the armies the picture was entirely different. The same multitudes of unaccustomed men, restrained by the orderly elements of a laborious peasant population, standardised by military discipline, and inspired by contagious enthusiasm, heroically supported privations, disdained perils, and contributed to form that fabulous strain which triumphed over the most redoubtable troops in Europe.

These facts are among those which should always be invoked to show the force of discipline. It transforms men. Liberated from its influence, peoples and armies become barbarian hordes.

This truth is daily and increasingly forgotten. Ignoring the fundamental laws of collective logic, we give way more and more to shifting popular impulses, instead of learning to direct them. The multitude must be shown the road to follow ; it is not for them to choose it.

# CHAPTER VII

## PSYCHOLOGY OF THE LEADERS OF THE REVOLUTION

1. *Mentality of the Men of the Revolution. The respective Influence of Violent and Feeble Characters.*

MEN judge with their intelligence, and are guided by their characters. To understand a man fully one must separate these two elements.

During the great periods of activity—and the revolutionary movements naturally belong to such periods—character always takes the first rank.

Having in several chapters described the various mentalities which predominate in times of disturbance, we need not return to the subject now. They constitute general types which are naturally modified by each man's inherited and acquired personality.

We have seen what an important part was played by the mystic element in the Jacobin mentality, and the ferocious fanaticism to which it led the sectaries of the new faith.

We have also seen that all the members of the Assemblies were not fanatics. These latter were even in the minority, since in the most sanguinary of the revolutionary assemblies the great majority was composed of timid and moderate men of neutral character. Before Thermidor the members of this

232

group voted from fear with the violent and after Thermidor with the moderate deputies.

In time of revolution, as at other times, these neutral characters, obeying the most contrary impulses, are always the most numerous. They are also as dangerous in reality as the violent characters. The force of the latter is supported by the weakness of the former.

In all revolutions, and in particularly in the French Revolution, we observe a small minority of narrow but decided minds which imperiously dominate an immense majority of men who are often very intelligent but are lacking in character

Besides the fanatical apostles and the feeble characters, a revolution always produces individuals who merely think how to profit thereby. These were numerous during the French Revolution. Their aim was simply to utilise circumstances so as to enrich themselves. Such were Barras, Tallien, Fouché, Barrère, and many more. Their politics consisted simply in serving the strong against the weak.

From the outset of the Revolution these "arrivists," as one would call them to-day, were numerous. Camille Desmoulins wrote in 1792 : "Our Revolution has its roots only in the egotism and self-love of each individual, of the combination of which the general interest is composed."

If we add to these indications the observations contained in another chapter concerning the various forms of mentality to be observed in times of political upheaval, we shall obtain a general idea of the character of the men of the Revolution. We shall now apply the principles already expounded to the most remarkable personages of the revolutionary period.

### 2. *Psychology of the Commissaries or Representatives "on Mission."*

In Paris the conduct of the members of the Convention was always directed, restrained, or excited by the action of their colleagues, and that of their environment.

To judge them properly we should observe them when left to themselves and uncontrolled, when they possessed full liberty. Such were the representatives who were sent " on mission " into the departments by the Convention.

The power of these delegates was absolute. No censure embarrassed them. Functionaries and magistrates had perforce to obey them.

A representative " on mission " "requisitions," sequestrates, or confiscates as seems good to him ; taxes, imprisons, deports, or decapitates as he thinks fit, and in his own district he is a pasha."

Regarding themselves as "pashas," they displayed themselves "drawn in carriages with six horses, surrounded by guards ; sitting at sumptuous tables with thirty covers, eating to the sound of music, with a following of players, courtezans, and mercenaries. . . ." At Lyons "the solemn appearance of Collot d'Herbois is like that of the Grand Turk. No one can come into his presence without three repeated requests ; a string of apartments precedes his reception-room, and no one approaches nearer than fifteen paces."

One can picture the immense vanity of these

dictators as they solemly entered the towns, surrounded by guards, men whose gesture was enough to cause heads to fall.

Petty lawyers without clients, doctors without patients, unfrocked clergymen, obscure attorneys, who had formerly known the most colourless of lives, were suddenly made the equals of the most powerful tyrants of history. Guillotining, drowning, shooting without mercy, at the hazard of their fancy, they were raised from their former humble condition to the level of the most celebrated potentates.

Never did Nero or Heliogabalus surpass in tyranny the representatives of the Convention. Laws and customs always restrained the former to a certain extent. Nothing restrained the commissaries

"Fouché," writes Taine, "lorgnette in hand, watched the butchery of 210 inhabitants of Lyons from his window. Collot, Laporte, and Fouché feasted on days of execution (*fusillades*), and at the sound of each discharge sprang up with cries of joy, waving their hats."

Among the representatives "on mission" who exhibit this murderous mentality we may cite as a type the ex-curé Lebon, who, having become possessed of supreme power, ravaged Arras and Cambrai. His example, with that of Carrier, contributes to show what man can become when he escapes from the yoke of law and tradition. The cruelty of the ferocious commissary was complicated by Sadism ; the scaffold was raised under his windows, so that he, his wife, and his helpers could rejoice in the carnage. At the foot of the guillotine a drinking-booth was established where the *sans-culottes* could come to drink. To amuse them the executioner would group on the pavement, in ridiculous attitudes, the naked bodies of the decapitated.

" The reading of the two volumes of his trial, printed at Amiens in 1795, may be counted as a nightmare. During twenty sessions the survivors of the hecatombs of Arras and Cambrai passed through the ancient hall of the bailiwick at Amiens, where the ex-member of the Convention was tried. What these phantoms in mourning related is unheard of. Entire streets dispeopled ; nonagenarians and girls of sixteen decapitated after a mockery of a trial ; death buffeted, insulted, adorned, rejoiced in ; executions to music ; battalions of children recruited to guard the scaffold ; the debauchery, the cynicism, the refinements of an insane satrap ; a romance by Sade turned epic ; it seems, as we watch the unpacking of these horrors, that a whole country, long terrorised, is at last disgorging its terror and revenging itself for its cowardice by overwhelming the wretch there, the scapegoat of an abhorred and vanished system."

The only defence of the ex-clergyman was that he had obeyed orders. The facts with which he was reproached had long been known, and the Convention had in no wise blamed him for them.

I have already spoken of the vanity of the deputies " on mission," who were suddenly endowed with a power greater than that of the most powerful despots ; but this vanity is not enough to explain their ferocity.

That arose from other sources. Apostles of a severe faith, the delegates of the Convention, like the inquisitors of the Holy Office, could feel, can have felt, no pity for their victims. Freed, moreover, from all the bonds of tradition and law, they could give rein to the most savage instincts that primitive animality has left in us.

Civilisation restrains these instincts, but they never die. The need to kill which makes the hunter is a permanent proof of this. M. Cunisset-Carnot has expressed in the following lines the grip of this hereditary tendency, which, in the pursuit of the most harmless game, re-awakens the barbarian in every hunter :—

" The pleasure of killing for killing's sake is, one may say, universal; it is the basis of the hunting instinct, for it must be admitted that at present, in civilised countries, the need to live no longer counts for anything in its propagation. In reality we are continuing an action which was imperiously imposed upon our savage ancestors by the harsh necessities of existence, during which they had either to kill or die of hunger, while to-day there is no longer any legitimate excuse for it. But so it is, and we can do nothing ; probably we shall never break the chains of a slavery which has bound us for so long. We cannot prevent ourselves from feeling an intense, often passionate, pleasure in shedding the blood of animals towards whom, when the love of the chase possesses us, we lose all feeling of pity. The gentlest and prettiest creatures, the song-birds, the charm of our springtime, fall to our guns or are choked in our snares, and not a shudder of pity troubles our pleasure at seeing them terrified, bleeding, writhing in the horrible suffering we inflict on them, seeking to flee on their poor broken paws or desperately beating their wings, which can no longer support them. . . . The excuse is the impulse of that imperious atavism which the best of us have not the strength to resist."

At ordinary times this singular atavism, restrained by fear of the laws, can only be exercised on animals. When codes are no longer operative it immediately applies itself to man, which is why so many terrorists took an intense pleasure in killing. Carrier's remark concerning the joy he felt in contemplating the faces of his victims during their torment is very typical. In many civilised men ferocity is a restrained instinct. but it is by no means eliminated.

### 3. *Danton and Robespierre.*

Danton and Robespierre represented the two principal personages of the Revolution. I shall say little of the former : his psychology, besides being simple, is familiar. A club orator firstly, impulsive and violent, he showed himself always ready to excite the people. Cruel only in his speeches, he often regretted their effects. From the outset he shone in the first rank, while his future rival, Robespierre, was vegetating almost in the lowest.

At one given moment Danton became the soul of the Revolution, but he was deficient in tenacity and fixity of conduct. Moreover, he was needy, while Robespierre was not. The continuous fanaticism of the latter defeated the intermittent efforts of the former. Nevertheless, it was an amazing spectacle to see so powerful a tribune sent to the scaffold by his pale, venemous enemy and mediocre rival.

Robespierre, the most influential man of the Revolution and the most frequently studied, is yet the least explicable. It is difficult to understand the prodigious influence which gave him the power of life and death, not only over the enemies of the Revolution but also over colleagues who could not have been considered as enemies of the existing Government.

We certainly cannot explain the matter by saying with Taine that Robespierre was a pedant lost in abstractions, nor by asserting with the Michelet that he succeeded on account of his principles, nor by repeating with his contemporary Williams that "one of the secrets of his government was to take men marked by opprobrium or soiled with crime as stepping-stones to his ambition."

It is impossible to regard his eloquence as the cause of his success. His eyes protected by goggles, he painfully read his speeches, which were composed of cold and indefinite abstractions. The Assembly contained orators who possessed an immensely superior talent, such as Danton and the Girondists; yet it was Robespierre who destroyed them.

We have really no acceptable explanation of the ascendancy which the dictator finally obtained. Without influence in the National Assembly, he gradually became the master of the Convention and of the Jacobins. "When he reached the Committee of Public Safety he was already," said Billaud-Varennes, "the most important person in France."

"His history," writes Michelet, "is prodigious, far more marvellous than that of Bonaparte. The threads, the wheels, the preparation of forces, are far less visible. It is an honest man, an austere but pious figure, of middling talents, that shoots up one morning, borne upward by I know not what cataclysm. There is nothing like it in the *Arabian*

239

# The Psychology of Revolution

*Nights.* And in a moment he goes higher than the throne. He is set upon the altar. Astonishing story!"

Certainly circumstances helped him considerably. People turned to him as to the master of whom all felt the need. But then he was already there, and what we wish to discover is the cause of his rapid ascent. I would willingly suppose in him the existence of a species of personal fascination which escapes us to-day. His successes with women might be quoted in support of this theory. On the days when he speaks "the passages are choked with women . . . there are seven or eight hundred in the tribunes, and with what transports they applaud! At the Jacobins, when he speaks there are sobs and cries of emotion, and men stamp as though they would bring the hall down." A young widow, Mme. de Chalabre, possessed of sixteen hundred pounds a year, sends him burning love-letters and is eager to marry him.

We cannot seek in his character for the causes of his popularity. A hypochondriac by temperament, of mediocre intelligence, incapable of grasping realities, confined to abstractions, crafty and dissimulating, his prevailing note was an excessive pride which increased until his last day. High priest of a new faith, he believed himself sent on earth by God to establish the reign of virtue. He received writings stating "that he was the Messiah whom the Eternal Being had promised to reform the world."

Full of literary pretensions, he laboriously polished his speeches. His profound jealousy of other orators or men of letters, such as Camille Desmoulins, caused their death.

# Psychology of the Leaders of Revolution

"Those who were particularly the objects of the tyrant's rage," writes the author already cited, "were the men of letters. With regard to them the jealousy of a colleague was mingled with the fury of the oppressor; for the hatred with which he persecuted them was caused less by their resistance to his despotism than by their talents, which eclipsed his."

The contempt of the dictator for his colleagues was immense and almost unconcealed. Giving audience to Barras at the hour of his toilet, he finished shaving, spitting in the direction of his colleague as though he did not exist, and disdaining to reply to his questions.

He regarded the *bourgeoisie* and the deputies with the same hateful disdain. Only the multitude found grace in his eyes. "When the sovereign people exercises its power," he said, "we can only bow before it. In all it does all is virtue and truth, and no excess, error, or crime is possible."

Robespierre suffered from the persecution mania. That he had others' heads cut off was not only because he had a mission as an apostle, but because he believed himself hemmed in by enemies and conspirators. "Great as was the cowardice of his colleagues where he was concerned," writes M. Sorel, "the fear he had of them was still greater."

His dictatorship, absolute during five months, is a striking example of the power of certain leaders. We can understand that a tyrant backed by an army can easily destroy whom he pleases, but that a single man should succeed in sending to death a large number of his equals is a thing that is not easily explained.

# The Psychology of Revolution

The power of Robespierre was so absolute that he was able to send to the Tribunal, and therefore to the scaffold, the most eminent deputies: Desmoulins, Hébert, Danton, and many another. The brilliant Girondists melted away before him. He attacked even the terrible Commune, guillotined its leaders, and replaced it by a new Commune obedient to his orders.

In order to rid himself more quickly of the men who displeased him he induced the Convention to enact the law of Prairial, which permitted the execution of mere suspects, and by means of which he had 1,373 heads cut off in Paris in forty-nine days. His colleagues, the victims of an insane terror, no longer slept at home; scarcely a hundred deputies were present at sessions. David said : " I do not believe twenty of us members of the Mountain will be left."

It was his very excess of confidence in his own powers and in the cowardice of the Convention that lost Robespierre his life. Having attempted to make them vote a measure which would permit deputies to be sent before the Revolutionary Tribunal, which meant the scaffold, without the authorisation of the Assembly, on an order from the governing Committee, several Montagnards conspired with some members of the Plain to overthrow him. Tallien, knowing himself marked down for early execution, and having therefore nothing to lose, accused him loudly of tyranny. Robespierre wished to defend himself by reading a speech which he had long had in hand, but he learned to his cost that although it is possible to destroy men in the name of logic it is not possible to lead an assembly by means of logic. The shouts of the conspirators drowned his voice; the cry "Down with the tyrant!" quickly repeated, thanks to mental contagion, by many of the members present, was enough to complete his downfall. Without losing a moment the Assembly decreed his accusation.

The Commune having wished to save him, the Assembly outlawed him. Struck by this magic formula, he was definitely lost.

"This cry of outlawry," writes Williams, "at this period produced the same effect on a Frenchman as the cry of pestilence; the outlaw became civilly excommunicated, and it was as though men believed that they would be contaminated passing through the air which he had breathed. Such was the effect it produced upon the gunners who had trained their cannon against the Convention. Without receiving further orders, merely on hearing that the Commune was 'outside the law,' they immediately turned their batteries about."

Robespierre and all his band—Saint-Just, the president of the Revolutionary Tribunal, the mayor of the Commune, &c.,—were guillotined on the 10th of Thermidor to the number of twenty-one. Their execution was followed on the morrow by a fresh batch of seventy Jacobins, and on the next day by thirteen. The Terror, which had lasted ten months, was at an end.

The downfall of the Jacobin edifice in Thermidor is one of the most curious psychological events of the revolutionary period. None of the Montagnards who had worked for the downfall of Robespierre had for a moment dreamed that it would mark the end of the Terror.

# The Psychology of Revolution

Tallien, Barras, Fouché, &c., overthrew Robespierre as he had overthrown Hébert, Danton, the Girondists, and many others. But when the acclamations of the crowd told them that the death of Robespierre was regarded as having put an end to the Terror they acted as though such had been their intention. They were the more obliged to do so in that the Plain—that is, the great majority of the Assembly—which had allowed itself to be decimated by Robespierre, now rebelled furiously against the system it had so long acclaimed even while it abhorred it. Nothing is more terrible than a body of men who have been afraid and are afraid no longer. The Plain revenged itself for being terrorised by the Mountain, and terrorised that body in turn.

The servility of the colleagues of Robespierre in the Convention was by no means based upon any feeling of sympathy for him. The dictator filled them with an unspeakable alarm, but beneath the marks of admiration and enthusiasm which they lavished on him out of fear was concealed an intense hatred. We can gather as much by reading the reports of various deputies inserted in the *Moniteur* of August 11, 15, and 29, 1794, and notably that on "the conspiracy of the triumvirs, Robespierre, Couthon, and Saint-Just." Never did slaves heap such invectives on a fallen master.

We learn that "these monsters had for some time been renewing the most horrible prescriptions of Marius and Sulla." Robespierre is represented as a most frightful scoundrel; we are assured that "like Caligula, he would soon have asked the French people to worship his horse . . . He sought security in the execution of all who aroused his slightest suspicion."

These reports forget to add that the power of Robespierre obtained no support, as did that of the Marius and Sulla to whom they allude, from a powerful army, but merely from the repeated adhesion of the members of the Convention. Without their extreme timidity the power of the dictator could not have lasted a single day.

Robespierre was one of the most odious tyrants of history, but he is distinguished from all others in that he made himself a tyrant without soldiers.

We may sum up his doctrines by saying that he was the most perfect incarnation, save perhaps Saint-Just, of the Jacobin faith, in all its narrow logic, its intense mysticism, and its inflexible rigidity. He has admirers even to-day. M. Hamel describes him as " the martyr of Thermidor." There has been some talk of erecting a monument to him. I would willingly subscribe to such a purpose, feeling that it is useful to preserve proofs of the blindness of the crowd, and of the extraordinary docility of which an assembly is capable when the leader knows how to handle it. His statue would recall the passionate cries of admiration and enthusiasm with which the Convention acclaimed the most threatening measures of the dictator, on the very eve of the day when it was about to cast him down.

4. *Fouquier-Tinville, Marat, Billaud-Varenne, &c.*

I shall devote a paragraph to certain revolutionists who were famous for the development of their most sanguinary instincts. Their ferocity was complicated by other sentiments, by fear and hatred, which could but fortify it.

Fouquier-Tinville, the public prosecutor of the Revolutionary Tribunal, was one of those who have left the most sinister memories. This magistrate, formerly reputed for his kindness, and who became the bloodthirsty creature whose memory evokes such repulsion, has already served me as an example in other works, when I have wished to show the transformation of certain natures in time of revolution.

Needy in the extreme at the moment of the fall of the monarchy, he had everything to hope from a social upheaval and nothing to lose. He was one of those men whom a period of disorder will always find ready to sustain it.

The Convention abandoned its powers to him. He had to pronounce upon the fate of nearly two thousand accused, among whom were Marie-Antoinette, the Girondists, Danton, Hébert, &c. He had all the suspects brought before him executed, and did not scruple to betray his former protectors. As soon as one of them fell into his power—Camille Desmoulins, Danton, or another—he would plead against him.

Fouquier-Tinville had a very inferior mind, which the Revolution brought to the top. Under normal conditions, hedged about by professional rules, his destiny would have been that of a peaceable and obscure magistrate. This was precisely the lot of his deputy, or substitute, at the Tribunal, Gilbert-Liendon. " He should," writes M. Durel, " have inspired the same horror as his colleague, yet he completed his career in the upper ranks of the Imperial magistracy."

246

# Psychology of the Leaders of Revolution

One of the great benefits of an organised society is that it does restrain these dangerous characters, whom nothing but social restraints can hold.

Fouquier-Tinville died without understanding why he was condemned, and from the revolutionary point of view his condemnation was not justifiable. Had he not merely zealously executed the orders of his superiors? It is impossible to class him with the representatives who were sent into the provinces, who could not be supervised. The delegates of the Convention examined all his sentences and approved of them up to the last. If his cruelty and his summary fashion of trying the prisoners before him had not been encouraged by his chiefs, he could not have remained in power. In condemning Fouquier-Tinville, the Convention condemned its own frightful system of government. It understood this fact, and sent to the scaffold a number of Terrorists whom Fouquier-Tinville had merely served as a faithful agent.

Beside Fouquier-Tinville we may set Dumas, who presided over the Revolutionary Tribunal, and who also displayed an excessive cruelty, which was whetted by an intense fear. He never went out without two loaded pistols, barricaded himself in his house, and only spoke to visitors through a wicket. His distrust of everybody, including his own wife, was absolute. He even imprisoned the latter, and was about to have her executed when Thermidor arrived.

Among the men whom the Convention brought to light, Billaud-Varenne was one of the wildest and most brutal. He may be regarded as a perfect type of bestial ferocity.

" In these hours of fruitful anger and heroic anguish

# The Psychology of Revolution

he remained calm, acquitting himself methodically of his task—and it was a frightful task : he appeared officially at the massacres of the Abbaye, congratulated the assassins, and promised them money ; upon which he went home as if he had merely been taking a walk. We see him as president of the Jacobin Club, president of the Convention, and member of the Committee of Public Safety ; he drags the Girondists to the scaffold : he drags the queen thither, and his former patron, Danton, said of him, ' Billaud has a dagger under his tongue.' He approves of the cannonades at Lyons, the drownings at Nantes, the massacres at Arras ; he organises the pitiless commission of Orange ; he is concerned in the laws of Prairial ; he eggs on Fouquier-Tinville ; on all decrees of death is his name, often the first ; he signs before his colleagues ; he is without pity, without emotion, without enthusiasm ; when others are frightened, hesitate, and draw back, he goes his way, speaking in turgid sentences, ' shaking his lion's mane '—for to make his cold and impassive face more in harmony with the exuberance that surrounds him he now decks himself in a yellow wig which would make one laugh were it on any but the sinister head of Billaud-Varenne. When Robespierre, Saint-Just, and Couthon are threatened in turn, he deserts them and goes over to the enemy, and pushes them under the knife. . . . Why ? What is his aim ? No one knows ; he is not in any way ambitious ; he desires neither power nor money."

I do not think it would be difficult to answer why. The thirst for blood, of which we have already spoken, and which is very common among certain criminals,

# Psychology of the Leaders of Revolution

perfectly explains the conduct of Billaud-Varennes. Bandits of this type kill for the sake of killing, as sportsmen shoot game—for the very pleasure of exercising their taste for destruction. In ordinary times men endowed with these homicidal tendencies refrain, generally from fear of the policeman and the scaffold. When they are able to give them free vent nothing can stop them. Such was the case with Billaud-Varenne and many others.

The psychology of Marat is rather more complicated, not only because his craving for murder was combined with other elements—wounded self-love, ambition, mystic beliefs, &c.—but also because we must regard him as a semi-lunatic, affected by megalomania, and haunted by fixed ideas.

Before the Revolution he had advanced great scientific pretensions, but no one attached much importance to his maunderings. Dreaming of place and honour, he had only obtained a very subordinate situation in the household of a great noble. The Revolution opened up an unhoped-for future. Swollen with hatred of the old social system which had not recognised his merits, he put himself at the head of the most violent section of the people. Having publicly glorified the massacres of September, he founded a journal which denounced everybody and clamoured incessantly for executions.

Speaking continually of the interests of the people, Marat became their idol. The majority of his colleagues heartily despised him. Had he escaped the knife of Charlotte Corday, he certainly would not have escaped that of the guillotine.

# The Psychology of Revolution

## 5. *The Destiny of those Members of the Convention who survived the Revolution.*

Beside the members of the Convention whose psychology presents particular characteristics there were others—Barras, Fouché, Tallien, Merlin de Thionville, &c.—completely devoid of principles or belief, who only sought to enrich themselves.

They sought to build up enormous fortunes out of the public misery. In ordinary times they would have been qualified as simple scoundrels, but in perods of revolution all standards of vice and virtue seem to disappear.

Although a few Jacobins remained fanatics, the majority renounced their convictions as soon as they had obtained riches, and became the faithful courtiers of Napoleon. Cambacérès, who, on addressing Louis XVI. in prison, called him Louis Capet, under the Empire required his friends to call him " Highness " in public and " Monseigneur " in private, thus displaying the envious feeling which accompanied the craving for equality in many of the Jacobins.

" The majority of the Jacobins," writes M. Madelin "were greatly enriched, and like Chabot, Bazire, Merlin, Barras, Boursault, Tallien, Barrère, &c., possessed *châteaux* and estates. Those who were not wealthy as yet were soon to become so. . . In the Committee of the year III. alone the staff of the Thermidorian party comprised a future prince, 13 future counts, 5 future barons, 7 future senators of the Empire, and 6 future Councillors of State, and beside them in the Convention there were, between the future Duke of Otranto to the future Count Regnault, no less than

50 democrats who fifteen years later possessed titles, coats of arms, plumes, carriages, endowments, entailed estates, hotels, and *châteaux*. Fouché died worth £600,000."

The privileges of the *ancien régime* which had been so bitterly decried were thus very soon re-established for the benefit of the *bourgeoisie*. To arrive at this result it was necessary to ruin France, to burn entire provinces, to multiply suffering, to plunge innumerable families into despair, to overturn Europe, and to destroy men by the hundred thousand on the field of battle.

In closing this chapter we will recall what we have already said concerning the possibility of judging the men of this period.

Although the moralist is forced to deal severely with certain individuals, because he judges them by the types which society must respect if it is to succeed in maintaining itself, the psychologist is not in the same case. His aim is to understand, and criticism vanishes before a complete comprehension.

The human mind is a very fragile mechanism, and the marionettes which dance upon the stage of history are rarely able to resist the imperious forces which impel them. Heredity, environment, and circumstances are imperious masters. No one can say with certainty what would have been his conduct in the place of the men whose actions he endeavours to interpret.

## BOOK III

*THE CONFLICT BETWEEN ANCESTRAL INFLU-
ENCES AND REVOLUTIONARY PRINCIPLES*

## CHAPTER I

### THE LAST CONVULSIONS OF ANARCHY—THE DIRECTORY

1. *The Psychology of the Directory.*

As the various revolutionary assemblies were composed in part of the same men, one might suppose that their psychology would be very similar.

At ordinary periods this would have been so, for a constant environment means constancy of character. But when circumstances change as rapidly as they did under the Revolution, character must perforce transform itself to adapt itself thereto. Such was the case with the Directory.

The Directory comprised several distinct assemblies: two large chambers, consisting of different categories of deputies, and one very small chamber, which consisted of the five Directors.

The two larger Assemblies remind one strongly of the Convention by their weakness. They were no longer forced to obey popular riots, as these were energetically prevented by the Directors, but they yielded without discussion to the dictatorial injunctions of the latter.

The first deputies to be elected were mostly moderates. Everyone was weary of the Jacobin tyranny. The new Assembly dreamed of rebuilding the ruins with which France was covered, and establishing a liberal government without violence.

But by one of those fatalities which were a law of the Revolution, and which prove that the course of events is often superior to men's wills, these deputies, like their predecessors, may be said always to have done the contrary of what they wished to do. They hoped to be moderate, and they were violent; they wanted to eliminate the influence of the Jacobins, and they allowed themselves to be led by them; they thought to repair the ruins of the country and they succeeded only in adding others to them; they aspired to religious peace, and they finally persecuted and massacred the priests with greater rigour than during the Terror.

The psychology of the little assembly formed by the five Directors was very different from that of the Chamber of Deputies. Encountering fresh difficulties daily, the directors were forced to resolve them, while the large Assemblies, without contact with realities, had only their aspirations.

The prevailing thought of the Directors was very simple. Highly indifferent to principles, they wished above all to remain the masters of France. To attain that result they did not shrink from resorting to the most illegitimate measures, even annulling the elections of a great number of the departments when these embarrassed them.

# The Psychology of Revolution

Feeling themselves incapable of reorganising France, they left her to herself. By their despotism they contrived to dominate her, but they never governed her Now, what France needed more than anything at this juncture was to be governed.

The convention has left behind it the reputation of a strong Government, and the Directory that of a weak Government. The contrary is true: it was the Directory that was the strong Government.

Psychologically we may readily explain the difference between the Government of the Directory and that of the preceding Assemblies by recalling the fact that a gathering of six hundred to seven hundred persons may well suffer from waves of contagious enthusiasm, as on the night of the 4th of August, or even impulses of energetic will-power, such as that which launched defiance against the kings of Europe. But such impulses are too ephemeral to possess any great force. A committee of five members, easily dominated by the will of one, is far more susceptible of continuous resolution—that is, of perseverance in a settled line of conduct.

The Government of the Directory proved to be always incapable of governing, but it never lacked a strong will. Nothing restraining it, neither respect for law nor consideration for the citizens, nor love of the public welfare, it was able to impose upon France a despotism more crushing than that of any Government since the beginning of the Revolution, not excepting the Terror.

Although it utilised methods analogous to those of the Convention, and ruled France in the most tyrannical manner, the Directory, no more than the Convention, was never the master of France.

# The Last Convulsions of Anarchy

This fact, which I have already noted, proves once more the impotence of material constraint to dominate moral forces. It cannot be too often repeated that the true guide of mankind is the moral scaffolding erected by his ancestors.

Accustomed to live in an organised society, supported by codes and respected traditions, we can with difficulty represent to ourselves the condition of a nation deprived of such a basis. As a general thing we only see the irksome side of our environment, too readily forgetting that society can exist only on condition of imposing certain restraints, and that laws, manners, and custom constitute a check upon the natural instincts of barbarism which never entirely perishes.

The history of the Convention and the Directory which followed it shows plainly to what degree disorder may overcome a nation deprived of its ancient structure, and having for guide only the artificial combinations of an insufficient reason.

2. *Despotic Government of the Directory. Recrudescence of the Terror.*

With the object of diverting attention, occupying the army, and obtaining resources by the pillage of neighbouring countries, the Directors decided to resume the wars of conquest which had succeeded under the Convention.

These continued during the life time of the Directory. The armies won a rich booty, especially in Italy.

Some of the invaded populations were so simple as to suppose that these invasions were undertaken in their interest. They were not long in discovering that all military operations were accompanied by crushing taxes and the pillage of churches, public treasuries, &c.

The final consequence of this policy of conquest was the formation of a new coalition against France, which lasted until 1801.

Indifferent to the state of the country and incapable of reorganising it, the Directors were principally concerned in struggling against an incessant series of conspiracies in order to keep in power.

This task was enough to occupy their leisure, for the political parties had not disarmed. Anarchy had reached such a point that all were calling for a hand powerful enough to restore order. Everyone felt, the Directors included, that the republican system could not last much longer.

Some dreamed of re-establishing royalty, others the Terrorist system, while others waited for a general. Only the purchasers of the national property feared a change of Government.

The unpopularity of the Directory increased daily, and when in May, 1797, the third part of the Assembly had to be renewed, the majority of those elected were hostile to the system.

The Directors were not embarrassed by a little thing like that. They annulled the elections in 49 departments ; 154 of the new deputies were invalidated and expelled, 53 condemned to deportation. Among these latter figured the most illustrious names of the Revolution : Portalis, Carnot, Tronson du Coudray, &c.

To intimidate the electors, military commissions condemned to death, rather at random, 160 persons, and sent to Guiana 330, of whom half speedily died.

# The Last Convulsions of Anarchy

The *emigrés* and priests who had returned to France were violently expelled. This was known as the *coup d'État* of Fructidor.

This *coup*, which struck more especially at the moderates, was not the only one of its kind; another quickly followed. The Directors, finding the Jacobin deputies too numerous, annulled the elections of sixty of them.

The preceding facts displayed the tyrannical temper of the Directors, but this appeared even more plainly in the details of their measures. The new masters of France also proved to be as bloodthirsty as the most ferocious deputies of the Terror.

The guillotine was not re-established as a permanency, but replaced by deportation under conditions which left the victims little chance of survival. Sent to Rochefort in cages of iron bars, exposed to all the severities of the weather, they were then packed into boats.

"Between the decks of the *Décade* and the *Bayonnaise*," says Taine, "the miserable prisoners, suffocated by the lack of air and the torrid heat, bullied and fleeced, died of hunger or asphyxia, and Guiana completed the work of the voyage: of 193 taken thither by the *Décade* 39 were left alive at the end of twenty-two months; of 120 taken by the *Bayonnaise* 1 remained."

Observing everywhere a Catholic renascence, and imagining that the clergy were conspiring against them, the Directors deported or sent to the galleys in one year 1,448 priests, to say nothing of a large number who were summarily executed. The Terror was in reality completely re-established.

# The Psychology of Revolution

The autocratic despotism of the Directory was exercised in all the branches of the administration, notably the finances. Thus, having need of six hundred million francs, it forced the deputies, always docile, to vote a progressive impost, which yielded, however, only twelve millions. Being presently in the same condition, it decreed a forced loan of a hundred millions, which resulted in the closing of workshops, the stoppage of business, and the dismissal of domestics. It was only at the price of absolute ruin that forty millions could be obtained.

To assure itself of domination in the provinces the Directory caused a so-called law of hostages to be passed, according to which a list of hostages, responsible for all offences, was drawn up in each commune.

It is easy to understand what hatred such a system provoked. At the end of 1799 fourteen departments were in revolt and forty-six were ready to rise. If the Directory had lasted the dissolution of society would have been complete.

For that matter, this dissolution was far advanced. Finances, administration, everything was crumbling. The receipts of the Treasury, consisting of depreciated *assignats* fallen to a hundredth part of their original value, were negligible. Holders of Government stock and officers could no longer obtain payment.

France at this time gave travellers the impression of a country ravaged by war and abandoned by its inhabitants. The broken bridges and dykes and ruined buildings made all traffic impossible. The roads, long deserted, were infested by brigands. Certain departments could only be crossed at the price of buying a safe-conduct from the leaders of these bands. Industry and commerce were annihilated. In Lyons 13,000 workshops and mills out of 15,000 had been forced to close. Lille, Havre, Bordeaux, Lyons, Marseilles, &c., were like dead cities. Poverty and famine were general.

The moral disorganisation was no less terrible. Luxury and the craving for pleasure, costly dinners, jewels, and extravagant households were the appanage of a new society composed entirely of stock-jobbers, army contractors, and shady financiers enriched by pillage. They gave Paris that superficial aspect of luxury and gaiety which has deluded so many historians of this period, because the insolent prodigality displayed covered the general misery.

The chronicles of the Directory as told in books help to show us of what lies the web of history is woven. The theatre has lately got hold of this period, of which the fashions are still imitated. It has left the memory of a joyous period of re-birth after the gloomy drama of the Terror. In reality the drama of the Directory was hardly an improvement on the Terror and was quite as sanguinary. Finally, it inspired such loathing that the Directors, feeling that it could not last, sought themselves for the dictator capable of replacing it and also of protecting them.

### 3. *The Advent of Bonaparte.*

We have seen that at the end of the Directory the anarchy and disorganisation were such that every one was desperately calling for the man of energy capable of re-establishing order. As early as 1795 a number of deputies had thought for a moment of re-establishing royalty. Louis XVIII., having been tactless enough to declare that he would restore the *ancien régime* in its entirety, return all property to its original owners, and punish the men of the Revolution, was immediately thrown over. The senseless expedition of Quiberon finally alienated the supporters of the future sovereign. The royalists gave a proof during the whole of the Revolution of an incapacity and a narrowness of mind which justified most of the measures taken against them.

The monarchy being impossible, it was necessary to find a general. Only one existed whose name carried weight—Bonaparte. The campaign in Italy had just made him famous. Having crossed the Alps, he had marched from victory to victory, penetrated to Milan and Venice, and everywhere obtained important war contributions. He then made towards Vienna, and was only twenty-five leagues from its gates when the Emperor of Austria decided to sue for peace.

But great as was his renown, the young general did not consider it sufficient. To increase it he persuaded the Directory that the power of England could be shaken by an invasion of Egypt, and in May, 1798, he embarked at Toulon.

This need of increasing his prestige arose from a very sound psychological conception which he clearly expounded at St. Helena :—

" The most influential and enlightened generals had long been pressing the general of Italy to take steps to place himself at the head of the Republic. He refused ; he was not yet strong enough to walk quite alone. He had ideas upon the art of governing and upon what was necessary to a great nation which

# The Last Convulsions of Anarchy

were so different from those of the men of the Revolution and 'the assemblies that, not being able to act alone, he feared to compromise his character. He determined to set out for Egypt, but resolved to reappear if circumstances should arise to render his presence useful or necessary."

Bonaparte did not stay long in Egypt. Recalled by his friends, he landed at Frejus, and the announcement of his return provoked universal enthusiasm. There were illuminations everywhere. France collaborated in advance in the *coup d'État* prepared by two Directors and the principal ministers. The plot was organised in three weeks. Its execution on the 18th of Brumaire was accomplished with the greatest ease.

All parties experienced the greatest delight at being rid of the sinister gangs who had so long oppressed and exploited the country. The French were doubtless about to enter upon a despotic system of government, but it could not be so intolerable as that which had been endured for so many years.

The history of the *coup d'État* of Brumaire justifies all that we have already said of the impossibility of forming exact judgments of events which apparently are fully understood and attested by no matter how many witnesses.

We know what ideas people had thirty years ago concerning the *coup* of Brumaire. It was regarded as a crime committed by the ambition of a man who was supported by his army. As a matter of fact the army played no part whatever in the affair. The little body of men who expelled the few recalcitrant deputies were not soldiers even, but the gendarmes of the Assembly itself. The true author of the *coup d'État* was the Government itself, with the complicity of all France.

### 4. *Causes of the Duration of the Revolution.*

If we limit the Revolution to the time necessary for the conquest of its fundamental principles—equality before the law, free access to public functions, popular sovereignty, control of expenditures, &c.—we may say that it lasted only a few months. Towards the middle of 1789 all this was accomplished, and during the years that followed nothing was added to it, yet the Revolution lasted much longer.

Confining the duration to the dates admitted by the official historians, we see it persisting until the advent of Bonaparte, a space of some ten years.

Why did this period of disorganisation and violence follow the establishment of the new principles? We need not seek the cause in the foreign war, which might on several occasions have been terminated, thanks to the divisions of the allies and the constant victories of the French; neither must we look for it in the sympathy of Frenchmen for the revolutionary Government. Never was rule more cordially hated and despised than that of the Assemblies. By its revolts as well as by its repeated votes a great part of the nation displayed the horror with which it regarded the system.

This last point, the aversion of France for the revolutionary *régime*, so long misunderstood, has been well displayed by recent historians. The author of the last book published on the Revolution, M. Madelin, has well summarised their opinion in the following words:—

# The Last Convulsions of Anarchy

" As early as 1793 a party by no means numerous had seized upon France, the Revolution, and the Republic. Now, three-quarters of France longed for the Revolution to be checked, or rather delivered from its odious exploiters ; but these held the unhappy country by a thousand means. . . . As the Terror was essential to them if they were to rule, they struck at whomsoever seemed at any given moment to be opposed to the Terror, were they the best servants of the Revolution."

Up to the end of the Directory the government was exercised by Jacobins, who merely desired to retain, along with the supreme power, the riches they had accumulated by murder and pillage, and were ready to surrender France to any one who would guarantee them free possession of these. That they negotiated the *coup d'État* of Brumaire with Napoleon was due simply to the fact that they had not been able to realise their wishes with regard to Louis XVIII.

But how explain the fact that a Government so tyrannical and so dishonoured was able to survive for so many years ?

It was not merely because the revolutionary religion still survived in men's minds, nor because it was forced on them by means of persecution and bloodshed, but especially, as I have already stated, on account of the great interest which a large portion of the population had in maintaining it.

This point is fundamental. If the Revolution had remained a theoretical religion, it would probably have been of short duration. But the belief which had just been founded very quickly emerged from the domain of pure theory.

263

# The Psychology of Revolution

The Revolution did not confine itself to despoiling the monarchy, the nobility, and the clergy of their powers of government. In throwing into the hands of the *bourgeoisie* and the large numbers of peasantry the wealth and the employments of the old privileged classes it had at the same stroke turned them into obstinate supporters of the revolutionary system. All those who had acquired the property of which the nobles and clergy had been despoiled had obtained lands and *châteaux* at low prices, and were terrified lest the restoration of the monarchy should force them to make general restitution.

It was largely for these reasons that a Government which, at any normal period, would never have been endured, was able to survive until a master should re-establish order, while promising to maintain not only the moral but also the material conquests of the Revolution. Bonaparte realised these anxieties, and was promptly and enthusiastically welcomed. Material conquests which were still contestable and theoretical principles which were still fragile were by him incorporated in institutions and the laws. It is an error to say that the Revolution terminated with his advent. Far from destroying it, he ratified and consolidated it.

# CHAPTER II

## THE RESTORATION OF ORDER. THE CONSULAR REPUBLIC

### 1. *How the Work of the Revolution was Confirmed by the Consulate.*

THE history of the Consulate is as rich as the preceding period in psychological material. In the first place it shows us that the work of a powerful individual is superior to that of a collectivity. Bonaparte immediately replaced the bloody anarchy in which the Republic had for ten years been writhing by a period of order. That which none of the four Assemblies of the Revolution had been able to realise, despite the most violent oppression, a single man accomplished in a very short space of time.

His authority immediately put an end to all the Parisian insurrections and the attempts at monarchical resistance, and re-established the moral unity of France, so profoundly divided by intense hatreds. Bonaparte replaced an unorganised collective despotism by a perfectly organised individual despotism. Everyone gained thereby, for his tyranny was infinitely less heavy than that which had been endured for ten long years. We must suppose, moreover, that it was unwelcome to very few, as it was very soon accepted with immense enthusiasm.

# The Psychology of Revolution

We know better to-day than to repeat with the old historians that Bonaparte overthrew the Republic. On the contrary, he retained of it all that could be retained, and never would have been retained without him, by establishing all the practicable work of the Revolution—the abolition of privileges, equality before the law, &c.—in institutions and codes of law. The Consular Government continued, moreover, to call itself the Republic.

It is infinitely probable that without the Consulate a monarchical restoration would have terminated the Directory, and would have wiped out the greater part of the work of the Revolution. Let us suppose Bonaparte erased from history. No one, I think, will imagine that the Directory could have survived the universal weariness of its rule. It would certainly have been overturned by the royalist conspiracies which were breaking out daily, and Louis XVIII. would probably have ascended the throne. Certainly he was to mount it sixteen years later, but during this interval Bonaparte gave such force to the principles of the Revolution, by establishing them in laws and customs, that the restored sovereign dared not touch them, nor restore the property of the returned *emigrés*.

Matters would have been very different had Louis XVIII. immediately followed the Directory. He would have brought with him all the absolutism of the *ancien régime*, and fresh revolutions would have been necessary to abolish it. We know that a mere attempt to return to the past overthrew Charles X.

It would be a little ingenuous to complain of the

tyranny of Bonaparte. Under the *ancien régime* Frenchmen had supported every species of tyranny, and the Republic had created a despotism even heavier than that of the monarchy. Despotism was then a normal condition, which aroused no protest save when it was accompanied by disorder.

A constant law of the psychology of crowds shows them as creating anarchy, and then seeking the master who will enable them to emerge therefrom. Bonaparte was this master.

### 2. *The Reorganisation of France by the Consulate.*

Upon assuming power Bonaparte undertook a colossal task. All was in ruins; all was to be rebuilt. On the morrow of the *coup* of Brumaire he drafted, almost single-handed, the Constitution destined to give him the absolute power which was to enable him to reorganise the country and to prevail over the factions. In a month it was completed.

This Constitution, known as that of the year VIII., survived, with slight modifications, until the end of his reign. The executive power was the attribute of three Consuls, two of whom possessed a consultative voice only. The first Consul, Bonaparte, was therefore sole master of France. He appointed ministers, councillors of state, ambassadors, magistrates, and other officials, and decided upon peace or war. The legislative power was his also, since only he could initiate the laws, which were subsequently submitted to three Assemblies—the Council of State, the Tribunate, and the Legislative Corps. A fourth Assembly,

# The Psychology of Revolution

the Senate, acted effectually as the guardian of the Constitution.

Despotic as he was and became, Bonaparte always called the other Consuls about him before proceeding with the most trivial measure. The Legislative Corps did not exercise much influence during his reign, but he signed no decrees of any kind without first discussing them with the Council of State. This Council, composed of the most enlightened and learned men of France, prepared laws, which were then presented to the Legislative Corps, which could criticise them very freely, since voting was secret. Presided over by Bonaparte, the Council of State was a kind of sovereign tribunal, judging even the actions of ministers.[1]

The new master had great confidence in this Council, as it was composed more particularly of

[1] Napoleon naturally often overruled the Council of State, but by no means always did so. In one instance, reported in the *Mémorial de Sainte-Hélene*, he was the only one of his own opinion, and accepted that of the majority in the following terms: "Gentlemen, matters are decided here by majority, and being alone, I must give way; but I declare that in my conscience I yield only to form. You have reduced me to silence, but in no way convinced me."

Another day the Emperor, interrupted three times in the expression of his opinion, addressed himself to the speaker who had just interrupted him: "Sir, I have not yet finished; I beg you to allow me to continue. After all, it seems to me that every one has a perfect right to express his opinion here."

"The Emperor, contrary to the accepted opinion, was so far from absolute, and so easy with his Council of State, that he often resumed a discussion, or even annulled a decision, because one of the members of the Council had since, in private, given him fresh reasons, or had urged that the Emperor's personal opinion had influenced the majority."

# The Restoration of Order

eminent jurists, each of whom dealt with his own speciality. He was too good a psychologist not to entertain the greatest suspicion of large and incompetent assemblies of popular origin, whose disastrous results had been obvious to him during the whole of the Revolution.

Wishing to govern for the people, but never with its assistance, Bonaparte accorded it no part in the government, reserving to it only the right of voting, once for all, for or against the adoption of the new Constitution. He only in rare instances had recourse to universal suffrage. The members of the Legislative Corps recruited themselves, and were not elected by the people.

In creating a Constitution intended solely to fortify his own power, the First Consul had no illusion that it would serve to restore the country. Consequently, while he was drafting it he also undertook the enormous task of the administrative, judicial, and financial reorganisation of France. The various powers were centralised in Paris. Each department was directed by a prefect, assisted by a consul-general; the *arrondissement* by a sub-prefect, assisted by a council; the commune by a mayor, assisted by a municipal council. All were appointed by the ministers, and not by election, as under the Republic.

This system, which created the omnipotent State and a powerful centralisation, was retained by all subsequent Governments and is preserved to-day. Centralisation being, in spite of its drawbacks, the only means of avoiding local tyrannies in a country profoundly divided within itself, has always been maintained.

# The Psychology of Revolution

This organisation, based on a profound knowledge of the soul of the French people, immediately restored that tranquillity and order which had for so long been unknown.

To complete the mental pacification of the country, the political exiles were recalled and the churches restored to the faithful.

Continuing to rebuild the social edifice, Bonaparte busied himself also with the drafting of a code, the greater part of which consisted of customs borrowed from the *ancien régime*. It was, as has been said, a sort of transition or compromise between the old law and the new.

Considering the enormous task accomplished by the First Consul in so short a time, we realise that he had need, before all, of a Constitution according him absolute power. If all the measures by which he restored France had been submitted to assemblies of attorneys, he could never have extricated the country from the disorder into which it had fallen.

The Constitution of the year VIII. obviously transformed the Republic into a monarchy at least as absolute as the "Divine right" monarchy of Louis XIV. Being the only Constitution adapted to the needs of the moment, it represented a psychological necessity.

### 3. Psychological Elements which determined the Success of the Work of the Consulate

All the external forces which act upon men— economic, historical, geographical, &c.—may be finally translated into psychological forces. These psychological forces a ruler must understand in order to govern. The Revolutionary Assemblies were completely ignorant of them; Bonaparte knew how to employ them.

The various Assemblies, the Convention notably, were composed of conflicting parties. Napoleon understood that to dominate them he must not belong to any one of these parties. Very well aware that the value of a country is disseminated among the superior intelligences of the various parties, he tried to utilise them all. His agents of government—ministers, priests, magistrates, &c.— were taken indifferently from among the Liberals, Royalists, Jacobites, &c., having regard only to their capacities.

While accepting the assistance of men of the *ancien régime*, Bonaparte took care to make it understood that he intended to maintain the fundamental principles of the Revolution. Nevertheless many Royalists rallied round the new Government.

One of the most remarkable feats of the Consulate, from the psychological point of view, was the restoration of religious peace. France was far more divided by religious disagreement than by political differences. The systematic destruction of a portion of the Vendée had almost completely terminated the struggle by force of arms, but without pacifying men's minds. As only one man, and he the head of Christianity, could assist in this pacification, Bonaparte did not hesitate to treat with him. His concordat was the work of a real psychologist, who knew that moral forces do not use violence, and the great danger of persecuting such. While conciliating the clergy he contrived to place them under his own domination. The bishops were to be appointed and remunerated by the State, so that he would still be master.

The religious policy of Napoleon had a bearing which escapes our modern Jacobins. Blinded by their narrow fanaticism, they do not understand that to detach the Church from the Government is to create a state within the State, so that they are liable to find themselves opposed by a formidable caste, directed by a master outside France, and necessarily hostile to France. To give one's enemies a liberty they did not possess is extremely dangerous. Never would Napoleon, nor any of the sovereigns who preceded him, have consented to make the clergy independent of the State, as they have become to-day.

The difficulties of Bonaparte the First Consul were far greater than those he had to surmount after his coronation. Only a profound knowledge of men enabled him to triumph over them. The future master was far from being the master as yet. Many departments were still in insurrection. Brigandage persisted, and the Midi was ravaged by the struggles of partisans. Bonaparte, as Consul, had to conciliate and handle Talleyrand, Fouché, and a number of generals who thought themselves his equal. Even his brothers conspired against his power. Napoleon, as Emperor, had no hostile party to face, but as Consul he had to combat all the parties and to hold the balance equal among them. This must indeed have been a difficult task, since during the last century very few Governments have succeeded in accomplishing it.

The success of such an undertaking demanded an extremely subtle mixture of finesse, firmness, and

# The Restoration of Order

diplomacy. Not feeling himself powerful enough as yet, Bonaparte the Consul made a rule, according to his own expression, "of governing men as the greater number wish to be governed." As Emperor he often managed to govern them according to his own ideal.

We have travelled a long way since the time when historians, in their singular blindness, and great poets, who possessed more talent than psychology, would hold forth in indignant accents against the *coup d'État* of Brumaire. What profound illusions underlay the assertion that "France lay fair in Messidor's great sun"! And other illusions no less profound underlay such verdicts as that of Victor Hugo concerning this period. We have seen that the "Crime of Brumaire" had as an enthusiastic accomplice, not only the Government itself but the whole of France, which it delivered from anarchy.

One may wonder how intelligent men could so misjudge a period of history which is nevertheless so clear. It was doubtless because they saw events through their own convictions, and we know what transformations the truth may suffer for the man who is imprisoned in the valleys of belief. The most luminous facts are obscured, and the history of events is the history of his dreams.

The psychologist who desires to understand the period which we have so briefly sketched can only do so if, being attached to no party, he stands clear of the passions which are the soul of parties. He will never dream of recriminating a past which was dictated by such imperious necessities. Certainly Napoleon has cost France dear : his epic was terminated by two invasions, and there was yet to be a third, whose consequences are felt even to-day, when the prestige which he exerted even from the tomb set upon the throne the inheritor of his name.

All these events are narrowly connected in their origin. They represent the price of that capital phenomenon in the evolution of a people, a change of ideal. Man can never make the attempt to break suddenly with his ancestors without profoundly affecting the course of his own history.

# CHAPTER III

POLITICAL CONSEQUENCES OF THE CONFLICT
BETWEEN TRADITIONS AND REVOLUTIONARY
PRINCIPLES DURING THE LAST CENTURY

1. *The Psychological Causes of the continued
Revolutionary Movements to which France has
been subject.*

IN examining, in a subsequent chapter, the evolution
of revolutionary ideas during the last century, we
shall see that during more than fifty years they very
slowly spread through the various strata of society.

During the whole of this period the great majority
of the people and the *bourgeoisie* rejected them, and
their diffusion was effected only by a very limited
number of apostles. But their influence, thanks
principally to the faults of Governments, was sufficient
to provoke several revolutions. We shall examine
these briefly when we have examined the
psychological influences which gave them birth.

The history of our political upheavals during the
last century is enough to prove, even if we did not
yet realise the fact, that men are governed by their
mentalities far more than by the institutions which
their rulers endeavour to force upon them.

The successive revolutions which France has
suffered have been the consequences of struggles

between two portions of the nation whose mentalities are different. One is religious and monarchical and is dominated by long ancestral influences; the other is subjected to the same influences, but gives them a revolutionary form.

From the commencement of the Revolution the struggle between contrary mentalities was plainly manifested. We have seen that in spite of the most frightful repression insurrections and conspiracies lasted until the end of the Directory. They proved that the traditions of the past had left profound roots in the popular soul. At a certain moment sixty departments were in revolt against the new Government, and were only repressed by repeated massacres on a vast scale.

To establish some sort of compromise between the *ancien régime* and the new ideals was the most difficult of the problems which Bonaparte had to resolve. He had to discover institutions which would suit the two mentalities into which France was divided. He succeeded, as we have seen, by conciliatory measures, and also by dressing very ancient things in new names.

His reign was one of those rare periods of French history during which the mental unity of France was complete.

This unity could not outlive him. On the morrow of his fall all the old parties reappeared, and have survived until the present day. Some attach themselves to traditional influences; others violently reject them.

If this long conflict had been between believers and the indifferent, it could not have lasted, for indifference is always tolerant; but the struggle was really between two different beliefs. The lay Church very soon assumed a religious aspect, and its pretended rationalism has become, especially in recent years, a barely attenuated form of the narrowest clerical spirit. Now, we have shown that no conciliation is possible between dissimilar religious beliefs. The clericals when in power could not therefore show themselves more tolerant towards freethinkers than these latter are to-day toward the clericals.

These divisions, determined by differences of belief, were complicated by the addition of the political conceptions derived from those beliefs.

Many simple souls have for long believed that the real history of France began with the year I. of the Republic. This rudimentary conception is at last dying out. Even the most rigid revolutionaries renounce it,[1] and are quite willing to recognise that the past was something better than an epoch of black barbarism dominated by low superstitions.

The religious origin of most of the political beliefs held in France inspires their adepts with an inextinguishable hatred which always strikes foreigners with amazement.

"Nothing is more obvious, nothing is more certain," writes Mr. Barret-Wendell, in his book on France, "than this fact: that not only have the

[1] We may judge of the recent evolution of ideas upon this point by the following passage from a speech by M. Jaurès, delivered in the Chamber of Deputies: "The greatness of to-day is built of the efforts of past centuries. France is not contained in a day nor in an epoch, but in the succession of all days, all periods, all her twilights and all her dawns."

royalists, revolutionaries, and Bonapartists always been mortally opposed to one another, but that, owing to the passionate ardour of the French character, they have always entertained a profound intellectual horror for one another. Men who believe themselves in possession of the truth cannot refrain from affirming that those who do not think with them are instruments of error.

" Each party will gravely inform you that the advocates of the adverse cause are afflicted by a dense stupidity or are consciously dishonest. Yet when you meet these latter, who will say exactly the same things as their detractors, you cannot but recognise, in all good faith, that they are neither stupid nor dishonest."

This reciprocal execration of the believers of each party has always facilitated the overthrow of Governments and ministers in France. The parties in the minority will never refuse to ally themselves against the triumphant party. We know that a great number of revolutionary Socialists have been elected to the present Chamber only by the aid of the monarchists, who are still as unintelligent as they were at the time of the Revolution.

Our religious and political differences do not constitute the only cause of dissension in France. They are held by men possessing that particular mentality which I have already described under the name of the revolutionary mentality. We have seen that each period always presents a certain number of individuals ready to revolt against the established order of things, whatever that may be, even though it may realise all their desires.

# Traditions and Revolutionary Principles

The intolerance of the parties in France, and their desire to seize upon power, are further favoured by the conviction, so prevalent under the Revolution, that societies can be remade by means of laws. The modern State, whatever its leader, has inherited in the eyes of the multitudes and their leaders the mystic power attributed to the ancient kings, when these latter were regarded as an incarnation of the Divine will. Not only the people is inspired by this confidence in the power of Government; all our legislators entertain it also.[1]

Legislating always, politicians never realise that as institutions are effects, and not causes, they have no virtue in themselves. Heirs to the great revolutionary illusion, they do not see that man is created by a past whose foundations we are powerless to reshape.

The conflict between the principles dividing France, which has lasted more than a century, will doubtless continue for a long time yet, and no one can foresee what fresh upheavals it may engender. No doubt if before our era the Athenians could have divined that their social dissensions would have led to the enslavement of Greece, they would have renounced them; but how could they have foreseen as much? M. Guiraud justly writes : " A generation of men

[1] After the publication of an article of mine concerning legislative illusions, I received from one of our most eminent politicians, M. Boudenot the senator, a letter from which I extract the following passage : "Twenty years passed in the Chamber and the Senate have shown me how right you are. How many times I have heard my colleagues say : 'The Government ought to prevent this, order that,' &c. What would you have? there are fourteen centuries of monarchical atavism in our blood."

# The Psychology of Revolution

very rarely realises the task which it is accomplishing. It is preparing for the future ; but this future is often the contrary of what it wishes."

## 2. *Summary of a Century's Revolutionary Movement in France.*

The psychological causes of the revolutionary movements which France has seen during the past century having been explained, it will now suffice to present a summary picture of these successive revolutions.

The sovereigns in coalition having defeated Napoleon, they reduced France to her former limits, and placed Louis XVIII., the only possible sovereign, on the throne.

By a special charter the new king accepted the position of a constitutional monarch under a representative system of government. He recognised all the conquests of the Revolution : the civil Code, equality before the law, liberty of worship, irrevocability of the sale of national property, &c. The right of suffrage, however, was limited to those paying a certain amount in taxes.

This liberal Constitution was opposed by the ultra-royalists. Returned *emigrés*, they wanted the restitution of the national property, and the re-establishment of their ancient privileges.

Fearing that such a reaction might cause a new revolution, Louis XVIII. was reduced to dissolving the Chamber. The election having returned moderate deputies, he was able to continue to govern with the same principles, understanding very well that any attempt to govern the French by the *ancien régime* would be enough to provoke a general rebellion.

# Traditions and Revolutionary Principles

Unfortunately, his death, in 1824, placed Charles X., formerly Comte d'Artois, on the throne. Extremely narrow, incapable of understanding the new world which surrounded him, and boasting that he had not modified his ideas since 1789, he prepared a series of reactionary laws—a law by which an indemnity of forty millions sterling was to be paid to *emigrés*; a law of sacrilege ; and laws establishing the rights of primogeniture, the preponderance of the clergy, &c.

The majority of the deputies showing themselves daily more opposed to his projects, in 1830 he enacted Ordinances dissolving the Chamber, suppressing the liberty of the Press, and preparing for the restoration of the *ancien régime*.

The effect was immediate. This autocratic action provoked a coalition of the leaders of all parties. Republicans, Bonapartists, Liberals, Royalists—all united in order to raise the Parisian populace. Four days after the publication of the Ordinances the insurgents were masters of the capital, and Charles X. fled to England.

The leaders of the movement—Thiers, Casimir-Perier, La Fayette, &c.—summoned to Paris Louis-Philippe, of whose existence the people were scarcely aware, and declared him king of the French.

Between the indifference of the people and the hostility of the nobles, who had remained faithful to the legitimate dynasty, the new king relied chiefly upon the *bourgeoisie*. An electoral law having reduced the electors to less than 200,000, this class played an exclusive part in the government.

The situation of the sovereign was not easy. He had to struggle simultaneously against the legitimist supporters of Henry V. the grandson of Charles X., and the Bonapartists, who recognised as their head Louis-Napoleon, the Emperor's nephew, and finally against the republicans.

By means of their secret societies, analogous to the clubs of the Revolution, the latter provoked numerous riots at various intervals between 1830 and 1840, but these were easily repressed.

The clericals and legitimists, on their side, did not cease their intrigues. The Duchess de Berry, the mother of Henry V., tried in vain to raise the Vendée. As to the clergy, their demands finally made them so intolerable that an insurrection broke out, in the course of which the palace of the archbishop of Paris was sacked.

The republicans as a party were not very dangerous, as the Chamber sided with the king in the struggle against them. The minister Guizot, who advocated a strong central power, declared that two things were indispensable to government—" reason and cannon." The famous statesman was surely somewhat deluded as to the necessity or efficacy of reason.

Despite this strong central power, which in reality was not strong, the republicans, and above all the Socialists, continued to agitate. One of the most influential, Louis Blanc, claimed that it was the duty of the Government to procure work for every citizen. The Catholic party, led by Lacordaire and Monta-lembert, united with the Socialists—as to-day in Belgium—to oppose the Government.

A campaign in favour of electoral reform ended in 1848 in a fresh riot, which unexpectedly overthrew Louis-Philippe.

# Traditions and Revolutionary Principles

His fall was far less justifiable than that of Charles X. There was little with which he could be reproached. Doubtless he was suspicious of universal suffrage, but the French Revolution had more than once been quite suspicious of it. Louis-Philippe not being, like the Directory, an absolute ruler, could not, as the latter had done, annul unfavourable elections.

A provisional Government was installed in the Hôtel de Ville, to replace the fallen monarchy. It proclaimed the Republic, established universal suffrage, and decreed that the people should proceed to the election of a National Assembly of nine hundred members.

From the first days of its existence the new Government found itself the victim of socialistic manœuvres and riots.

The psychological phenomena observed during the first Revolution were now to be witnessed again. Clubs were formed, whose leaders sent the people from time to time against the Assembly, for reasons which were generally quite devoid of common sense—for example, to force the Government to support an insurrection in Poland, &c.

In the hope of satisfying the Socialists, every day more noisy and exigent, the Assembly organised national workshops, in which the workers were occupied in various forms of labour. In these 100,000 men cost the State more than £40,000 weekly. Their claim to receive pay without working for it forced the Assembly to close the workshops.

This measure was the origin of a formidable insurrection, 50,000 workers revolting. The Assembly, terrified, confided all the executive powers to General Cavaignac. There was a four-days battle with the insurgents, during which three generals and the Archbishop of Paris were killed; 3,000 prisoners were deported by the Assembly to Algeria, and revolutionary Socialism was annihilated for a space of fifty years.

These events brought Government stock down from 116 to 50 francs. Business was at a standstill. The peasants, who thought themselves threatened by the Socialists, and the *bourgeois*, whose taxes the Assembly had increased by half, turned against the Republic, and when Louis-Napoleon promised to re-establish order he found himself welcomed with enthusiasm. A candidate for the position of President of the Republic, who according to the new Constitution must be elected by the whole body of citizens, he was chosen by 5,500,000 votes.

Very soon at odds with the Chamber, the prince decided on a *coup d'État*. The Assembly was dissolved; 30,000 persons were arrested, 10,000 deported, and a hundred deputies were exiled.

This *coup d'État*, although summary, was very favourably received, for when submitted to a plebiscite it received 7,500,000 votes out of 8,000,000.

On the 2nd of November, 1852, Napoleon had himself named Emperor by an even greater majority. The horror which the generality of Frenchmen felt for demagogues and Socialists had restored the Empire.

In the first part of its existence it constituted an absolute Government, and during the latter half a liberal Government. After eighteen years of rule the Emperor was overthrown by the revolution of the

4th of September, 1870, after the capitulation of Sedan.

Since that time revolutionary movements have been rare; the only one of importance was the revolution of March, 1871, which resulted in the burning of many of the monuments of Paris and the execution of about 20,000 insurgents.

After the war of 1870 the electors, who, amid so many disasters, did not know which way to turn, sent a great number of Orleanist and legitimist deputies to the Constituent Assembly. Unable to agree upon the establishment of a monarchy, they appointed M. Thiers President of the Republic, later replacing him by Marshal Mac-Mahon. In 1876 the new elections, like all those that have followed, sent a majority of republicans to the Chamber.

The various assemblies which have succeeded to this have always been divided into numerous parties, which have provoked innumerable changes of ministry.

However, thanks to the equilibrium resulting from this division of parties, we have for forty years enjoyed comparative quiet. Four Presidents of the Republic have been overthrown without revolution, and the riots that have occurred, such as those of Champagne and the Midi, have not had serious consequences.

A great popular movement, in 1888, did nearly overthrow the Republic for the benefit of General Boulanger, but it has survived and triumphed over the attacks of all parties.

Various reasons contribute to the maintenance of the present Republic. In the first place, of the conflicting factions none is strong enough to crush the rest. In the second place, the head of the State being purely decorative, and possessing no power, it is impossible to attribute to him the evils from which the country may suffer, and to feel sure that matters would be different were he overthrown. Finally, as the supreme power is distributed among thousands of hands, responsibilities are so disseminated that it would be difficult to know where to begin. A tyrant can be overthrown, but what can be done against a host of little anonymous tyrannies?

If we wished to sum up in a word the great transformations which have been effected in France by a century of riots and revolutions, we might say that individual tyranny, which was weak and therefore easily overthrown, has been replaced by collective tyrannies, which are very strong and difficult to destroy. To a people avid of equality and habituated to hold its Governments responsible for every event individual tyranny seemed insupportable, while a collective tyranny is readily endured, although generally much more severe.

The extension of the tyranny of the State has therefore been the final result of all our revolutions, and the common characteristic of all systems of government which we have known in France. This form of tyranny may be regarded as a racial ideal, since successive upheavals of France have only fortified it. Statism is the real political system of the Latin peoples, and the only system that receives all suffrages. The other forms of government—republic, monarchy, empire—represent empty labels, powerless shadows.

# PART III

## THE RECENT EVOLUTION OF THE REVOLUTIONARY PRINCIPLES

# CHAPTER I

## THE PROGRESS OF DEMOCRATIC BELIEFS SINCE THE REVOLUTION

### 1. *Gradual Propagation of Democratic Ideas after the Revolution.*

IDEAS which are firmly established, incrusted, as it were, in men's minds, continue to act for several generations. Those which resulted from the French Revolution were, like others, subject to this law.

Although the life of the Revolution as a Government was short, the influence of its principles was, on the contrary, very long-lived. Becoming a form of religious belief, they profoundly modified the orientation of the sentiments and ideas of several generations.

Despite a few intervals, the French Revolution has continued up to the present, and still survives. The *rôle* of Napoleon was not confined to overturning the world, changing the map of Europe, and remaking the exploits of Alexander. The new rights of the people, created by the Revolution and established by its institutions, have exercised a profound influence. The military work of the conqueror was soon dissolved, but the revolutionary principles which he contributed to propagate have survived him.

# The Psychology of Revolution

The various restorations which followed the Empire caused men at first to become somewhat forgetful of the principles of the Revolution. For fifty years this propagation was far from rapid. One might almost have supposed that the people had forgotten them. Only a small number of theorists maintained their influence. Heirs to the "simplicist" spirit of the Jacobins, believing, like them, that societies can be remade from top to bottom by the laws, and persuaded that the Empire had only interrupted the task of revolution, they wished to resume it.

While waiting until they could recommence, they attempted to spread the principles of the Revolution by means of their writings. Faithful imitators of the men of the Revolution, they never stopped to ask if their schemes for reform were in conformity with human nature. They too were erecting a chimerical society for an ideal man, and were persuaded that the application of their dreams would regenerate the human species.

Deprived of all constructive power, the theorists of all the ages have always been very ready to destroy. Napoleon at St. Helena stated that "if there existed a monarchy of granite the idealists and theorists would manage to reduce it to powder."

Among the galaxy of dreamers such as Saint-Simon, Fourier, Pierre Leroux, Louis Blanc, Quinet, &c., we find that only Auguste Comte understood that a transformation of manners and ideas must precede political reorganisation.

Far from favouring the diffusion of democratic ideas, the projects of reform of the theorists of this period merely impeded their progress. Communistic

# The Progress of Democratic Beliefs

Socialism, which several of them professed would restore the Revolution, finally alarmed the *bourgeoisie* and even the working-classes. We have already seen that the fear of their ideas was one of the principal causes of the restoration of the Empire.

If none of the chimerical lucubrations of the writers of the first half of the nineteenth century deserve to be discussed, it is none the less interesting to examine them in order to observe the part played by religious and moral ideas which to-day are regarded with contempt. Persuaded that a new society could not, any more than the societies of old, be built up without religious and moral beliefs, the reformers were always endeavouring to found such beliefs.

But on what could they be based? Evidently on reason. By means of reason men create complicated machines : why not therefore a religion and a morality, things which are apparently so simple? Not one of them suspected the fact that no religious or moral belief ever had rational logic as its basis. Auguste Comte saw no more clearly. We know that he founded a so-called positivist religion, which still has a few followers. Scientists were to form a clergy directed by a new Pope, who was to replace the Catholic Pope.

All these conceptions—political, religious, or moral —had, I repeat, no other results for a long time than to turn the multitude away from democratic principles.

If these principles did finally become widespread, it was not on account of the theorists, but because new conditions of life had arisen. Thanks to the discoveries of science, industry developed and led to the erection of immense factories. Economic necessities increasingly dominated the wills of Governments and the people and finally created a favourable soil for the extension of Socialism, and above all of Syndicalism, the modern forms of democratic ideas.

## 2. The Unequal Influence of the Three Fundamental Principles of the Revolution.

The heritage of the Revolution is summed up in its entirety in the one phrase—*Liberty, Equality, and Fraternity*. The principle of equality, as we have seen, has exerted a powerful influence, but the two others did not share its lot.

Although the sense of these terms seems clear enough, they were comprehended in very different fashions according to men and times. We know that the various interpretation of the same words by persons of different mentality has been one of the most frequent causes of the conflicts of history.

To the member of the Convention liberty signified merely the exercise of its unlimited despotism. To a young modern "intellectual" the same word means a general release from everything irksome : tradition, law, superiority, &c. To the modern Jacobin liberty consists especially in the right to persecute his adversaries.

Although political orators still occasionally mention liberty in their speeches, they have generally ceased to evoke fraternity. It is the conflict of the different classes and not their alliance that they teach to-day. Never did a more profound hatred divide the various strata of society and the political parties which lead them.

# The Progress of Democratic Beliefs

But while liberty has become very doubtful and fraternity has completely vanished, the principle of equality has grown unchecked. It has been supreme in all the political upheavals of which France has been the stage during the last century, and has reached such a development that our political and social life, our laws, manners, and customs are at least in theory based on this principle. It constitutes the real legacy of the Revolution. The craving for equality, not only before the law, but in position and fortune, is the very pivot of the last product of democracy : Socialism. This craving is so powerful that it is spreading in all directions, although in contradiction with all biological and economic laws. It is a new phase of the interrupted struggle of the sentiments against reason, in which reason so rarely triumphs.

### 2. *The Democracy of the "Intellectuals" and Popular Democracy.*

All ideas that have hitherto caused an upheaval of the world of men have been subject to two laws : they evolve slowly, and they completely change their sense according to the mentalities in which they find reception.

A doctrine may be compared to a living being. It subsists only by process of transformation. The books are necessarily silent upon these variations, so that the phase of things which they establish belongs only to the past. They do not reflect the image of the living, but of the dead. The written statement of a doctrine often represents the most negligible side of that doctrine.

# The Psychology of Revolution

I have shown in another work how institutions, arts, and languages are modified in passing from one people to another, and how the laws of these transformations differ from the truth as stated in books. I allude to this matter now merely to show why, in examining the subject of democratic ideas, we occupy ourselves so little with the text of doctrines, and seek only for the psychological elements of which they constitute the vestment, and the reactions which they provoke in the various categories of men who have accepted them.

Modified rapidly by men of different mentalities, the original theory is soon no more than a label which denotes something quite unlike itself.

Applicable to religious beliefs, these principles are equally so to political beliefs. When a man speaks of democracy, for example, must we inquire what this word means to various peoples, and also whether in the same people there is not a great difference between the democracy of the "intellectuals" and popular democracy.

In confining ourselves now to the consideration of this latter point we shall readily perceive that the democratic ideas to be found in books and journals are purely the theories of literary people, of which the people know nothing, and by the application of which they would have nothing to gain. Although the working-man possesses the theoretical right of passing the barriers which separate him from the upper classes by a whole series of competitions and examinations, his chance of reaching them is in reality extremely slight.

The democracy of the lettered classes has no other

# The Progress of Democratic Beliefs

object than to set up a selection which shall recruit the directing classes exclusively from themselves. I should have nothing to say against this if the selection were real. It would then constitute the application of the maxim of Napoleon: "The true method of government is to employ the aristocracy, but under the forms of democracy."

Unhappily the democracy of the "intellectuals" would simply lead to the substitution of the Divine right of kings by the Divine right of a petty oligarchy, which is too often narrow and tyrannical. Liberty cannot be created by replacing a tyranny.

Popular democracy by no means aims at manufacturing rulers. Dominated entirely by the spirit of equality and the desire to ameliorate the lot of the workers, it rejects the idea of fraternity, and exhibits no anxiety in respect of liberty. No government is conceivable to popular democracy except in the form of an autocracy. We see this, not only in history, which shows us that since the Revolution all despotic Governments have been vigorously acclaimed, but also in the autocratic fashion in which the workers' trades unions are conducted.

This profound distinction between the democracy of the lettered classes and popular democracy is far more obvious to the workers than to the intellectuals. In their mentalities there is nothing in common ; the two classes do not speak the same language. The syndicalists emphatically assert to-day that no alliance could possibly exist between them and the politicians of the *bourgeoisie*. This assertion is strictly true.

It was always so, and this, no doubt, is why popular

democracy, from Plato's to our own times, has never been defended by the great thinkers.

This fact has greatly struck Emile Faguet. "Almost all the thinkers of the nineteenth century," he says, "were not democrats. When I was writing my *Politiques et moralistes du XIX^e siècle* this was my despair. I could not find one who had been a democrat; yet I was extremely anxious to find one so that I could give the democratic doctrine as formulated by him."

The eminent writer might certainly have found plenty of professional politicians, but these latter rarely belong to the category of thinkers.

## 2. *Natural Inequalities and Democratic Equalisation.*

The difficulty of reconciling democratic equalisation with natural inequalities constitutes one of the most difficult problems of the present hour. We know what are the desires of democracy. Let us see what Nature replies to these demands.

The democratic ideas which have so often shaken the world from the heroic ages of Greece to modern times are always clashing with natural inequalities. Some observers have held, with Helvetius, that the inequality between men is created by education.

As a matter of fact, Nature does not know such a thing as equality. She distributes unevenly genius, beauty, health, vigour, intelligence, and all the qualities which confer on their possessors a superiority over their fellows.

No theory can alter these discrepancies, so that democratic doctrines will remain confined to words until the laws of heredity consent to unify the capacities of men.

Can we suppose that societies will ever succeed in establishing artificially the equality refused by Nature?

A few theorists have believed for a long time that education might effect a general levelling. Many years of experience have shown the depth of this illusion.

It would not, however, be impossible for a triumphant Socialism to establish equality for a time by rigorously eliminating all superior individuals. One can easily foresee what would become of a people that had suppressed its best individuals while surrounded by other nations progressing by means of their best individuals.

Not only does Nature not know equality, but since the beginning of the ages she has always realised progress by means of successive differentiations—that is to say, by increasing inequalities. These alone could raise the obscure cell of the early geological periods to the superior beings whose inventions were to change the face of the earth.

The same phenomenon is to be observed in societies. The forms of democracy which select the better elements of the popular classes finally result in the creation of an intellectual aristocracy, a result the contrary of the dream of the pure theorists, to beat down the superior elements of society to the level of the inferior elements.

On the side of natural law, which is hostile to theories of equality, are the conditions of modern progress. Science and industry demand more and

# The Psychology of Revolution

more considerable intellectual efforts, so that mental inequalities and the differences of social condition which spring from them cannot but become accentuated.

We therefore observe this striking phenomenon : as laws and institutions seek to level individuals the progress of civilisation tends still further to differentiate them. From the peasant to the feudal baron the intellectual difference was not great, but from the working-man to the engineer it is immense and is increasing daily.

Capacity being the principal factor of progress, the capable of each class rise while the mediocre remain stationary or sink. What could laws do in the face of such inevitable necessities?

In vain do the incapable pretend that, representing number, they also represent force. Deprived of the superior brains by whose researches all workers profit, they would speedily sink into poverty and anarchy.

The capital *rôle* of the elect in modern civilisation seems too obvious to need pointing out. In the case of civilised nations and barbarian peoples, which contain similar averages of mediocrities, the superiority of the former arises solely from the superior minds which they contain. The United States have understood this so thoroughly that they forbid the immigration of Chinese workers, whose capacity is identical with that of American workers, and who, working for lower wages, tend to create a formidable competition with the latter. Despite these evidences we see the antagonism between the multitude and the elect increasing day by day. At no period were the elect more necessary, yet never were they supported with such difficulty.

# The Progress of Democratic Beliefs

One of the most solid foundations of Socialism is an intense hatred of the elect. Its adepts always forget that scientific, artistic, and industrial progress, which creates the strength of a country and the prosperity of millions of workers, is due solely to a small number of superior brains.

If the worker makes three times as much to-day as he did a hundred years ago, and enjoys commodities then unknown to great nobles, he owes it entirely to the elect.

Suppose that by some miracle Socialism had been universally accepted a century ago. Risk, speculation, initiative—in a word, all the stimulants of human activity—being suppressed, no progress would have been possible, and the worker would have remained as poor as he was. Men would merely have established that equality in poverty desired by the jealousy and envy of a host of mediocre minds. Humanity will never renounce the progress of civilisation to satisfy so low an ideal.

# CHAPTER II

## THE RESULTS OF DEMOCRATIC EVOLUTION

### 1. *The Influence upon Social Evolution of Theories of no Rational Value.*

WE have seen that natural laws do not agree with the aspirations of democracy. We know, also, that such a statement has never affected doctrines already in men's minds. The man led by a belief never troubles about its real value.

The philosopher who studies a belief must obviously discuss its rational content, but he is more concerned with its influences upon the general mind.

Applied to the interpretation of all the great beliefs of history, the importance of this distinction is at once evident. Jupiter, Moloch, Vishnu, Allah, and so many other divinities, were, no doubt, from the rational point of view, mere illusions, yet their effect upon the life of the peoples has been considerable.

The same distinction is applicable to the beliefs which prevailed during the Middle Ages. Equally illusory, they nevertheless exercised as profound an influence as if they had corresponded with realities.

If any one doubts this, let him compare the domination of the Roman Empire and that of the Church of Rome. The first was perfectly real and tangible, and implied no illusion. The second, while its foundations were entirely chimerical, was fully as powerful. Thanks to it, during the long night of the Middle Ages, semi-barbarous peoples acquired those social bonds and restraints and that national soul without which there is no civilisation.

The power possessed by the Church proves, again, that the power of certain illusions is sufficiently great to create, at least momentarily, sentiments as contrary to the interests of the individual as they are to that of society—such as the love of the monastic life, the desire for martyrdom, the crusades, the religious wars, &c.

The application to democratic and socialistic ideas of the preceding considerations shows that it matters little that these ideas have no defensible basis. They impress and influence men's minds, and that is sufficient. Their results may be disastrous in the extreme, but we cannot prevent them.

The apostles of the new doctrines are quite wrong in taking so much trouble to find a rational basis for their aspirations. They would be far more convincing were they to confine themselves to making affirmations and awakening hopes. Their real strength resides in the religious mentality which is inherent in the heart of man, and which during the ages has only changed its object.

Later on we shall consider from a philosophical point of view various consequences of the democratic evolution whose course we see accelerating. We may say in respect of the Church in the Middle Ages that it had the power of profoundly influencing the mentality of men. Examining certain results of the democratic doctrines, we shall see that the power of these is no less than that of the Church.

## 2. *The Jacobin Spirit and the Mentality created by Democratic Beliefs.*

Existing generations have inherited, not only the revolutionary principles but also the special mentality which achieves their success.

Describing this mentality when we were examining the Jacobin spirit, we saw that it always endeavours to impose by force illusions which it regards as the truth. The Jacobin spirit has finally become so general in France and in other Latin countries that it has affected all political parties, even the most conservative. The *bourgeoisie* is strongly affected by it, and the people still more so.

This increase of the Jacobin spirit has resulted in the fact that political conceptions, institutions, and laws tend to impose themselves by force. Syndicalism, peaceful enough in other countries, immediately assumed in France an uncompromising and anarchical aspect, which betrayed itself in the shape of riots, *sabotage*, and incendiarism.

Not to be repressed by timid Governments, the Jacobin spirit produces melancholy ravages in minds of mediocre capacity. At a recent congress of railway men a third of the delegates voted approval of *sabotage*, and one of the secretaries of the Congress began his speech by saying : " I send all *saboteurs* my fraternal greeting and all my admiration."

This general mentality engenders an increasing anarchy. That France is not in a permanent state of anarchy is, as I have already remarked, due to

# The Results of Democratic Evolution

the fact that the parties by which she is divided produce something like equilibrium. They are animated by a mortal hatred for one another, but none of them is strong enough to enslave its rivals.

This Jacobin intolerance is spreading to such an extent that the rulers themselves employ without scruple the most revolutionary tactics with regard to their enemies, violently persecuting any party that offers the least resistance, and even despoiling it of its property. Our rulers to-day behave as the ancient conquerors used ; the vanquished have nothing to hope from the victors.

Far from being peculiar to the lower orders, intolerance is equally prominent among the ruling classes. Michelet remarked long ago that the violence of the cultivated classes is often greater than that of the people. It is true that they do not break the street lamps, but they are ready enough to cause heads to be broken. The worst violence of the revolution was the work of cultivated *bourgeoisie*— professors, lawyers, &c., possessors of that classical education which is supposed to soften the manners.

It has not done so in these days, any more than it did of old. One can make sure of this by reading the advanced journals, whose contributors and editors are recruited chiefly from among the professors of the University.

Their books are as violent as their articles, and one wonders how such favourites of fortune can have secreted such stores of hatred.

One would find it hard to credit them did they assure us that they were consumed by an intense passion for altruism. One might more readily admit that apart from a narrow religious mentality the hope of being remarked by the mighty ones of the day, or of creating a profitable popularity, is the only possible explanation of the violence recommended in their written propaganda.

I have already, in one of my preceding works, cited some passages from a book written by a professor at the College of France, in which the author incites the people to seize upon the riches of the *bourgeoisie*, whom he furiously abuses, and have arrived at the conclusion that a new revolution would readily find among the authors of such books the Marats, Robespierres, and Carriers whom it might require.

The Jacobin religion—above all in its Socialist form—has all the power of the ancient faiths over feeble minds. Blinded by their faith, they believe that reason is their guide, but are really actuated solely by their passions and their dreams.

The evolution of democratic ideas has thus produced not only the political results already mentioned, but also a considerable effect upon the mentality of modern men.

If the ancient dogmas have long ago exhausted their power, the theories of democracy are far from having lost theirs, and we see their consequences increasing daily. One of the chief results has been the general hatred of superiority.

This hatred of whatever passes the average in social fortune or intelligence is to-day general in all classes, from the working-classes to the upper strata of the *bourgeoisie*. The results are envy, detraction, and a love of attack, of raillery, of persecution, and a habit of attributing all actions to low motives, of refusing to believe in probity, disinterestedness, and intelligence.

# The Results of Democratic Evolution

Conversation, among the people as among the most cultivated Frenchmen, is stamped with the craze for abasing and abusing everything and everyone. Even the greatest of the dead do not escape this tendency. Never were so many books written to depreciate the merit of famous men, men who were formerly regarded as the most precious patrimony of their country.

Envy and hatred seem from all time to have been inseparable from democratic theories, but the spread of these sentiments has never been so great as to-day. It strikes all observers.

"There is a low demagogic instinct," writes M. Bourdeau, "without any moral inspiration, which dreams of pulling humanity down to the lowest level, and for which any superiority, even of culture, is an offence to society. . . it is the sentiment of ignoble equality which animated the Jacobin butchers when they struck off the head of a Lavoisier or a Chénier."

This hatred of superiority, the most prominent element in the modern progress of Socialism, is not the only characteristic of the new spirit created by democratic ideas.

Other consequences, although indirect, are not less profound. Such, for example, are the progress of "statism," the diminution of the power of the *bourgeoisie*, the increasing activity of financiers, the conflict of the classes, the vanishing of the old social constraints, and the degradation of morality.

All these effects are displayed in a general insubordination and anarchy. The son revolts against the father, the employee against his patron, the soldier against his officers. Discontent, hatred, and envy reign throughout.

305

# The Psychology of Revolution

A social movement which continues is necessarily like a machine in movement which accelerates its motion. We shall therefore find that the results of this mentality will become yet more important. It is betrayed from time to time by incidents whose gravity is daily increasing—railway strikes, postmen's strikes, explosions on board ironclads, &c. *A propos* of the destruction of the *Liberté*, which cost more than two million pounds and slew two hundred men in the space of a minute, an ex-Minister of Marine, M. de Lanessan, expresses himself as follows :—

"The evil that is gnawing at our fleet is the same as that which is devouring our army, our public administrations, our parliamentary system, our governmental system, and the whole fabric of our society. This evil is anarchy—that is to say, such a disorder of minds and things that nothing is done as reason would dictate, and no one behaves as his professional or moral duty should require him to behave."

On the subject of the catastrophe of the *Liberté*, which followed that of the *Iéna*, M. Felix Roussel said, in a speech delivered as president of the municipal council of Paris :—

"The causes of the evil are not peculiar to our day. The evil is more general, and bears a triple name : irresponsibility, indiscipline, and anarchy."

These quotations, which state facts with which everyone is familiar, show that the staunchest upholders of the republican system themselves recognise the progress of social disorganisation.[1]   Everyone

---

[1] This disorder is the same in all the Government departments. Interesting examples will be found in a report of M. Dausset to the Municipal Council :—

sees it, while he is conscious of his own impotence to change anything. It results, in fact, from mental influences whose power is greater than that of our wills.

### 3. *Universal Suffrage and its Representatives.*

Among the dogmas of democracy perhaps the most fundamental of all and the most attractive is that of universal suffrage. It gives the masses the idea of equality, since for a moment at least rich and poor, learned and ignorant, are equal before the electoral urn. The minister elbows the least of his servants, and during this brief moment the power of one is as great as the others.

All Governments, including that of the Revolution, have feared universal suffrage. At a first glance, indeed, the objections which suggests themselves are numerous. The idea that the multitude could usefully choose the men capable of governing, that individuals of indifferent morality, feeble knowledge, and narrow

"The service of the public highways, which ought above all to be noted for its rapid execution, is, on the contrary, the very type of red-tape, bureaucratic, and ink-slinging administration, possessing men and money and wasting both in tasks which are often useless, for lack of order, initiative, and method—in a word, of organisation."

Speaking then of the directors of departments, each of whom works as he pleases, and after his own fashion, he adds :—

"These important persons completely ignore one another; they prepare and execute their plans without knowing anything of what their neighbours are doing; there is no one above them to group and co-ordinate their work." This is why a road is often torn up, repaired, and then torn up again a few days later, because the departments dealing with the supply of water, gas, electricity, and the sewers are mutually jealous, and never attempt to work together. This anarchy and indiscipline naturally cost enormous sums of money, and a private firm which operated in this manner would soon find itself bankrupt.

# The Psychology of Revolution

minds should possess, by the sole fact of number, a certain talent for judging the candidate proposed for its selection is surely a shocking one.

From a rational point of view the suffrage of numbers is to a certain extent justified if we think with Pascal.

" Plurality is the best way, because it is visible and has strength to make itself obeyed ; it is, however, the advice of the less able."

As universal suffrage cannot in our times be replaced by any other institution, we must accept it and try to adapt it. It is accordingly useless to protest against it or to repeat with the queen Marie Caroline, at the time of her struggle with Napoleon : " Nothing is more dreadful than to govern men in this enlightened century, when every cobbler reasons and criticises the Government."

To tell the truth, the objections are not always as great as they appear. The laws of the psychology of crowds being admitted, it is very doubtful whether a limited suffrage would give a much better choice of men than that obtained by universal suffrage.

These same psychological laws also show us that so-called universal suffrage is in reality a pure fiction. The crowd, save in very rare cases, has no opinion but that of its leaders. Universal suffrage really represents the most limited of suffrages.

There justly resides its real danger. Universal suffrage is made dangerous by the fact that the leaders who are its masters are the creatures of little local committees analogous to the clubs of the Revolution. The leader who canvasses for a mandate is chosen by them.

# The Results of Democratic Evolution

Once nominated, he exercises an absolute local power, on condition of satisfying the interests of his committees. Before this necessity the general interest of the country disappears almost totally from the mind of the elected representative.

Naturally the committees, having need of docile servants, do not choose for this task individuals gifted with a lofty intelligence nor, above all, with a very high morality. They must have men without character, without social position, and always docile.

By reason of these necessities the servility of the deputy in respect of these little groups which patronise him, and without which he would be no one, is absolute. He will speak and vote just as his committee tells him. His political ideal may be expressed in a few words : it is to obey, that he may retain his post.

Sometimes, rarely indeed, and only when by name or position or wealth he has a great prestige, a superior character may impose himself upon the popular vote by overcoming the tyranny of the impudent minorities which constitute the local committees.

Democratic countries like France are only apparently governed by universal suffrage. For this reason is it that so many measures are passed which do not interest the people and which the people never demanded. Such were the purchase of the Western railways, the laws respecting congregations, &c. These absurd manifestations merely translated the demands of fanatical local committees, and were imposed upon deputies whom they had chosen.

We may judge of the influence of these committees when we see moderate deputies forced to patronise the anarchical destroyers of arsenals, to ally themselves with anti-militarists, and, in a word, to obey the most atrocious demands in order to ensure re-election. The will of the lowest elements of democracy has thus created among the elected representatives manners and a morality which we can but recognise are of the lowest. The politician is the man in public employment, and as Nietzsche says :—

"Where public employment begins there begins also the clamour of the great comedians and the buzzing of venomous flies. . . . The comedian always believes in that which makes him obtain his best effects, in that which impels the people to believe in him. To-morrow he will have a new faith, and the day after to-morrow yet another. . . . All that is great has its being far from public employment and glory."

### 4. *The Craving for Reforms.*

The craze for reforms imposed suddenly by means of decrees is one of the most disastrous conceptions of the Jacobin spirit, one of the formidable legacies left by the Revolution. It is among the principal factors of all the incessant political upheavals of the last century in France.

One of the psychological causes of this intense thirst for reforms arises from the difficulty of determining the real causes of the evils complained of. The need of explanation creates fictitious causes of the simplest nature. Therefore the remedies also appear simple.

For forty years we have incessantly been passing reforms, each of which is a little revolution in itself. In spite of all these, or rather because of them, the

# The Results of Democratic Evolution

French have evolved almost as little as any race in Europe.

The slowness of our actual evolution may be seen if we compare the principal elements of our social life—commerce, industry, &c.—with those of other nations. The progress of other nations—of the Germans especially—then appears enormous, while our own has been very slow.

Our administrative, industrial, and commercial organisation is considerably out of date, and is no longer equal to our new needs. Our industry is not prospering; our marine is declining. Even in our own colonies we cannot compete with foreign countries, despite the enormous pecuniary subventions accorded by the State. M. Cruppi, an ex-Minister of Commerce, has insisted on this melancholy decline in a recent book. Falling into the usual errors, he believed it easy to remedy this inferiority by new laws.

All politicians share the same opinion, which is why we progress so slowly. Each party is persuaded that by means of reforms all evils could be remedied. This conviction results in struggles such as have made France the most divided country in the world and the most subject to anarchy.

No one yet seems to understand that individuals and their methods, not regulations, make the value of a people. The efficacious reforms are not the revolutionary reforms but the trifling ameliorations of every day accumulated in course of time. The great social changes, like the great geological changes, are effected by the daily addition of minute causes. The economic history of Germany during the last forty years proves in a striking manner the truth of this law.

Many important events which seem to depend more or less on hazard—as battles, for example— are themselves subject to this law of the accumulation of small causes. No doubt the decisive struggle is sometimes terminated in a day or less, but many minute efforts, slowly accumulated, are essential to victory. We had a painful experience of this in 1870, and the Russians have learned it more recently. Barely half an hour did Admiral Togo need to annihilate the Russian fleet, at the battle of Tsushima, which finally decided the fate of Japan, but thousands of little factors, small and remote, determined that success. Causes not less numerous engendered the defeat of the Russians—a bureaucracy as complicated as ours, and as irresponsible; lamentable material, although paid for by its weight in gold; a system of graft at every degree of the social hierarchy, and general indifference to the interests of the country.

Unhappily the progress in little things which by their total make up the greatness of a nation is rarely apparent, produces no impression on the public, and cannot serve the interests of politicians at elections. These latter care nothing for such matters, and permit the accumulation, in the countries subject to their influence, of the little successive disorganisations which finally result in great downfalls.

5. *Social Distinctions in Democracies and Democratic Ideas in Various Countries.*

When men were divided into castes and differentiated chiefly by birth, social distinctions were generally accepted as the consequences of an unavoidable natural law.

As soon as the old social divisions were destroyed the distinctions of the classes appeared artificial, and for that reason ceased to be tolerated.

The necessity of equality being theoretical, we have seen among democratic peoples the rapid development of artificial inequalities, permitting their possessors to make for themselves a plainly visible supremacy. Never was the thirst for titles and decorations so general as to-day.

In really democratic countries, such as the United States, titles and decorations do not exert much influence, and fortune alone creates distinctions. It is only by exception that we see wealthy young American girls allying themselves to the old names of the European aristocracy. They are then instinctively employing the only means which will permit a young race to acquire a past that will establish its moral framework.

But in a general fashion the aristocracy that we see springing up in America is by no means founded on titles and decorations. Purely financial, it does not provoke much jealousy, because every one hopes one day to form part of it.

When, in his book on democracy in America, Toqueville spoke of the general aspiration towards equality he did not realise that the prophesied equality would end in the classification of men founded exclusively on the number of dollars possessed by them. No other exists in the United States, and it will doubtless one day be the same in Europe.

# The Psychology of Revolution

At present we cannot possibly regard France as a democratic country save on paper, and here we feel the necessity, already referred to, of examining the various ideas which in different countries are expressed by the word "democracy."

Of truly democratic nations we can practically mention only England and the United States. There, democracy occurs in different forms, but the same principles are observed—notably, a perfect toleration of all opinions. Religious persecutions are unknown. Real superiority easily reveals itself in the various professions which any one can enter at any age if he possesses the necessary capacity. There is no barrier to individual effort.

In such countries men believe themselves equal because all have the idea that they are free to attain the same position. The workman knows he can become foreman, and then engineer. Forced to begin on the lower rungs of the ladder instead of high up the scale, as in France, the engineer does not regard himself as made of different stuff to the rest of mankind. It is the same in all professions. This is why the class hatred, so intense in Europe, is so little developed in England and America.

In France the democracy is practically non-existent save in speeches. A system of competitions and examinations, which must be worked through in youth, firmly closes the door upon the liberal professions, and creates inimical and separate classes.

The Latin democracies are therefore purely theoretical. The absolutism of the State has replaced monarchical absolutism, but it is no less severe. The

# The Results of Democratic Evolution

aristocracy of fortune has replaced that of birth, and its privileges are no less considerable.

Monarchies and democracies differ far more in form than in substance. It is only the variable mentality of men that varies their effects. All the discussions as to various systems of government are really of no interest, for these have no special virtue of themselves. Their value will always depend on that of the people governed. A people effects great and rapid progress when it discovers that it is the sum of the personal efforts of each individual and not the system of government that determines the rank of a nation in the world.

# CHAPTER III

## THE NEW FORMS OF DEMOCRATIC BELIEF

1. *The Conflict between Capital and Labour.*
WHILE our legislators are reforming and legislating at
hazard, the natural evolution of the world is slowly
pursuing its course. New interests arise, the economic
competition between nation and nation increases in
severity, the working-classes are bestirring themselves,
and on all sides we see the birth of formidable problems which the harangues of the politicians will never
resolve.

Among these new problems one of the most complicated will be the problem of the conflict between
labour and capital. It is becoming acute even in
such a country of tradition as England. Working-
men are ceasing to respect the collective contracts
which formerly constituted their charter, strikes are
declared for insignificant motives, and unemployment
and pauperism are attaining disquieting proportions.

In America these strikes would finally have affected
all industries but that the very excess of the evil
created a remedy. During the last ten years the
industrial leaders have organised great employers'
federations, which have become powerful enough to
force the workers to submit to arbitration.

The labour question is complicated in France by

316

# The New Forms of Democratic Belief

the intervention of numerous foreign workers, which the stagnation of our population has rendered necessary.[1] This stagnation will also make it difficult for France to contend with her rivals, whose soil will soon no longer be able to nourish its inhabitants, who, following one of the oldest laws of history, will necessarily invade the less densely peopled countries.

These conflicts between the workers and employers of the same nation will be rendered still more acute by the increasing economic struggle between the Asiatics, whose needs are small, and who can therefore produce manufactured articles at very low prices, and the Europeans, whose needs are many. For twenty-five years I have laid stress upon this point. General Hamilton, ex-military attaché to the Japanese army, who foresaw the Japanese victories long before the outbreak of hostilities, writes as follows in an essay translated by General Langlois :—

" The Chinaman, such as I have seen him in Manchuria, is capable of destroying the present type of worker of the white races. He will drive him off the face of the earth. The Socialists, who preach equality to the labourer, are far from thinking what would be the practical result of carrying out their theories. Is it, then, the destiny of the white races to disappear in the long run ? In my humble opinion

[1] Population of the Great Powers :—

|  |  | 1789. | 1906. |
|---|---|---|---|
| Russia ... | ... | 28,000,000 | 129,000,000 |
| Germany ... | ... | 28,000,000 | 57,000,000 |
| Austria ... | ... | 18,000,000 | 44,000,000 |
| England ... | ... | 12,000,000 | 40,000,000 |
| France ... | ... | 26,000,000 | 39,000,000 |

this destiny depends upon one single factor : Shall we or shall we not have the good sense to close our ears to speeches which present war and preparation for war as a useless evil?

"I believe the workers must choose. Given the present constitution of the world, they must cultivate in their children the military ideal, and accept gracefully the cost and trouble which militarism entails, or they will be let in for a cruel struggle for life with a rival worker of whose success there is not the slightest doubt. There is only one means of refusing Asiatics the right to emigrate, to lower wages by competition, and to live in our midst, and that is the sword. If Americans and Europeans forget that their privileged position is held only by force of arms, Asia will soon have taken her revenge."

We know that in America the invasion of Chinese and Japanese, owing to the competition between them and the workers of white race, has become a national calamity. In Europe the invasion is commencing, but has not as yet gone far. But already Chinese emigrants have formed important colonies in certain centres—London, Cardiff, Liverpool, &c. They have provoked several riots by working for low wages. Their appearance has always lowered salaries.

But these problems belong to the future, and those of the present are so disquieting that it is useless at the moment to occupy ourselves with others.

2. *The Evolution of the Working-Classes and the Syndicalist Movement.*

The most important democratic problem of the day will perhaps result from the recent development of the working-class engendered by the Syndicalist or Trades Union movement.

The aggregation of similar interests known as Syndicalism has rapidly assumed such enormous developments in all countries that it may be called world-wide. Certain corporations have budgets comparable to those of small States. Some German leagues have been cited as having saved over three millions sterling in subscriptions.

The extension of the labour movement in all countries shows that it is not, like Socialism, a dream of Utopian theorists, but the result of economic necessities. In its aim, its means of action, and its tendencies, Syndicalism presents no kinship with Socialism. Having sufficiently explained it in my *Political Psychology*, it will suffice here to recall in a few words the difference between the two doctrines.

Socialism would obtain possession of all industries, and have them managed by the State, which would distribute the products equally between the citizens. Syndicalism, on the other hand, would entirely eliminate the action of the State, and divide society into small professional groups which would be self-governing.

Although despised by the Syndicalists and violently attacked by them, the Socialists are trying to ignore the conflict, but it is rapidly becoming too obvious to be concealed. The political influence which the Socialists still possess will soon escape them.

If Syndicalism is everywhere increasing at the expense of Socialism, it is, I repeat, because this corporative movement, although a renewal of the past, synthetises certain needs born of the specialisation of modern industry.

We see its manifestations under a great variety of circumstances. In France its success has not as yet been as great as elsewhere. Having taken the revolutionary form already mentioned, it has fallen, at least for the time being, into the hands of the anarchists, who care as little for Syndicalism as for any sort of organisation, and are simply using the new doctrine in an attempt to destroy modern society. Socialists, Syndicalists, and anarchists, although directed by entirely different conceptions, are thus collaborating in the same eventual aim—the violent suppression of the ruling classes and the pillage of their wealth.

The Syndicalist doctrine does not in any way derive from the principles of Revolution. On many points it is entirely in contradiction with the Revolution. Syndicalism represents rather a return to certain forms of collective organisation similar to the guilds or corporations proscribed by the Revolution. It thus constitutes one of those federations which the Revolution condemned. It entirely rejects the State centralisation which the Revolution established.

Syndicalism cares nothing for the democratic principles of liberty, equality, and fraternity. The Syndicalists demand of their members an absolute discipline which eliminates all liberty.

Not being as yet strong enough to exercise mutual tyranny, the syndicates so far profess sentiments in respect of one another which might by a stretch be called fraternal. But as soon as they are sufficiently powerful, when their contrary interests will necessarily enter into conflict, as during the Syndicalist period of the old Italian republics—Florence and Siena, for example—the present fraternity will speedily be forgotten, and equality will be replaced by the despotism of the most powerful.

Such a future seems near at hand. The new power is increasing very rapidly, and finds the Governments powerless before it, able to defend themselves only by yielding to every demand—an odious policy, which may serve for the moment, but which heavily compromises the future.

It was, however, to this poor recourse that the English Government recently resorted in its struggle against the Miners' Union, which threatened to suspend the industrial life of England. The Union demanded a minimum wage for its members, but they were not bound to furnish a minimum of work.

Although such a demand was inadmissible, the Government agreed to propose to Parliament a law to sanction such a measure. We may profitably read the weighty words pronounced by Mr. Balfour before the House of Commons :—

"The country has never in its so long and varied history had to face a danger of this nature and this importance.

"We are confronted with the strange and sinister spectacle of a mere organisation threatening to paralyse—and paralysing in a large measure—the commerce and manufactures of a community which lives by commerce and manufacture.

"The power possessed by the miners is in the present state of the law almost unlimited. Have we ever seen the like of it? Did ever feudal baron exert a comparable tyranny? Was there ever an American trust which served the rights which it holds from the law with such contempt of the general interest? The very degree of perfection to which we have brought our laws, our social organisation, the mutual relation between the various professions and industries, exposes us more than our predecessors in ruder ages to the grave peril which at present threatens society. . . . We are witnesses at the present moment of the first manifestation of the power of elements which, if we are not heedful, will submerge the whole of society. . . . The attitude of the Government in yielding to the injunction of the miners gives some appearance of reality to the victory of those who are pitting themselves against society."

3. *Why certain modern Democratic Governments are gradually being transformed into Governments by Administrative Castes.*

Anarchy and the social conflicts resulting from democratic ideas are to-day impelling some Governments towards an unforeseen course of evolution which will end by leaving them only a nominal power. This development, of which I shall briefly denote the effects, is effected spontaneously under the stress of those imperious necessities which are still the chief controlling power of events.

The Governments of democratic countries to-day consist of the representatives elected by universal suffrage. They vote laws, and appoint and dismiss ministers chosen from themselves, and provisionally entrusted with the executive power. These ministers are naturally often replaced, since a vote will do it.

# The New Forms of Democratic Belief

Those who follow them, belonging to a different party, will govern according to different principles.

It might at first seem that a country thus pulled to and fro by various influences could have no continuity or stability. But in spite of all these conditions of instability a democratic Government like that of France works with fair regularity. How explain such a phenomenon?

Its interpretation, which is very simple, results from the fact that the ministers who have the appearance of governing really govern the country only to a very limited extent. Strictly limited and circumscribed, their power is exercised principally in speeches which are hardly noticed and in a few inorganic measures.

But behind the superficial authority of ministers, without force or duration, the playthings of every demand of the politician, an anonymous power is secretly at work whose might is continually increasing the administrations. Possessing traditions, a hierarchy, and continuity, they are a power against which, as the ministers quickly realise, they are incapable of struggling.[1] Responsibility is so divided in the administrative machine that a minister may never find himself opposed by any person of importance. His momentary impulses are checked by a network of regulations, customs, and decrees, which are continually quoted to him, and which he knows so little that he dare not infringe them.

This diminution of the power of democratic Govern-

---

[1] The impotence of ministers in their own departments has been well described by one of them, M. Cruppi, in a recent book. The most ardent wishes of the minister being immediately paralysed by his department, he promptly ceases to struggle against it.

# The Psychology of Revolution

ments can only develop. One of the most constant laws of history is that of which I have already spoken : immediately any one class becomes preponderant— nobles, clergy, army, or the people—it speedily tends to enslave others. Such were the Roman armies, which finally appointed and overthrew the emperors ; such were the clergy, against whom the kings of old could hardly struggle ; such were the States General, which at the moment of Revolution speedily absorbed all the powers of government, and supplanted the monarchy.

The caste of functionaries is destined to furnish a fresh proof of the truth of this law. Preponderant already, they are beginning to speak loudly, to make threats, and even to indulge in strikes, such as that of the postmen, which was quickly followed by that of the Government railway employees. The administrative power thus forms a little State within the State, and if its present rate of revolution continues it will soon constitute the only power in the State. Under a Socialist Government there would be no other power. All our revolutions would then have resulted in stripping the king of his powers and his throne in order to bestow them upon the irresponsible, anonymous and despotic class of Government clerks.

To foresee the issue of all the conflicts which threaten to cloud the future is impossible. We must steer clear of pessimism as of optimism ; all we can say is that necessity will always finally bring things to an equilibrium. The world pursues its way without bothering itself with our speeches, and sooner or later we manage to adapt ourselves to the variations of our environment. The difficulty is to do so without too much friction, and above all to resist the chimerical conceptions of dreamers. Always powerless to re-organise the world, they have often contrived to upset it.

Athens, Rome, Florence, and many other cities which formerly shone in history, were victims of these terrible theorists. The results of their influence has always been the same—anarchy, dictatorship, and decadence.

But such lessons will not affect the numerous Catilines of the present day. They do not yet see that the movements unchained by their ambitions threaten to submerge them. All these Utopians have awakened impossible hopes in the mind of the crowd, excited their appetites, and sapped the dykes which have been slowly erected during the centuries to restrain them.

The struggle of the blind multitudes against the elect is one of the continuous facts of history, and the triumph of popular sovereignties without counter-poise has already marked the end of more than one civilisation. The elect create, the plebs destroys. As soon as the first lose their hold the latter begins its precious work.

The great civilisations have only prospered by dominating their lower elements. It is not only in Greece that anarchy, dictatorship, invasion, and, finally, the loss of independence has resulted from the despotism of a democracy. Individual tyranny is always born of collective tyranny. It ended the first cycle of the greatness of Rome; the Barbarians achieved the second.

# CONCLUSIONS

THE principal revolutions of history have been studied in this volume. But we have dealt more especially with the most important of all—that which for more than twenty years overwhelmed all Europe, and whose echoes are still to be heard.

The French Revolution is an inexhaustible mine of psychological documents. No period of the life of humanity has presented such a mass of experience, accumulated in so short a time.

On each page of this great drama we have found numerous applications of the principles expounded in my various works, concerning the transitory mentality of crowds and the permanent soul of the peoples, the action of beliefs, the influence of mystic, affective, and collective elements, and the conflict between the various forms of logic.

The Revolutionary Assemblies illustrate all the known laws of the psychology of crowds. Impulsive and timid, they are dominated by a small number of leaders, and usually act in a sense contrary to the wishes of their individual members.

The Royalist Constituent Assembly destroyed an ancient monarchy; the humanitarian Legislative Assembly allowed the massacres of September. The same pacific body led France into the most formidable campaigns.

326

# Conclusions

There were similar contradictions during the Convention. The immense majority of its members abhorred violence. Sentimental philosophers, they exalted equality, fraternity, and liberty, yet ended by exerting the most terrible despotism.

The same contradictions were visible during the Directory. Extremely moderate in their intentions at the outset, the Assemblies were continually effecting bloodthirsty *coups d'état*. They wished to re-establish religious peace, and finally sent thousands of priests into imprisonment. They wished to repair the ruins which covered France, and only succeeded in adding to them.

Thus there was always a complete contradiction between the individual wills of the men of the revolutionary period and the deeds of the Assemblies of which they were units.

The truth is that they obeyed invisible forces of which they were not the masters. Believing that they acted in the name of pure reason, they were really subject to mystic, affective, and collective influences, incomprehensible to them, and which we are only to-day beginning to understand.

Intelligence has progressed in the course of the ages, and has opened a marvellous outlook to man, although his character, the real foundation of his mind, and the sure motive of his actions, has scarcely changed. Overthrown one moment, it re-appears the next. Human nature must be accepted as it is.

The founders of the Revolution did not resign themselves to the facts of human nature. For the first time in the history of humanity they attempted to transform men and society in the name of reason.

Never was any undertaking commenced with such chances of success. The theorists, who claimed to effect it, had a power in their hands greater than that of any despot.

Yet, despite this power, despite the success of the armies, despite Draconian laws and repeated *coups d'état*, the Revolution merely heaped ruin upon ruin, and ended in a dictatorship.

Such an attempt was not useless, since experience is necessary to the education of the peoples. Without the Revolution it would have been difficult to prove that pure reason does not enable us to change human nature, and, consequently, that no society can be rebuilt by the will of legislators, however absolute their power.

Commenced by the middle classes for their own profit, the Revolution speedily became a popular movement, and at the same time a struggle of the instinctive against the rational, a revolt against all the constraints which make civilisation out of barbarism. It was by relying on the principle of popular sovereignty that the reformers attempted to impose their doctrines. Guided by leaders, the people intervened incessantly in the deliberations of the Assemblies, and committed the most sanguinary acts of violence.

The history of the multitudes during the Revolution is eminently instructive. It shows the error of the politicians who attribute all the virtues to the popular soul.

# Conclusions

The facts of the Revolution teach us, on the contrary, that a people freed from social constraints, the foundations of civilisation, and abandoned to its instinctive impulses, speedily relapses into its ancestral savagery. Every popular revolution which succeeds in triumphing is a temporary return to barbarism. If the Commune of 1871 had lasted, it would have repeated the Terror. Not having the power to kill so many people, it had to confine itself to burning the principal monuments of the capital.

The Revolution represents the conflict of psychological forces liberated from the bonds whose function it is to restrain them. Popular instincts, Jacobin beliefs, ancestral influences, appetites, and passions unloosed, all these various influences engaged in a furious mutual conflict for the space of ten years, during which time they soaked France in blood and covered the land with ruins.

Seen from a distance, this seems to be the whole upshot of the Revolution. There was nothing homogeneous about it. One must resort to analysis before one can understand and grasp the great drama and display the impulses which continually actuated its heroes. In normal times we are guided by the various forms of logic—rational, affective, collective, and mystic—which more or less perfectly balance one another. During seasons of upheaval they enter into conflict, and man is no longer himself.

We have by no means undervalued in this work the importance of certain acquisitions of the Revolution in respect of the rights of the people. But with many

# The Psychology of Revolution

other historians, we are forced to admit that the prize gained at the cost of such ruin and bloodshed would have been obtained at a later date without effort, by the mere progress of civilisation. For a few years gained, what a load of material disaster, what moral disintegration! We are still suffering as a result of the latter. These brutal pages in the book of history will take long to efface : they are not effaced as yet.

Our young men of to-day seem to prefer action to thought. Disdaining the sterile dissertations of the philosophers, they take no interest in vain speculation concerning matters whose essential nature remains unknown.

Action is certainly an exce..ent thing, and all real progress is a result of action, but it is only useful when properly directed. The men of the Revolution were assuredly men of action, yet the illusions which they accepted as guides led them to disaster.

Action is always hurtful when, despising realities, it professes violently to change the course of events. One cannot experiment with society as with apparatus in a laboratory. Our political upheavals show us what such social errors may cost.

Although the lesson of the Revolution was extremely categorical, many unpractical spirits, hallucinated by their dreams, are hoping to recommence it. Socialism, the modern synthesis of this hope, would be a regression to lower forms of evolution, for it would paralyse the greatest sources of our activity. By replacing individual initiative and responsibility by collective initiative and responsibility mankind would descend several steps on the scale of human values.

# Conclusions

The present time is hardly favourable to such experiments. While dreamers are pursuing their dreams, exciting appetites and the passions of the multitude, the peoples are every day arming themselves more powerfully. All feel that amid the universal competition of the present time there is no room for weak nations.

In the centre of Europe a formidable military Power is increasing in strength, and aspiring to dominate the world, in order to find outlets for its goods, and for an increasing population, which it will soon be unable to nourish.

If we continue to shatter our cohesion by intestine struggles, party rivalries, base religious persecutions, and laws which fetter industrial development, our part in the world will soon be over. We shall have to make room for peoples more solidly knit, who have been able to adapt themselves to natural necessities instead of pretending to turn back upon their course. The present does not repeat the past, and the details of history are full of unforeseen consequences; but in their main lines events are conditioned by eternal laws.

# INDEX

*(Names of Historians, etc., cited in italics.)*

# Index

334

# Index

# Index

# Index